"Not for me, Clive"

Clive Tyldesley

"Not for me, Clive"

Stories from the Voice of Football

HEADLINE

First published in 2021
by HEADLINE PUBLISHING GROUP

1

Cataloguing in Publication Data is available from the British Library

Hardback ISBN 978 1 4722 8128 9

Designed and typeset by EM&EN
Printed and bound in Great Britain by Clays Ltd, Elcograf S.p.A.

MIX
Paper from
responsible sources
FSC® C104740

Headline's policy is to use papers that are natural, renewable and recyclable products and made from wood grown in well-managed forests and other controlled sources. The logging and manufacturing processes are expected to conform to the environmental regulations of the country of origin.

HEADLINE PUBLISHING GROUP
An Hachette UK Company
Carmelite House
50 Victoria Embankment
London EC4Y 0DZ

www.headline.co.uk
www.hachette.co.uk

For the incomparable Mrs T . . .

and anybody else that has had to live with

someone trying to write their first book

At the peak of my playing career.

I have written every word you're about to read
and I'm afraid I swear too much.
Apologies in advance for when I do.

CONTENTS

INTRO

Football changes everything.

It changes how we feel, how we think, how we behave. It turns us into someone else.

I was a teenage Manchester United fan during the early 1970s. A conscientious grammar school boy heading for university with the chance of a career in the professions . . . until I set off for the match.

When the 'football special' train pulled out of Victoria Station on a Saturday morning, I turned into that 'someone else'. I didn't know the lippy kids off the Wythenshawe estate that I shared the carriage and the cause with. I never will. But for a few short hours, I was one of them. One of us.

It's a beautiful game but 'us' versus 'them' is the essence of the sport. You can love football but that love is tossed and blown by defeat. You love your team first. It's tribal.

Except I did love something else. I loved the idea of commentating on my team, on every team. I loved it even more than United. I ditched the girl next door for the diva on the silver screen.

It was a crush. Something to fall ever deeper in love with. A romance, an ambition, a calling. A different 'someone else'.

Like all true romances, it was irrational and intoxicating, it was tangled and foolish, it became addictive and occasionally heartbreaking and it kept on changing.

Two United goals inside two minutes changed it in 1999. A teenage Evertonian called Rooney twisted the plot in 2002. Three Liverpool goals in less than six minutes changed everything again in 2005. Hello, hello.

Moments. Mere blinks of wide eyes. Football happens in heartbeats.

Hurst's second, Maradona's first. Moments, millimetres, fractions, infractions. You never know when they are coming, but you know when they are gone because everything is different in their wake. In a breath, Beckham is walking, Keegan is slumped, Solskjaer is celebrating.

Meeting those moments is my job. Seeing them, saying them, spelling out the difference they have just made. It's all I've ever wanted to do. Probably all I can do. I don't put up shelves.

The best part of the job is doing it. The ultimate workplace is one that you want to go to every day. The second best part of the job is the extraordinary people that I spend my working life with.

Some you will know, others you won't, but football is one of the last, great meritocracies of contemporary life. The only way that you can succeed as a performer in football is to be good enough. Billionaires can buy their way into football clubs but not into football teams.

It is the most populated rat race on the planet. Millions of people want to be great footballers, but only a gifted handful truly are.

INTRO

Spending time in the company of the 'greats' of football like Sir Alex Ferguson, Bill Shankly, Brian Clough and Sir Kenny Dalglish has changed everything for me, and probably for you too if you've got this far. Read on.

1

DENIS

Denis Law was my boyhood hero. Not every choice that I've made in my life has been a good one but that was a great one.

Heroes are not meant to be admired or respected, they are there to be loved. And I loved Denis. Still do.

As a fan of Sir Matt Busby's Manchester United, I was not short of seducers. But Bobby Charlton had always been my dad's favourite player and George Best's exploding fame rocketed him beyond my stratosphere. Denis was on planet Earth with me. The King of planet Earth.

That was me he was saluting each and every time he scored a goal in front of the adoring Stretford End. Just me.

Sometimes, I could only catch a subliminal glimpse of his gloating smile and raised arm and index finger pointing to the sky amid the cascading bodies spilling down the shallow terrace steps around me, but he was always looking at me. We had a thing going.

I had a thing going with Diana Rigg too. It was a different kind of thing but it was still just between me and her. Like the Mona Lisa, pin-ups and poster boys follow us round the room with their eyes. No one else understands but we know, don't we?

Sport, cinema and music are all about creating idols. A 12 year old's relationship with today's idols has been rebooted and reset by social and tabloid media, but it's still a romance, still a flight of fancy and fantasy, still a thing.

I did wonder whether or not to tell Denis about our thing when he cadged a cigarette off me in the Goodison Park press room ten years later. It didn't seem like the right time. But, to my eternal relief, the BBC radio co-commentator that had replaced the valorous champion inside his slight frame turned out to be an eminently likeable man. Denis has always remained on the planet.

Imagine meeting your hero and not liking them. I once sat on a sports panel where a member of the audience asked us which famous person had turned out to be the biggest disappointment on meeting them. Before I could begin to think up a diplomatic reply, Steve Rider just blurted out, 'Jack Nicklaus'.

I had never heard Steve say a bad word about anyone, but he may even have answered this inquiry before the question was fully out. He didn't offer an explanation or illustrative anecdote, he didn't condemn the great American golfer any further, he just raised the microphone to his mouth and coolly answered. Next question.

Denis has never disappointed me. Not even when he backheeled a goal for City at Old Trafford on the day United were relegated in 1974. He didn't break my heart, the stooges in red did that. They had been doing it all season. I probably celebrated the international goals he scored against England. It was unconditional love.

The single biggest change in football during my 45 years in broadcasting is the widening of the distance between the professionals and their public. You just don't see your team's centre-back in Sainsbury's anymore.

During his time as England manager, Roy Hodgson was forced to publicly apologise to Rio Ferdinand for discussing his selection with a couple of passengers in a London tube carriage. The apology was as genuine as it was merited, but part of me was buoyed by the idea of an England manager still travelling by underground in 2012, mixing with his public.

The real sadness is that the conversation found its way into the papers in the first place. The single biggest cause of that single biggest change in football is the breakdown in trust between the game and its media. Our essential role as sports journalists is to provide a link between the doers and their watchers. We are granted access to the performers in order to ask the supporters' questions on their behalf, to ask Roy Hodgson if he intends to pick Rio Ferdinand in his next squad or not.

What a strange state of affairs we have reached when a couple of fans happen to break through the cordon and get to ask a manager directly for once, and then promptly report his answer to the press.

Fifteen minutes of fame. We all want it. No wonder every conversation between football professionals is now held behind a hand covering their mouths from prying lip readers. We will turn our national game into an underground activity if we don't back off.

The mobile phone has changed the relationship between hero and follower. Or the camera phone to be more precise. The scribbled autograph is antique. Face recognition is now needed for evidential proof of encounter. The selfie is merely

Exhibit A, the minimum requirement. A shout out, a personal birthday greeting or a proposal of marriage are the least a cornered celebrity can offer when staring up into a cracked iPhone screen in video mode.

At the last World Cup, I took the 20-minute stroll from our Moscow hotel to the ITV studios in Red Square with Ryan Giggs. He must have posed for at least fifty selfies en route. Remarkably, he took most of the snaps himself. As each applicant began to match our businesslike pace and move up alongside for the inevitable ask, Ryan simply, silently took the phone from their grasp, framed the shot, smiled the smile, pressed the white circle and handed the device back to them.

Not once did he break stride or break the thread of the conversation that we were holding about Gareth Southgate's midfield options. It was one of the finest displays of male multi-tasking I've ever seen. I suspect that when his many admirers downloaded their images to Facebook, most of them were wearing goggle-eyed, shocked expressions at the sheer slickness of the operation.

Roy Keane is less slick in these situations. He never says 'no' to a request but he likes a debate first.

'Can I get a selfie with you please, Roy?'

'Why do you want a photo with me?'

'So I can tell my friends I've met you.'

'Won't they believe you if you just tell them?'

'I don't know. Maybe.'

'I mean, do your friends not trust you? Do you tell them things that aren't true?'

'No, not really.'

'So why don't you just tell them? If they are real friends, they'll believe you, won't they?'

'I guess.'

It's at this point that Lee Dixon or someone usually steps in to point out that the transaction could have been completed thirty seconds ago without the third-degree interrogation. Roy rests his case, flashes a playful grin and poses for the picture.

He did get his comeuppance in Warsaw during the 2012 Euros. A passing supporter stopped Roy and Adrian Chiles as they were walking through the city and began to pull his phone from his bag for the requisite request.

'Oh, thank you,' said the stranger breathlessly combing his hair with his hand and frantically trying to improve his dishevelled look. With that, he handed his phone to Roy, put an arm around Adrian's shoulder and said his cheeses into the device that a bewildered Roy was now pointing at the two of them. The fan had no idea who his award-winning photographer was.

Roy does have a point. Why do we need photographic confirmation that we have not dreamt our brief excursion to Hollywood? What is wrong with the dream, with gazing and gawping at our idea of greatness from a distance? Why do we feel a compulsion to climb up onto the stage? Even 'P' list celebrities like me get followed by an amateur paparazzi.

I have developed a worryingly pathological hatred of strangers that randomly step out of the throng, offer a hand to shake and then say, 'You don't remember me, do you?' I mean, I like a quiz as much as anyone but these mystery guests immediately force you into an embarrassing corner from which you can only escape by apologetically answering, 'No, I'm sorry you'll have to remind me.'

The really annoying ones then say, 'No, I didn't think you would' before feigning a retreat to the anonymity from whence they came, leaving me to pursue them with further pleas for atonement. One thing that everyone should know about television is, we can't see you through the screen.

While security fences and bodyguards have put a greater distance between the millionaire baller and the man in Row Z, the level of exposure that contemporary media affords famous players breeds a kind of familiarity that many fans can't contain. I notice it when I am walking towards a stadium in the company of a recognisable face.

'Hey, Wrighty, what do you think today?'

'Oi, Dicko, got any spares?'

'Keano, Keano, brought your boots?'

Most of the salutations are friendly enough. They are shouted heartily and warmly without any malice. They are just so pally and cocksure. You wouldn't hail your postman in such a chummy fashion as he walked up your street and yet we feel a kind of ownership over the players we pay to watch.

It's not necessarily a bad thing but no footballer in his right mind would turn down a selfie request without very good reason now. The PR penalties are too great.

Personality assessments and character references are formed on the sketchy evidence of these brief encounters. The Google Translate version of 'I met Clive Tyldesley once but he was very rude and totally ignored me' is 'I once nodded and smiled at Clive Tyldesley in the waiting area at A&E but he just clutched his injured knee and grimaced.'

All that growing fame ensures is that more and more people will get you wrong.

Denis would have been no good at all in the selfie age. He never kept still long enough for a photo opportunity.

Every picture of him that I pinned to my wall had a blur on it somewhere. He was too quick for the lens. A flashing, dashing player, all of his moving parts were forever activated. Even if he was walking back to catch his breath after another burst of pent-up, agitated energy, he would be wryly smiling, defiantly arguing or gesturing, wagging a finger, talking to the referee, chiding an opponent. I doubt he ever slept for more than a couple of hours at a time. He was the most fabulous fidget.

For those of you for whom Denis Law is just a name, he was a goal scorer and much more. Forty-six goals in his second season at Old Trafford (still a club record – sorry Cristiano). Nobody has scored more goals for Scotland. All kinds of goals. Left foot, right foot, long-range, close-range, knifing volleys, neck-ricking headers, gravity-defying overhead kicks. All scored with a flourish and a flamboyance.

Denis was dramatic. His movement was as sharp and pointed as his angled features. A sweep of fair hair bouncing along aboard his animated face. His heart beating boldly on a sleeve, always pulled over hands that clung religiously to the white cuffs on his red shirt until . . . until he scored and thrust one or both of them skywards towards the heavens that he carried me to.

Shirt out of his shorts specifically in defiance of my dad, he lacked some of the natural grace of his slaloming team-mates, Charlton and Best. Instead, a Denis solo run was an urgent, darting, jagging foray into enemy territory. Somehow, he was never quite balanced or set, so time after time his slender silhouette had to twist and contort in order to deliver the pass or the finish that his predatory instincts and racing imagination had seen coming from way back. Denis played at the stretch, on the limits.

Who would I compare him to of a later vintage? He was somewhere in the vicinity of Ian Wright and Robbie Fowler. Maybe a diet version of Diego Costa.

I was taken to Wembley for the first big adventure of my football life in 1963. I can remember Dad touching a hundred on the M1 and I can recall the Corona Cherryade and the Crunchie bars better than the FA Cup final itself. I was eight. I had my own priorities.

But Denis must have known I was there. He scored the first goal in United's 3–1 win over Leicester and was denied a hat-trick only by a post and a goal-line clearance. I have learnt all this by watching the highlights of the match over and over. My lasting image is of Denis following the ball into the net after David Herd sealed it with the third goal. He picked it up and strutted away, arm triumphantly raised, before tossing the ball into the far yonder as if to say 'game over'. The Lawman.

Westerns and war movies shaped much of my boyhood thinking. For someone that has turned out to be so devoutly 'anti-gun', I spent a lot of my formative years running around firing imaginary bullets at playmates. The heroism of my dad's generation was fashioned on battlefields and my rich imagination was forever taking me behind enemy lines to pull off daring rescue missions and bring Emma Peel safely home to her wardrobe of leather catsuits. She never failed to show me her gratitude.

At the age of 12, female beauty alone was not enough to turn my head. A woman needed to be able to show some commando qualities in order to join my fantasy harem. *The Avengers* and the Bond movies provided suitable candidates galore. Pussy Galore. The two most ogled bedroom posters of the day featured Ursula Andress emerging from the sea in *Doctor No* and Raquel Welch's strident pose from *One Million Years BC*. One carried a knife, the other a spear. That was good enough for me.

In 1965, my parents separated and I swapped the family home just outside Bury for a stark boarding house dormitory at Kirkham Grammar School, near Blackpool. My visits to Old Trafford were duly rationed to school holidays and exeat weekends. Sometimes the outcome of an important midweek match was not revealed until the morning paper was delivered to the junior common room. The act of nervously unfolding the back page was a sporting drama in itself. I still get a shiver now just thinking about it.

I was given a small transistor radio that I occasionally smuggled into bed with me to listen to Brian Moore and Maurice Edelston's BBC radio commentaries via a tiny ear-piece. Any such nefarious activity after 'lights out' was painfully punishable. The house master's wooden cane and the head boy's heavy training shoe were the prices I paid for following my team back then. The hooked cane left fearful ridged marks on my derrière. Any kind of corporal punishment is brutal and inexcusable. Is now, was then.

I can't say the thrill of hearing Peter Jones bring a United goal to vivid colourful life was actually worth the stinging wounds but there is a mysterious sorcery about radio transmissions that no amount of television camera angles and slow-motion replays can match. During my early weeks as a broadcaster, the programme controller at my first radio station chastised me for mentioning that a member of the cleaning staff had entered the lonely studio during a late-night music show.

'Don't talk about anything real,' he lectured me. 'You'll break the spell.'

'What spell?' I asked.

'Watch *Play Misty for Me*,' he replied cryptically.

Directing a rookie radio presenter to a psychological thriller in which a fictional DJ gets stalked by a psychopathic woman is probably not the most considered advice – particularly given my show didn't end until 2 am – but Clint Eastwood's cornily dated character captures the seductively mysterious nature of a radio persona that is heard but never seen.

A rich, hypnotic radio voice can put the sightless listener under their spell. The rules of engagement change. The reliance is greater, the dependency heightened. A blind faith is afforded to the radio broadcaster akin to that of the volunteer who is coaxed from the audience during a magic show.

The point that my boss was making to me about the person emptying the studio bins is that nobody really wants a conjurer's trick explaining to them. Radio broadcasts to the mind's eye only. I have always tried to spare the listener the practical problems of a poorly-located commentary position or particularly cold weather. The detail of your own circumstances is not relevant to them. Protect that secret spell.

The great radio commentators get you to close your eyes and follow them to wherever they want to lead you. They take you out of your world into the one that they are creating with their verbal paints and brushes. It can be a bewitching and enchanting world with the right tonsils at the mike.

Radio commentators should not be illusionists. A colleague once said to me of Peter Jones that he can 'make a terrible game sound like a great one'. I doubt it. He was too good a journalist to do that. With the stronger relationship with the audience comes a greater responsibility to tell it like it is, to be as measured as you are mesmeric. You are a reporter, not a propagandist.

The one cardinal sin of radio commentary is to sound like a terrible game is wasting your time, to give the impression that you've got better things to do than watch the rubbish in front of you. One of Peter's successors at BBC Radio was especially guilty of that. We should never forget how lucky we are to do a job that all of our audience would give their right arms for.

The next game that I work on may be the most important game of your season or of your life. It is my professional duty to make sure that it feels every bit as special and individual to me. If my diary ever filled to the point that I found it difficult to care as much about the next one as I did about the previous one, I would take a break.

Football commentary is all I ever wanted to do. Still is.

My starry, stolen nights with those first radio commentators I heard must have been a catalyst for my ambitions. Hindsight is an illuminating thing, and sometimes we trace too straight a line between our influences and our fate, but I'm sure I owe a debt of gratitude to Messrs Jones, Butler, Edelston, Clarke and Moore for my crazy ambitions.

I worked alongside Brian Moore for two years in the mid-1990s. He was a class act both as a broadcaster and as a man.

Because I would have given my Duncan Fearnley cricket bat, my Civil War bubble gum cards and my entire stamp collection for the opportunity to broadcast just sixty seconds of commentary during my teens, I remain as precious about every minute of airtime to this day. Realising those ambitions has never marked down the value I place on a platform to connect with people.

To waste that time in meandering rambles and mindless banter is a crime. To be an editor that cocks a deaf ear to bland blah broadcasting is worse still. Air time should be measured in impact, not minutes. It's got to count, it's got to connect, it's got to command attention.

I receive daily DMs and emails from young people with the same ambitions that I once dreamily entertained when I listened to Brian after lights out. The power of communication should only fall into the hands of those with an appetite to use it to inspire the next generation of dreamers.

You are fast-tracked towards 'manhood' in a boarding house of 60 students covering seven school years. Because I was always in the company of older boys, I was always under their influence. A long list of life-adjusting evolutionary developments happened to me way before they were scheduled to . . . smoking, drinking, swearing, heavy petting, The Doors, *The Graduate*, *The Prisoner*, Cream, Three-card brag, *Barbarella*, *Men Only*, rugby songs . . . all in no particular order, all bloody great discoveries at the time.

My virginity disappeared in messy, fumbled, bungled stages but took its final leave of me at the age of 16 on a canvas groundsheet under a bivouac I constructed from a bent sapling as part of an army cadet exercise to survive a night under the stars. The earth moved only because it was a bit muddy.

Meanwhile, my newly-acquired wandering eye had hit upon a love rival to Denis. A younger model. Brian Kidd was nine years his junior. More my age.

Football loyalties are stubbornly rooted in one sense but flightily fickle in another. We can go off players, even our own players, particularly our own players after a few frustrating performances. I never went off Denis altogether but once Kiddo had announced himself with his 19th birthday goal in the 1968 European Cup final, he was a suitor for my affections.

Neither Denis nor I were at Wembley for United's crowning victory over Benfica. He watched it from a hospital bed following knee surgery, I listened to it from a school bed under a thick linen sheet. The next time we were together at Old Trafford a few months later, my torn devotions were shared by my fellow Stretford Enders.

When the cry of 'Who's that king?' went up from some throaty cheerleader at the core of the mass congregation, some answered 'Denis Law', then others would counter 'Brian Kidd'. It wasn't a split of Blair–Brown proportions but it was a sign that a changing of the guard might be afoot, a natural and organic change, the best kind. I thought I would be 'United Forever', but I always knew that Law and Kidd wouldn't.

My own match-day routine was undergoing organic development too. Dad took me to my first United game on

14 November 1959, aged five. I didn't go to a match without him until I was 15. For many years, we watched side-by-side from the Main Stand Paddock that ran along the length of Old Trafford. We clambered onto the playing surface together to join the pitch invasion that followed the clinching of the title in 1967.

But I wanted to be a Stretford Ender. By 1969, I was one of the older boys leading the young ones astray at school. It was me that was introducing them to Led Zeppelin, Monty Python, *Straw Dogs*, Jenny Agutter bathing at a waterhole and all the other delicious vices that I had inherited from my seniors during my gawky early adolescence. I was ready to go it alone at Old Trafford.

I still travelled to the games with Dad, but at 1 o'clock we went our separate ways. I was sponsored to the tune of my turnstile money and a little extra for a pie and some pop. That was often diverted in the direction of ten Embassy and a box of matches. I usually shared my cigarettes with neighbouring terrace-dwellers in a bid to get rid of all the fags and try to gain some temporary street cred. The truth is I never belonged on the Stretford End.

I was a middle-class grammar school boy on course for ten good O-level results. Like the St Martins College sculpture student that Jarvis Cocker sang about, I wanted to live like 'common people' for a few hours. So, I took on the disguise of some shelf-stacker from Salford and shouted abuse at Billy Bremner and Bobby Moore like I really hated them. I didn't really know how to hate anybody.

After a season or so of bobbing about helplessly on the human waves that rolled and surged and swayed until they broke and then plunged down the terracing like a thrill ride out of control, I retired to the small seated area at the rear of the massive stand behind Denis' favourite goal. I think he could just about see me but, better still, I could now see him.

It began to dawn on me when I re-joined my dad at the car in time to hear Bill Bothwell's match report on *Sports Report* that I had seen remarkably little of the game he was describing. As I sucked hard on another Trebor mint to try to overpower the scent of tobacco, I decided to sell up and leave the estates for good.

A lot has happened to me and everything since then, but I have no reason to believe that Mohamed Salah or Raheem Sterling are any less of a hero to today's young fans than Denis Law was to me. The unreal numbers that footballers can earn and the way their wealth is held against any of them that allow their public standards to slip below that of Mother Teresa puts a distance between the players and the realities of their supporters.

But, hey, George Best was caught in bed with a woman at the United team hotel around about the same time as I was starting to queue outside Hillsborough for the 1970 FA Cup semi-final. We don't truly expect or even want our heroes to live the same lives that we do. They are our gladiators, our dragons. They possess supernatural powers, they boldly go where nobody has been before. They can do no wrong. You can forgive them anything.

I have never quite understood why young footballers are supposed to set an example to their fans. They are carrying enough extra responsibilities just trying to win football matches before their time without being required to maintain the moral continence of the nation. Isn't that what parenting is for?

I fell under the spell of Jim Morrison in my adolescence but never so far that I ended up in a Paris cemetery before I was 28. By definition, heroes do things that we don't do.

Denis came down from Scotland to sign for Huddersfield Town as a 15 year old. Bill Shankly was the manager who gave him his debut at 16. He fathered him through his first lonesome days away from Aberdeen, prescribing a diet of milk and steak to fill out his skeletal frame and advising surgery to correct a squint eye that played on the teenager's confidence.

Ian St John once told me a story of Shankly becoming irritated with Denis' truancy. Weekend breaks granted to ease his homesickness were turning into whole weeks spent in hiding north of the border. A car was sent to bring him back to Yorkshire, and a ticking off was called for.

Shankly tried to rehearse the grave rebuke with his assistant manager, sending him from his office to knock at the door, then enter and face the music. Three times the assistant entered in the role of Denis, three times Bill began the final warning, three times he failed to find the right words of loud censure to the patient stand-in. The assistant took his leave ready for Act IV. Another knock on the door and in walked the player himself this time.

'Denis!' cried Bill striding across to give his blue-eyed boy a big hug. 'We've been worried about you. Great to see you back.' Some people are eternally pardonable.

I was just lucky to choose a boyhood hero that fitted the bill. Denis was no angel. He had a rogue tackle in his repertoire, he could be naughty or nice, he must have wound up opponents as much as he pumped up me and my quixotic vision of him punching the air in triumph. On the field, he was a bother, a nark, a nagging irritant . . . but always with a twinkle in his eye, always with an irresistible smile ready to break out across that unmistakable face.

That 80-year-old smile lit up the arena in Aberdeen that staged the 2019 BBC Sports Personality of the Year ceremony. Denis presented the award to Ben Stokes but not until he had made a disarming slip of the tongue and revelled in a cheeky exchange with Princess Anne on opening the envelope. He stole the show as usual.

CLIVE ROBERT TYLDESLEY

Born: 21/8/1954 Radcliffe, Greater Manchester

Prep school: Bury Grammar School (1959–65)

Secondary school: Kirkham Grammar School (1965–72)

I'm a Bury lad. I was born in Bealey's nursing home in neighbouring Radcliffe but I'm a Bury boy. Like Gary and Phil and Tracey Neville, like Kieran Trippier. Like Guy Garvey of Elbow, who is a bit of a contemporary hero to me now.

Looking back, I was always more likely to write songs than kick wingers. I was never an outstanding young sportsman but I was always the kid that wrote the match reports for the school magazine.

I was a 10-handicap golfer in my late teens. It was the rival passion to United in my dad's life and so I can remember the first time I beat him at golf as vividly as any goal that Denis Law scored. There really should be a plaque at Rossendale Golf Club marking the event.

When Tony Jacklin became the first home winner of the Open Championship for a generation in 1969, Dad and I walked every hole of his final two rounds with him at Royal Lytham. He had a flash of the Law twinkle in his eyes. I supported him like I supported my team. He was a headline act.

I was a child of Lancashire rather than a fully-fledged Manc. The parental home edged north from Bury up the Rossendale valley towards Haslingden, my schooling continued in Kirkham and a branch of the family settled in and around Morecambe on the southern fringes of the Lake District.

Lancashire boasted star-sprinkled county cricket and rugby union teams during my school days and I was a paying customer of both. Names like Clive Lloyd, Fran Cotton, Peter Lever, Tony Neary, Jack Simmons, Mike Slemen, Barry Wood, Steve Smith, David 'Bumble' Lloyd and Big Bill Beaumont won't have meant much in Salford but they were up there with the United players in my affections.

The Beatles were my other boyhood heroes and I cannot think of better possible influences on a child of 'impressionable age'. No attempt at trying to create a laboratory boyband since has come even close to the natural chemistry and sprouting alchemy of the rocket they fired up the backside of everything. I am so lucky to have been a kid that queued to buy the next Beatles single.

Never mind the images of screeching adolescent girls, the biggest noise they made was to drown out my parents' music, to shake rattle and roll Elvis away and put something of mine in its place. The Beatles were the soundtrack to my coming of age. Help!

2

UNCLE DAVE

Dave Russell was the manager of my hometown football club for eight years. I lived next door to him in Bury for seven of them. The first seven years of my life.

We weren't related but I called him 'uncle' and he treated me like family. His wife Gladys went with my mum on the bus to the nursing home for my arrival into the world on Saturday 21 August 1954.

Uncle Dave was watching Bury lose 3–2 at Lincoln, while my dad was at Old Trafford where United were beaten 3–1 by Portsmouth. Good news is always relative, but my birth was pretty much the best thing that happened to any of them that day.

I should have been a Bury fan, really. Mum took me to games at Gigg Lane before I was born. They played in the second tier of the English leagues at the time and we lived a ten-minute walk from the ground. I have no excuses, I just had a dad that went to watch the Busby Babes every week.

It was either Bob Stokoe or Bobby Charlton, and Dad bought me a red-and-white rattle to clinch the deal.

In fairness, Uncle Dave left Bury to take the manager's job at Tranmere as I was about to turn seven. He invited me to travel on the Rovers' team coach to a pre-season friendly at Chester that August. I was 'inside' football from the very start.

The game is different on the inside. I have never coached a team in my life, and I've never taken a shot at goal that truly mattered. The only full-time work I've ever done has been spent in the company of people whose livelihoods depend on the outcome of football matches.

Many of my most valued friends in the world are football professionals. Just as with Uncle Dave, I have come to know their families and share their highs and lows. I have attended their weddings and their children's weddings. I have been to far too many funerals in recent years.

If I had a pound for every time I've been asked, 'Who do you support, Clive?' I would be writing these rambles from a private island. The answer is simply, 'Them.' I support my friends. I have come to know what a 'W' and an 'L' mean to them. 'W's are what make them happy, make them secure.

'But you're a United fan, right?'

Nope. I used to be. And if you had told me as I trooped gloomily away from Wembley after Tommy Docherty's team had been beaten in the 1976 FA Cup final that I would ever feel as bad about a defeat of any other club then I would have started a heated argument with you.

My commitment to United had probably strengthened during the three years I spent at university in Nottingham. Armed with a driving licence and a little spending money from holiday jobs, I was able to travel to some away matches in addition to my regular trips to Old Trafford. During the sobering season that United spent in the Second Division, I only missed half-a-dozen games.

It was the hooligan era. Football was making headlines for all the wrong reasons, and those of us that were making those headlines knew it and played up to it. When I say 'us', I don't mean me. On the occasions that I chose to travel on board the 'football special' from Manchester Victoria, I was back in with the Wythenshawe crew only for a few escapist hours.

I remained the only conscientiously-objecting hoodlum in football. I might have passed for a delinquent with my standard-issue patchwork jumper and loons, tartan scarf knotted around my wrist and voice raised in tune with the menacing chant of the day. But that was where my own menace ended.

I was there in the landing crafts when the battle cry went up to signal the next enemy engagement and I saw the front-line troops surge forward with a clamorous roar like the first soldiers over the top at Passchendaele, but my role was merely to observe and marvel. Like a ruffian version of Wilfred Owen, I quietly chronicled events for posterity, always taking a strategic backward step at the first inevitable tinkle of broken glass.

Not that there was anything at all poetic about those orchestrated acts of terror. Nothing. Anyone that attempts to glamorise them either lived for them or didn't get close enough to them to get scared. I did. The recurring scraps and scuffles that broke out without warning around every ground filled me with dread. When the violence escalated into gruesome clashes between feuding gangs, nobody was safe.

I was somehow sufficiently smart and careful enough to stay out of harm's way, but I heard enough half-bricks crash against the window of my train carriage to know that survival was as much a matter of luck as judgement. 'We're going to wreck your town' was often the red army's overture on arrival in Bristol, Hull, York, Blackpool or wherever that strange promotion campaign took us. There were some dire days on the way back to the top flight. I struggle to find much in the way of sentimentality or romance looking back now.

Why was I there? Why did I run the risks involved? Because I was a United fan. And because that was the only way to be a United away fan in 1974. For home games, I still met up with my dad to join him amid the grumpy civility of the flat caps and hot Bovril drinks in the Paddock. My life was good. Since starting at university, it had been garnished by all manner of guilty pleasures I could previously only fantasise about. Following my team was a real-life fantasy that came complete with wicked villains and hairy escapes. It was an adventure that I was nearing the end of.

I should have been a much better footballer than I was. Not only did I live next door to Uncle Dave, I played outside with his son every day. Robin Russell went on to become a highly respected coach and youth development chief but I could only ever talk a good game.

In the Darwinian order of the grammar school boarding house, evolution demanded that you either honed a capacity to fight your way out of a corner, or talk your way out. As a bit of a wuss, talking was my natural selection.

It was a rugby school. I have never played football at any truly competitive level. If I ever refer to the difficulty of getting a clean strike on a spinning ball during a commentary, it is a knowledge that I have acquired partly on five-a-side courts in after-work kickabouts but mainly from listening intently to those that really know. I was in a privileged position to listen and learn from day one.

When Uncle Dave signed a goalkeeper from St Johnstone in 1955, the new signing and his wife came to live with us for a couple of months while they were house-hunting. I didn't learn a great deal from Roy MacLaren at the time. Maybe a little help with walking, I'm not sure. I was 11 months old.

Roy and Jessie MacLaren became firm family friends from that day, though. We went to stay with them when they moved on to Sheffield Wednesday. Roy was Tony Barton's assistant manager when Aston Villa lifted the European Cup in 1982. I had good teachers.

Our house in Bury was a relatively modest semi-detached property on busy Radcliffe Road. We were semi-attached to the Russells next door. Neither ever featured on *Through the Keyhole*. Their main selling point was that they backed onto the grounds of Bury Sports Club, a multi-sports facility with enough mown grass for Robin and me to chase a football without a care in the world for hour after hour until Gladys blew a whistle to summon us back to the nest for tea.

My mum insists that I was always commentating out loud as I played. Mums are not necessarily the most reliable witnesses to the precise detail of their children's paths through life, particularly mums of only children like me. But it is beyond dispute that at some stage of my childhood, I began to add a running commentary to my solo mazys across the back garden. Which child of football didn't?

While I watched all of my early live football with Dad, it was Mum that championed my broadcast ambitions. In 1970, she entered her 15-year-old son in a BBC competition to select a commentator to join Kenneth Wolstenholme and David Coleman at the World Cup in Mexico. She was suitably miffed when I didn't even make the final shortlist with Ed Stewart, Ian St John and the eventual winner, Idwal Robling.

When I finally did make it onto a BBC World Cup team in 1994, I had to stop Mum writing a 'told-you-so' to the director general. When you watch football from the outside, you look after your team. When you get inside football, you look after your own.

Martin O'Neill became my first firm friend when I worked my way inside and onto local radio in 1975. Nearly twenty years later, he was manager of Wycombe Wanderers for their first season in the Football League. They drew top-flight Norwich City in the third round of the FA Cup and I was selected to commentate on the game for *Match of the Day.*

Wycombe gave a good account of themselves but two Chris Sutton goals put them in their place. I wrapped up the commentary, voiced a 45-second report for *Grandstand*, recorded a couple of bland post-match interviews and made my way into the Directors' tea room to catch up with Martin's family. It soon became apparent that his wife, Geraldine, wasn't talking to me.

After a few uneasy minutes in the VIP lounge, I made my apologies and went hunting for Martin, who was still entertaining John Deehan and the Norwich staff in his office.

'My wife's not very happy with you,' he said the moment I was ushered through the door.

'I'm sorry, what have I done?'

'Don't be sorry. She's usually not very happy with me,' Martin grinned.

My post-match report for *Grandstand* was the problem. Other than a few 'oohs' and 'aahs', I felt Norwich had controlled the game pretty comfortably and won deservedly. The real problem was that I said so in those 45 seconds that Geraldine had heard on returning to the lounge.

'I don't disagree with your assessment,' explained Martin. 'I thought we played well but not quite well enough.'

'Which is exactly what I said,' I protested.

'Yeah, but Geraldine didn't see the game that way. And she thinks that because you're my friend you should be saying we were robbed.'

Like a compromised judge or a hometown referee, maybe I should have been stood down from the engagement. While the job calls for strict objectivity, total neutrality is more difficult for a reporter or commentator to strike. We probably try so hard to balance the noises coming from our hearts with the ones echoing round our heads that we err on the side of equitability. But perhaps the wife of the losing manager isn't best placed to decide.

Back in the day before good old-fashioned phone-in and Twitter abuse, disgruntled fans would often pen hand-written letters to under-performing managers. Some were even daft enough to head their complaints with a home address. Geraldine spent many a diligent hour thumbing through the phone directory so that Martin could call them personally with a counter-argument.

Imagine the honest High Wycombe roofer coming home from a hard day's graft to be handed the phone by his wife.

'Do you know a Martin O'Neill?'

An hour later the roofer still hadn't got a word in edgeways.

Blood is considerably thicker than water but friendships forged through sport are pretty compact too. I could have added a zero or two to the advance for this book if I felt inclined to tell every tale that I have been witness to. Or party to. The only two occasions in my adult life where I have been beyond regrettably drunk were in the company of footballers. Neil Ruddock was largely responsible for one, the England women's team of 1995 the other. You can fill in your own blanks.

There was an instance during my early local radio days when a well-known player had made an unhappy leap from back to front pages via an extra-marital rendezvous. It was enough for our news editor to contemplate the extraordinary step of promoting a sports story from the very end of the hourly bulletin to the top if I could secure an interview with the charlatan. He'd been told I knew him well.

I knew the player in question so well that he was secretly holed up at my house. Journalistic integrity had to take a leave of absence in this instance. I pleaded ignorance.

Everyone in my business has received tip-offs from sources too precious to reveal, often so precious because they are such good friends. Friendship accounts rarely fall into serious debt if the underlying trust remains intact. Credit gained over years of shared rapport is good credit of a kind that one bad act will rarely wipe out completely.

The time when a bond is strained or tested is the very time to try to reinforce it. Damnation should be a last resort, not a default response to something said or posted in haste. There will be nobody left on Twitter worth following if the cancellers prevail.

The Good Samaritan must have had some bad habits too. I have an innate suspicion of people with a religious certainty that their way is the only way. They create a judgement culture in which the sole alternative to right is wrong, in which you are either the chosen or the infidels, the saved or the damned. It's called social media.

Twitter is a lawless town in a Spaghetti Western where anyone can fire at anyone. There isn't a sheriff for miles around.

Its reach is overstated and under-representative of the nation's population and yet my business is as smitten by it as Donald Trump was. We report its findings like they are real life. We use it not so much as a source but THE source. We authenticate disinformation, we air the most random of grievances.

Fake news is our fault for not telling actual stories well enough. We leave gaping gaps for unsubstantiated sources to fill with their own brand of poison. The job of the mainstream media is surely to check and to challenge Twitter tales, not merely to recite them.

We decry Twitter abuse at its chilling poles but we report all the crackpot theories and rants that sit very comfortably in the same threads. It is a cheap and easy news agency for any platform in the click business. And, yes, I look at it every day.

I view it from the security of a great job, a loving family and a full life. Many others don't or can't. Social media is a vehicle for good but vehicles are only as safe as their drivers.

Like most forms of abuse, online abuse is collateral damage from a weapon of our own making. Like porn, like gambling, like first person shooter games, we create additives to human behaviour and act surprised when human nature cultivates them to grow out of control. Like we never saw any of this coming.

Football people become both accustomed to and hardened by damning judgements of their best efforts. Public abuse is just a danger of the workplace. It comes with a territory that football players, managers and commentators share. It bonds us like inmates on the same cell block.

Friendships formed inside football must be built to last. The naturally competitive nature of the game demands that. Close friends regularly play against one another for the sport's highest honours. Sometimes, one will take the other's place in the team, even the manager's chair. Circumstances place unique strains on relationships and put associates in difficult positions too. Divided loyalties in football are tricky.

Of all the games that I've ever commentated on, the 1986 FA Cup final may have been the biggest in my world. Not only were Everton and Liverpool deep-seated local rivals, they were the two best teams in the land at the time. They had contested the title race into its final furlong and now they were to meet at Wembley for what was still the most cherished trophy of all back then.

What lifted it up and beyond the Champions League finals and England World Cup games that I would later cover for television audiences of 20 million or more was that I knew all of the players in the final personally. They were my age, my mates. My commentary for the local station on Merseyside, Radio City, was not going to compete with BBC or ITV for an audience, but it was going to throw up all kinds of diversions and dilemmas to the voice resounding in my headphones. My own.

Distractions are a life essential. I wouldn't have met my wife and soulmate had she not distracted me from watching a schoolboy rugby match. The mind stagnates if it never wanders off in search of something better, something different, something enriching and enlivening. The precarious balance of sport dictates that one man's heady triumph is another's heartbreaking defeat. Observing those defining moments with an open microphone in your hand is a mental juggling act.

Life is like that. There is no substitute for the undiluted pleasure in stirring the vital senses that keep us human, but the natural elation of pleasure often generates counter emotions of envy, jealousy, and resentment in others. We've all been in that hotel room next to the one in which an exhibitionist couple are noisily re-enacting the entire *Fifty Shades* back catalogue. You can't help but want their bed to collapse.

The commentator's neutrality is seriously challenged in the wake of the orgasmic celebrations that follow an important football match. The 1986 cup final was unimaginably important to some of my best friends.

At the time, I occasionally frequented a nightclub in Birkenhead called *Atmosphere*. The owner, Julian Russell, was a friend of Peter Stringfellow, who ran London's most famous hot spot. Peter issued an invitation to the cup-winning team through Julian. All I had to do was guarantee that the FA Cup would find its way to *Stringfellows* nightclub before that Saturday night was out. I had the contacts.

My final task before leaving Wembley after the game was to check that Craig Johnston and Jan Molby were on message to deliver the deal. They asked me to join them at the Liverpool team banquet at their hotel near Marble Arch before travelling on to *Stringfellows* with them. I don't know if the cup ever made it. I had a better offer.

I had already taken up an invite to join the vanquished Everton players at their post-match bash next to Kensington Gardens. I was neither a blue nor a red. I just felt as though I would rather help drown the sorrows of my beaten pals than share the champagne of the celebrating ones. I didn't deserve to be with the cup winners. I played no part in their victory. I could play a better part in consoling good friends in need of it.

There is an understandable feeling among many fans on the outside that the players and managers on the inside of the game don't feel defeat like they do. Okay, we are occasionally presented with tabloid evidence to support that. Footballers drinking to forget under lairy headlines.

But I've seen far more eyewitness evidence of how deeply professional players do feel the hurt of defeat. Pride, vanity, ego, call it what you will. Most footballers have too much of it simply to brush off defeat like a pesky fly.

The physical difference between a manager two weeks before he is sacked and two weeks after the axe falls is graphic. The removal of the hair shirt and sackcloth suit that weighs them down during the final helpless days is cruelty to be kind. The end of their attempts to turn back tidal waves of tsunami proportions will seem like the end of their world for a hang-over day or ten, but then they start to shed their stresses and strains and suddenly lose years from their overall appearance and demeanour too. The only mystery is that they go back in.

Something they put in the beer and wine that managers ceremonially share in their offices after games needs testing. I have never met a losing manager that truly wants to break bread with the men they've been trading insults with for the previous couple of hours. And yet, once they start to drink from the same bottle, they all take a vow to come back for more of the same. I tell you, those drinks are spiked.

During my time in Liverpool, I made the acquaintance of Dave Jones. He was an underrated defender in an Everton team that very nearly took off under Billy Bingham, then Gordon Lee in the late 1970s. It says a lot about him that when he retired from playing, he didn't open a pub or a bookies but instead took a role in the care sector working with 'problem children' on his native Merseyside.

At the start of 2000, Dave was arrested on charges of child abuse. If you are not familiar with the case, the charges were not only dropped but the motives of some of the alleged victims were later challenged and exposed as fraudulent. Dave was innocent on all grounds; he should never have been asked to step inside a court room.

I had picked up our friendship during the stirring cup runs of his first manager's job at Stockport. He had moved on to Southampton by the time the original charges were brought and was duly suspended by the club. He endured a horrible eighteen months before his name was cleared. When the case was first scheduled for the Crown Court, his solicitor phoned me to ask if I would consider making a character reference on Dave's behalf. It wasn't needed in the end, but my answer was, 'Yes, certainly.' My opinion of him could hardly have been higher.

Four years later, Dave was managing Wolves and I was commentating on their game at West Ham. Defeat came with calls from a section of travelling supporters for Jones to be sacked. At best, he has always been a rather sombre-looking individual with an unusually soft scouse twang. Dave was in a particularly funereal mood for the post-match interview. He knew he was under pressure.

'Do you think you will still be manager of Wolverhampton Wanderers this time next week?' I heard myself asking. I'm not sure quite why I went that far. Maybe I thought that it was expected of me, to show that I could ask the tough questions. The ITV highlights programme was not aired until the following day so we always felt an onus to 'move the story on' from the match itself as we fished for meaningful quotes after the game.

Dave did his gracious best to find an answer of sorts, but when I ended the interview and the camera stopped rolling, he looked rather disdainfully up at me before departing with a sarcastic, 'Thanks a lot, pal. Thanks for that.'

He was the Wolves manager the following weekend and for another four matches before the club thanked him for his services. I didn't sack him but I poured another teaspoon of fuel onto the fire starting to envelop him. His pal, his friend of more than 15 years, his character reference. 'Thanks for that.'

I am nobody's idea of a foot-in-the-door reporter but I always try to carry out my job with a respect for journalistic principles, through sound editorial judgement. I have not asked another manager whether he or she thought they were about to be dismissed since I put the question to Dave Jones in 2004. What's the point? What does it achieve beyond etching a couple more worry lines onto a pale face as the camera zooms in? It's not like it's going to be their decision anyway.

I've never understood those questions that television reporters shout across Downing Street at the scurrying figure of a cabinet minister heading into Number 10 for some bad news on the reshuffle front. 'Are you being replaced Chancellor?' Wtf?

It's vanity broadcasting, it's getting your booming voice on the film clip, it's following a tradition as time-honoured and as useless as Prime Minister's Questions. Maybe I fell into the trap at Upton Park, maybe Dave should have just punched my lights out. That would have ended the speculation.

My personal friendship with Roy Hodgson was an even stronger one when I found myself commentating on England's exit from Euro 2016 at Iceland's hands in Nice. The ITV editor on duty for the match – another firm friend, Mark Demuth – was well aware that I'd enjoyed a trusting and rewarding friend-ship with Roy for several years. My wife and I have dined out with Roy and Sheila. They are both bright, engaging company.

Maybe that is why Mark felt the need to press his magic button and speak privately in my ear with three minutes of the match remaining and England 2–1 down. All I ask of an editor in those situations when I am trying to talk and listen at the same time is that whatever they have to say is succinct and considered.

'Defeat will make Roy's position untenable. You need to say that,' was the succinct and considered message from mission control. It was a timely reminder of something I already knew.

It would be pushing it to say that any tiny recess of my mind began to wander to fine wine and fine conversations with Roy and Sheila at that moment . . . but I didn't half want England to equalise. Yes, for my country and my television channel and for Gary Neville, who had also been a very supportive member of the coaching team and for a million other reasons besides.

But mainly for Roy. To save a friend from losing the job he cherished more than any other, to save me the pain of having to condemn his England career in front of 20 million viewers. I waited another couple of minutes before reaching for the black cap. Roy waited about as long after the match before falling on his sword. As commentators in a visual medium, we are charged not to say the things that the audience can already see. Sometimes we are required to do just that for emphasis.

Who do I support? Managers, mainly managers. My support moves with them from club to club: my support for the ones that are helpful, the ones that are not belittling, the ones that don't make every post-match interview a trial of your ability not to take a swing at them, the ones that are friendly, the ones that are friends.

When Gordon Strachan replaced my friend Gareth Southgate as Middlesbrough boss in 2009, I took great delight at his failure to get good results. I didn't really know Gordon then. I had been on the receiving end of a couple of his more contrary interview performances, but the instant dislike I took to him from far away was purely a measure of my sympathy and backing for Gareth.

As fate would have it, Gordon later became a good friend too. When I confessed to the evil hex with which I had attempted to jinx him, he totally understood. It's normal, it's natural, it's what happens on the inside.

When Gordon's Scotland team played Gareth's England in two vital qualifiers for the last World Cup, both men trusted me with top-secret advanced information on their line-ups. They knew I would not misuse it, because they knew I thought and acted like an insider.

Even in my little sub-culture, there is bound to be a rivalry between commentators for jobs, awards and plaudits that brings out the green-eyed worst in us. We all get on with each other mainly because we are united by the same fear of cocking up. A 'Colemanballs' communion.

We are not footballers or managers but we are on the inside of the game. Like the Denis Laws and Dave Russells, our well-being depends on each performance we give and other people's opinion of it.

While we retain some of the uncorrupted wonder that once led us to run around the garden shouting names out, we cross over to the dark side when football becomes our income stream. Our view is immediately inside looking out.

The laws of football are the same within the plumb white lines that mark out the pristine playing surface at Wembley as they are on the rolling contours of the council rec, but that is where the similarities between professional and amateur football end. One is played for fun, the other for fortune. One is entertainment, the other is business. You're either an insider or you're on the outside looking in.

The pro game tries to bridge the divide by branding itself as an entertainment business like music or cinema. It's not. Movie-goers don't turn up sporting studio colours, rock fans don't boo the support act. The paying customers at football grounds want entertaining but they also want to win. If they are forced to choose between the two, most of them will plump for that extra man in midfield. Sod the fantasy football.

You do occasionally hear supporters bemoaning the defensive style of their team, but you also hear fans of yo-yo clubs wishing that they were winning games in the Championship rather than losing every week in the Premier League. The pursuit of some kind of success is part of the binding contract you make with your chosen club whether you buy it or follow it. Better parking, cheaper seats and warmer Bovril are welcome extras but most fans will pay a little more to queue a bit longer to see a winning team.

Winning teams are created by shrewd recruitment. Football is a labour-intensive industry. It's played by human beings, not systems or philosophies. It is easy to waste money in football's marketplace but it is hard to spend well when you've got no money in the first place. The best players fetch the best prices and earn the best wages. Value for the money you invest in recruitment depends largely on how much money you've got and how much you can afford to waste on the occasional mistake.

So, the business model has got to work for a club to finance the purchase of the men and women that bring success. Selling your stadium's century-old name or selling a majority shareholding to a faceless foreign investment group are both classed as business models now. If winning football matches is central to the entertainment, then you'll need a fit and proper budget from your fit and proper owners. Business before pleasure. In football, the big dogs wag the tail.

Business insiders are conditioned to being hard-nosed and hard of hearing when their customers complain. The danger for broadcasters and journalists who are invited to become honorary insiders is that we start to think like them, that we privately develop the same lofty contempt for a public that doesn't quite understand the untold complexities of trying to bring success to them. We spend so much time in dressing-room corridors and press rooms talking football talk with football professionals that we can quickly lose touch with the reality of being a fan, lose contact with the soul of the very people we've been employed to serve. We become collaborators rather than correspondents.

Reading out a few tweets on air doesn't meet our responsibility to connect with our listeners and viewers in their language, on their terms. We need to step outside and see the game from their seat, their sofa. I watch and listen to a lot of TV and radio football. It's part of my job to. Seeing it from the other side of the screen is a critical touchstone for me. If I'm out on the circuit commentating on three or four games a week, I think there is a danger of me starting to miss the point of what I'm trying to do. My classroom for continuing to learn more about commentary and communication is my lounge at home, my teachers are my peers.

Confession. I mark every piece of work they do. I critique my own work even more closely. It's how I look to get better, to broaden my horizons, to stay relevant, to screen-grab the big picture.

The lockdowns and shutdowns of the past year cut us all off from a host of realities beyond our own. Just caring for our families and for ourselves was enough of a challenge to worry too much about that bigger picture. Televised football provided a distraction for people that enjoyed watching it but, even to someone that relies on the games being played for an income, covering them was a surreal and uncomfortable experience. I knew I was lucky to be there and for my voice to be echoing around the tumbleweed of a deserted stadium but I think I struggled to convey just how empty it felt, how sanitised it was.

I didn't want to be disrespectful to all of the initiatives and protocols that had been religiously followed in order to get this show on the road but a show is what it was. Football is a collective, not an assortment of distanced bubbles. It never felt quite right but I didn't know how to say it from my privileged position on the inside.

The default was to fawn and simper like Keats or Shelley over the impossible heartache of silent football without ever quite defining exactly how the game missed its fans. Yes, we missed the atmosphere, the sense of theatre, the sounds, the odours, the communal quickening of the pulse, the choreographed dance lines of support and the cyclonic roars that greeted a goal. But football missed the jeers and derision too. It missed the gathering unease and frustration with misplaced passes and misplaced optimism. It missed the fevered finger-pointing and rabid rants of disgust. It missed the scrutiny and sentence of people that had paid 'good money to watch this rubbish'. It missed advocacy and verification. It missed its jury.

I was often asked whether the absence of fans had changed my approach to commentary. It was a good question. But the more Ghost Town games I worked on, the less I thought about technique and whether I needed to adopt a more con-versational style in order to fill the natural pauses, and the more I wondered what the average football fan was making of yet another day of wall-to-wall games, another subscription, another diverse panel of pundits, another street poet with a pining ode to their banishment. All part of the show.

It was Jurgen Klopp that labelled football 'the most important of the least important things.' I think that was a good guide for editorialising the content we were putting out from barren stadia and off-tube voice-over booths, from the lonely planet we were whisked away to in order to narrate Project Restart.

I may be wrong but my Twitter feed suggested that the lighter touch of a commentator like Ally McCoist became the waft of fresh air that kept supporters' oxygen levels up until they could get back to their favourite inhaler and catch a breath of it for themselves. Football's importance is only relative at the best of times. At the worst of times, it is no more than a brief distraction. It was no time for pondering solemnity in commentary.

Ally can read a football match as well as any expert but he can read the room too. He can be irreverent and fond because football is there as an antidote to sombre, sober reality. It doesn't need to try to create its own out of VAR decisions, muscle fatigue or fixture pile-ups. Ally's love for the game is expressed with a smile and a wink and an 'I'll tell you what. . .' of enjoyment and marvel.

He is an insider. Ally has relied on football for a living as a player, manager and now broadcaster. His magic trick is simply an ability to take a step back and view his profession from the outside, to see it how the fans see it and so be able to represent them and their position when he picks up a microphone and goes back on the inside. If I changed and adapted to commentating on 'fake crowd' football, it was by trying to capture Ally's gentle and disarming perspective and not to risk patronising the most essential people in football, the people that football didn't realise just how much it would miss. The glorious outsiders. The fans who dream the dreams that furnish my collection of clichés.

The jarring contrast between dreams and realities was brought home to me with the demise of Bury Football Club in 2019. Many have stood on the same ledge, most have been somehow talked down. It is easy to be sad about the disappearance of my town from the reading of the classified results; it is as easy to become cynical.

Football finances are managed by hearts as much as heads. Or they are until they no longer add up. The black-and-white of the neat columns in the annual accounts make no mention of communal identity or social belonging. I feel regularly humbled by how many eulogies to lost loved ones make mention of the football team the deceased supported. This game, my business. It means so much to so many.

Any dreams that I entertained as I repeatedly rattled the hinges of the garage doors until my school shoes were scuffed from my shooting practice had nothing whatsoever to do with win bonuses or loyalty payments. I didn't want to play in a particular competition or for a chosen manager, I just wanted to play. The glory was in the game, not in the prize.

It is impossible to keep that innocence when football opens its doors to you. As soon as you peep behind the curtains at any event, your belief in magic is challenged. You see the wires and the workings, you see the discarded scenery and costumes, you see Santa without his beard.

Uncle Dave was the first person to take me backstage at a football club. As a child, you can barely take in the Gulliver proportions of the players that wrench your wrist with their handshakes, the vivid greenness of the grass as the grounds-man studiously mows his perfect strips, the equine clop of the players' studs on the concrete walkway to the pitch.

I still love the first glimpse of the inside of a stadium as I climb the steps from the concourse. It is one of those experiences that keeps the connection, keeps the consternation of the Bury boy that got to live and work in his Narnia. To carry a pass that takes you past the suspicious nod of the security guys and into the dressing-room area where even the cameras rarely get to roll is still a privilege.

Into the dreamland as far as the reality of introducing yourself to another new manager following another cruel sacking. Outside to in.

Dave Russell was one of the few managers afforded the luxury of choosing his own moment to 'move upstairs' after eight years in charge at Tranmere. He stayed with the club for as long again as general manager. There is a Dave Russell Suite at Prenton Park to this day. His son Robin is still a respected coaching consultant. Once an insider, always an insider.

So, when some wizened old Southampton scout introduced himself to the parents of a couple of lads in my son's Under-10s team many years ago, was it my place to flex my inside knowledge and shoot down their balloon before the burner had even ignited . . . to tell them that I didn't think their boys were quite good enough? Nah.

Uncle Dave didn't do anything like that to me and my fantasies when I was screaming 'and now Law finds Tyldesley' to a few rose trees and a couple of jumpers for goals in his garden in Bury. Insiders are there to create dreams for those on the outside, never to break them.

First team photo: (from right to left) Dad, Me, Auntie Gladys,
Uncle Dave, Robin.

CLIVE TYLDESLEY BSc

Industrial Economics (with Politics)

University of Nottingham 1972–75

I learnt nothing at university. Nothing and everything.

I didn't want to take Economics and I can't recall much of what I was taught. There were four media-related courses in the whole of the British further education system in 1972 and I couldn't get an offer from any of them. Now, there seem to be at least four at every university and college.

It was a wonderful time to be a student. All the tuition was free, all the major bands did varsity tours, all the girls were on the pill. If that makes me sound like a bit of a player, I may well have been guilty as charged back then. Hormone heavy, qualms light.

Joni Mitchell's tender eloquence managed to teach me a little about relationships but that doesn't mean that I didn't love shaking my long, lank hair to Ziggy Stardust too. Wham, bam, thank you ma'am. My recreational drugs were only ever Bulmers and B&H but I got high on the life of Riley.

Many undergraduates suffered a first-year plague of homesickness. I hadn't really known a family home for seven years. University was like boarding school with no rules and mixed dormitories. I was in late adolescent Disneyland. I went on every ride.

I volunteered for the social committee that booked all the union music gigs, I volunteered to edit the student newspaper and I volunteered to write the university comedy revue that we performed at a couple of Edinburgh Festivals. I created my own spare-time media course.

My dad was setting up his own business supplying oil to small factories around Manchester and he was gently trying to lead me in the direction of sales and marketing. I did a deal with him. If I couldn't crack a career in media within a year of graduating, I would bite the business bullet.

Before that year was out, Dad was standing in the press tent at the Open Championship listening to me interview the winner, Johnny Miller. I'd dodged that bullet forever.

Radio City, 1978. Diamond days.

3

CLOUGHIE

Brian Clough was my first manager.

I was never nearly good enough to play for him – or anyone else for that matter – but as Radio Trent's dedicated Nottingham Forest reporter, my life was ruled by his timekeeping and his moods throughout my first couple of years in broadcasting.

I spent many an hour waiting in the corridor outside his office for a word with him. If it ever actually came, it was usually 'no'. But If Cloughie said 'yes', the content was as spellbinding to listen to as it was scary to coax out of him. I was absolutely terrified of him, and I was in good company.

The best interview he gave me was in February 1976. The previous day, Brian had dramatically and surprisingly turned down an offer to return to Derby County. It was a difficult, emotional decision. I was asking him to explain it for a local radio station that covered the two cities closest to his family home.

After three minutes of heartfelt reasoning, his voice suddenly broke almost to a whimper at the end of a sentence and he leant across the two rotating wheels of the tape machine and pressed the 'Stop' button himself. 'And that, young man, is your out,' he said softly. I had asked questions that his head and his heart were offering conflicting answers to. Time to end the interview.

Brian Clough was a brazen performer when he was shooting the breeze with David Frost or Michael Parkinson, calling out Muhammad Ali to a prime-time audience. Cocky and pompous, his put-downs could be disdainful and demeaning. Old Big Head grew from a young big-mouth of a television pundit full of his own opinion and dismissive of others.

He could be rude, he could pick you apart until you fell to pieces in front of him. And yet the same man softly charmed my parents when he made a surprise appearance (in green sweat top and tracksuit bottoms) at the restaurant where I held my leaving-do. Surprise was his favourite weapon.

You learn a lot from the first football people you meet when you get 'inside track'. I remember an early interview I did with Martin O'Neill in the empty home team dressing-room after training one afternoon. Brian just happened to be walking down the corridor and overheard our conversation.

The next thing I knew, the manager had grabbed me roughly by the arm and was marching me out of the changing area in mid interview. We stopped at the open door for a lecture on trespassing.

'Son, are you in my team? Do you play for Nottingham Forest?' he began in that whiney, breathy tone of his.

'No, Mr Clough.'

'Then you don't come in my dressing-room. Understood?'

I've understood from that day forwards. I have crossed the threshold of many a dressing-room from Wembley to the Maracana but always with trepidation, always looking over my shoulder for another finger-wagging rebuke. He taught me a lot, he taught me without trying. I even graduated from 'son' to 'young man' after a few weeks in his domain. His favourite farewell was always, 'Be Good.' I sign autographs with the same message to this day and remember him every time I do.

Of all the great achievers in football that I've known and been around, Cloughie remains the greatest mystery to me. Maybe it's because he was the first mystery and I still had wide eyes and a narrow understanding of his profession in my rookie years. While he set his own rules about everything from dressing-room access to keeping your hands out of your pockets, he seemed to manage on the hoof, largely by instinct, almost by hunch. You never knew quite what was coming next with Brian Clough.

But did he?! Therein lies the rub.

On reflection, surprise is in itself a brilliant managerial strategy. Unease is a great motivator. Fear works in the short-term and even many of Brian's senior players shared my healthy fear of him.

My first boss in television could be a fearsome man but, once his reprimands became a matter of routine, they lost some of their shock value and potency. Making people feel ill at ease, making them jumpy, putting them on edge, off guard . . . that gives an executive more lasting control over his or her charges than high decibel brow-beating. Psychological control.

O'Neill was the brightest button in that dressing-room he got me chucked out of. His relationship with Cloughie was fascinating. People often ask if a great manager or player of yesteryear would have been as successful in contemporary football. As a unit of measure, it means nothing. You are trying to compare *Super Mario* with *Fortnite*. As a catalyst for whimsical discussion, it has an ongoing curiosity appeal.

I am not convinced that Brian Clough could have handled the modern footballer, but his handling of Martin O'Neill back in the mid-1970s may just challenge that view.

Varsity-educated, the erudite Irishman from an Ulster nationalist family was on the way to becoming a criminal lawyer when football came calling. Smart and witty, he would have made a scything barrister in adversarial courtroom jousts. Instead, he dropped out of Queen's University in Belfast to take on the case of trying to convince Cloughie that he was as good a player as O'Neill believed himself to be.

The trial ran throughout their six years together at Forest. The jury was never 'out' as such because, for the most part, Cloughie kept picking O'Neill in his teams. He just didn't give him much credit for the honours they won. If the manager's mental interrogation was part of a cunning plan to spur the player on, it worked a treat. Nobody grafted harder for his winners' medals.

It was almost as if he was constantly looking across to the touchline for the reward of one of those animated 'thumbs ups' that his great friend John Robertson seemed to get after every attack. He will tell you they rarely came.

Instead, O'Neill remembers the half-time barneys that he had with Cloughie as their two worlds collided. It was like he was forever trying to prove himself, maybe even prove the boss wrong. It was like Cloughie was forever testing Martin, daring him to crack and lash out. They worked together on that same narrow ledge season after season. Inspired man-management? That is the question.

O'Neill was not your average footballer. His manic fascination with criminal law did not drop off when he dropped out
of university. In 1982, he was part of a Norwich City squad that
arrived on Merseyside one September Friday evening to prepare for a match against Everton the next day. I was working
for a Liverpool radio station by then and he summoned me to
meet him at the team hotel.

Instead of a quiet coffee and catch-up, Martin sneaked out
of camp and directed me to drive to a dead-end back street
near Anfield. I had lived on Merseyside for five years by then,
but I had never heard of Wolverton Street. Why would I? I had
never studied the case of William Herbert Wallace and the
murder of his wife Julia in the sitting room of their house in
Wolverton Street in 1931. Martin knew the case like he had
prosecuted it.

Wallace's alibi was based on a meeting with a mysterious insurance agent in Menlove Gardens East around about
the time of the murder. Menlove Gardens East didn't exist.
Menlove Gardens West, North and South did, and Martin
and I visited them just to make sure. Then, we made our way
to the dimly-lit cul-de-sac where the tragic Mrs Wallace had
waited for her husband to return home. It looked like the set
from *10 Rillington Place.*

Martin stared at the murder house for a few moments, then
stepped out of my car for a closer look. A much closer look.
Next thing I knew, he was knocking at the door at 8 o'clock on
a Friday night and asking the residents if he could come inside
to inspect the modest parlour where Julia had been savagely
beaten to death more than 50 years earlier.

Am I painting a picture of an intense and insistent young

educated Irishman? Cloughie had a match on his hands with Martin O'Neill.

Brian had an innate suspicion of academic intelligence. It's not uncommon. It is almost inevitable in the sixth of nine children raised on Teesside through the World War II. He failed his 11-plus and admitted he didn't afford his school days the same attention and ambition that carried him into the England team and everything else that followed . . . followed despite his lack of an 'education.'

O'Neill's background is hardly typical but it is one of the great myths of our national game that footballers are 'thick.' Most of them possess a street wisdom that would get the better of a conclave of learned professors and scholars. You won't find a completed *Times* crossword in a Premier League dressing-room, but the Lord Chief Justice and the Vice-Chancellor of Oxford University wouldn't last a second in there.

To get by in the caustic, cutting language of football banter, you need to be light on your feet, to be sure of yourself, sure of your ability to give as good as you get. It is a savage jungle that tries to root out the weak before they can let the rest of the side down. The culture is not without its flaws and, sadly, it's not without its victims. It's changing but it's not changed. Manning up is still the default.

Brian demanded a level of old school manhood from those that worked under him, players and local radio reporters alike. The whole notion of such a primitive regime is considered antiquated and obsolete now, but it's not. Not in football. I think you'll find it is still 1980 in so many dressing-rooms at so many levels. There may be genuine efforts afoot to change all that but football can take some laboured dragging into its next era. Remodelling the time-honoured customs of the game is a slow and reluctant process. Look at VAR.

Not many of Cloughie's former players would tell you that they loved every minute they spent with him. One of the features of his management style was how much time he actually spent apart from his players. The boss's mid-season sunshine breaks were probably welcomed by one and all. He was a 'less is more' manager.

It was not unusual for him to stay away from the training ground until Friday of a match week. The players knew exactly what he wanted of them. His appearances hotfoot from the squash court were merely for emphasis, for impact. If your name was on his team-sheet, you had already bought into his ways. Or else.

The undisputed champions pick their fights. If ever Brian thought he was heading for a fight with even a new signing, the parting of the ways was swift and final. Stan Bowles, Asa Hartford, Justin Fashanu, Gary Megson. All gone in no time, all distinctive characters.

Not that he minded personality and presence in the players he rated. Larry Lloyd regularly tangled with the manager en route to his two European Cup winners' medals. He was repeatedly fined for breaking the rules of the establishment. It was some kind of loathe-hate relationship, but then how many of Cloughie's professional associations were a barrel of laughs, or ever meant to be?

The love, the respect, the gratitude came later. Few of us that enjoyed any level of connection with Brian will ever forget it or how we benefited from it. Like so many, Lloyd's career peaked under Cloughie in his thirties.

Recruitment was the key to many of the miracles that he somehow worked. The collection of unknowns and misfits that he pulled together for the epic voyage from the Second Division to European champions was like the cast of *The Magnificent Seven*, *The Italian Job* or *X-Men*. When someone shows a faith in you that you barely deserve, the debt is eternal.

Kenny Burns had a back-story from an early episode of *Taggart*. Liked a drink, liked a bet, liked a ruck etc. A craggy battering ram of a forward converted and honed into a polished gemstone of a central defender. From a 'previous job', John McGovern, Archie Gemmill and John O'Hare were recruited. Tony Woodcock had been farmed out on loan to Lincoln and Doncaster before getting the call, Garry Birtles was a carpet fitter playing part-time for Long Eaton United, Frank Clark was pushing 32 when he joined this vigilante group. You couldn't make it up.

Peter Taylor takes a lot of the credit for a lot of the above. If you knew Peter, taking credit came fairly naturally to him, but then so did unearthing rare football talent. The chemistry between a football manager and his faithful assistant should be the stuff of research doctorates. There is a thesis paper on the subject crying out to be written. Clough and Taylor were just better together. Beyond rationale but beyond doubt.

Peter was good to me. He was particularly good to me when Brian was away on one of his half-term holidays. All of a sudden, I didn't have to wait for an interview with the duty manager. Peter loved the sound of his own stuttering voice teasing us all about possible new signings. They were his chosen specialist subject and it was almost as if he enjoyed a little play while the big cat was away. My job was easier when

Brian was on a Spanish sunbed but not nearly as exciting or edifying.

Charisma is a misty, cryptic quality. A shroud of wonder. Cloughie was the centre of attention in every room he walked into. Aura. You never forgot time spent in his magnetic company. You always wanted more of it, wanted more of him however uncomfortable the last dose had been. As a broadcaster, I was straight in at the deep end.

My formal education ended at Nottingham University and my professional education began at Nottingham Forest in the same week. Radio Trent came on air the day I graduated in July 1975 and I read my first voice-over into a news bulletin three or four hours after shedding my cap and gown. I was as nervous as a virgin.

Most of my earliest broadcasts were as a late-night rock DJ for an audience whose mood music was endless guitar solos to consume midnight student feasts to but I always volunteered to help with anything on the sports front. That was where my heart was.

I pestered the station's programme controller, Bob Snyder, for months leading up to the launch date. Three weeks before I sat my finals, he called me at my shabby student house off Lenton Boulevard and began by telling me that I had to stop calling in at the studios every time I was in the city centre.

'We have got building work going on,' he said with an irritated air. 'I've got to put a stop to you just walking in here like you own the place. There's only one thing I can do, I'm afraid.'

Suddenly, it was me who was afraid. My employment-chasing policy of 'just keep knocking on doors until one opens' was about to slam one shut in my face. The one I most dearly wanted to get my foot in.

'I'm just going to have to offer you a job,' Bob said without changing tone.

'What?'

'A job. Broadcast assistant. You can say "yes" if you like.'

'Yes,' I spluttered over my Economics revision.

'Good. Now stay away until you've done your exams.'

'Er, what degree do I need?' I asked without thinking. My new boss roared with laughter on the other end of the phone.

'You don't need a degree to make tea.'

My tea was good enough to earn me a permanent post on the station's sports team within a couple of months of joining. Once I had played all of my favourite albums and failed to seduce any students with invitations to join me for my midnight show, I set my career course for becoming the next John Motson rather than the next Bob Harris.

Forest finished eighth in the Second Division during the first season that I began to wrap my tonsils around names like Barry Butlin and Bert Bowery. They were no more or less famous or important than Viv Anderson and Ian Bowyer at the time. They just never became European champions.

Neighbours Notts County actually finished higher in the table at the end of Clough's first full season in charge. They were managed by a delightfully weird and gnarled old Scot by the name of Jimmy Sirrel. He may just be the most difficult interviewee I've ever encountered.

'Why did you leave Les Bradd out of the team today, Jimmy?'

Endless pause.

'Why does a worm squirm?'

Answers like that would leave even Jeremy Paxman with nowhere to go.

Mercifully, I was detailed permanently to the Forest beat for the following season. Clough and Taylor were reunited that summer of 1976. Within four years they had only won and retained the European Cup. Messrs Bowyer, Anderson, McGovern, O'Hare, Robertson, Clark, Woodcock and O'Neill went the whole journey with them.

The football principles that were handed down by Cloughie changed little along the way. Those big personalities were allowed to direct and shape the character of the whole collective.

Of the many differences between football then and now, one of the strangest is how much noisier a match was in 1980. Talking is lauded as a vaunted skill by modern managers. The simple act of vibrating the voice box and speaking to a team-mate is rated as highly as pace or aerial prowess in the contemporary game.

In the twenty-first century, a 'talker' like Conor Coady or Jordan Henderson is singled out for praise simply by opening his mouth. In the twentieth century, most players never shut up. Maybe a 'Keane rant' will be revered like a 'Cruyff turn' in years to come.

It's probably a by-product of an era in which a conversation is held between tapping fingers rather than wagging tongues. We don't even take our eyes off our devices to cross a busy road. Today's players motivate one another via WhatsApp groups.

Clough teams were talking teams. His voice was inevitably the loudest and last in the conversation but that conversation ran from first to last whistle. Post-match analysis was not the kind that traced the blame trail for a lost goal via video review back to a misplaced pass five minutes earlier. Justice was meted out on the spot. Take your bollocking and move on.

To call it simple football is misleading because Forest could dazzle and delight but any attempt to sanctify their play or make it sound scholarly and scientific was given short and shrill shrift.

Nottingham is a city of less than 300,000 people. It has more of the feel of a market town than a major conurbation. Of communities of a similar size, only Eindhoven and Porto have welcomed European football's most prized possession to tour their streets since then. Each, once, not twice.

I left town in the spring of 1977 to join Merseyside's commercial station, Radio City. Liverpool were weeks away from lifting their first European Cup. Nottingham Forest was just a name on the pools coupon at the time. Eighteen months later, Clough's team had beaten Liverpool in a League Cup final and knocked the champions out of Europe. I was once turned away from the door of a popular scouse nightspot for being 'that Forest fan'. New battle lines had been dramatically drawn.

Cloughie was invited to the Radio Trent Christmas party in 1976. Not an invitation he was ever likely to take up, but I was coerced by my co-workers into going through with the formality of asking him.

'Will you all be having a few beers?' he enquired with a wearily knowing sigh.

'Yes,' I replied enthusiastically.

A warm smile came over his ruddy face as he peeled four £10 notes from a wad in his pocket and buried them in the palm of my hand.

'Get everyone a drink from me.'

And so, in the same sentence that I first chronicle his famed kindness, I also introduce the word 'drink' to this account of my encounters with Brian Clough.

Alcohol was the only opponent that ever gave him a good hiding. That is not my opinion, it is a matter of record. I saw his blotched complexion for myself, I heard his words slur, I remember the uneasy brume that wafted through the corridors at the City Ground on the days when the whisper was that 'he's been on it'. 'It' was all over his breath and his manner some afternoons. They were not the afternoons that you hung around.

I didn't ever feel that I was in a position to challenge him about his drinking, but that is a pretty miserable defence. I did once get laid into a couple of Forest committee members about the fact that it was allowed to go on to the ruination of a very special man, but then that was maybe just guilt. I think I gave them a piece of my belated mind after I'd had a couple of drinks myself. Enough said.

Nobody stopped him. I guess if his marvellous wife, Barbara, couldn't then it was a hopeless task. Brian knew it, admitted it but couldn't stop it either.

Judging people without reference to the context of the era in which they stumbled and fell is too easy, too convenient. I'm obviously not talking about Harvey Weinstein or Jimmy

Savile or Barry Bennell. Grim crimes are grim crimes in any generation. They hold up a cracked mirror to everyone of my age. We cannot and should not escape their stark reflection.

Historical judgements are formed on dangerous ground. If time and experience do not improve our understanding of how the earth turns, what the hell are we all doing on it in the first place? Experience bloody well should change our attitudes and practices.

Mistakes are a massive part of experience.

We cannot learn from our mistakes if the public punishment for them is always a life term. Forgiveness is part of progress. Compassion is a show of strength, not weakness.

I sometimes feel surrounded by jumped-up, self-appointed magistrates handing out on-the-spot fines for my every manoeuvre. One good deed deserves another virtue-signalling charge. Where did we suddenly attain the power to read the minds and motives of people we will never meet and summarily condemn them without any right to appeal?

These are uncertain times and yet the censure is so certain, so damning. After a decade of watching him, I can't make my mind up about David de Gea's keeping and yet total strangers are instantly and absolutely positive that I am a legitimate target on the strength of one phrase among the thousand I improvise during a commentary.

The best teachers in our lives ask questions of us, they don't deliver lectures and punishments. Any verdicts they reach about us are always open to retrial and the chance of redemption. They build bridges for us, not walls.

During the first lockdown in the Spring of 2020, people seemed to be looking out for one another more. We found renewed levels of appreciation, kindness and perspective. The world is a small place when the whole globe is under attack.

But it didn't take long for us to retreat back into our factions and self-interests. Opinions hardened again. Sides were picked for the next round of contests. Any and every comment was either a decree or it was viewed as shaming someone or something. The subsidence of centre ground has left us staring at one another across deep voids of intolerance. Blessed are the peacemakers but good luck with that.

In 1945, the people who saved the freedom of the world that my dad fought for drew their arbitrary lines across their maps and thought they had divvied up peaceful, lasting solutions. Of course, they made mistakes. Nobody had been called upon to do what they were doing before. Nothing that is any good has ever been created without mistakes.

Too many historical judgements are made by people that haven't been around for long enough to make their own mistakes and gather the experience that matures and eventually defines us. How will we all be judged in a hundred years when we have polluted the planet close to extinction? I tend to steer clear of retrospective judgements.

My main retrospective issue with Brian Clough's drink problem is that people still dine out on it, still tell the tales, still embroider the stories, still take the fee for their tawdry comedic value. I came across Brian again as part of ITV's backup team in London for the 1986 World Cup. He was a mess, a man to avoid. Recollections of his crass behaviour, of his faded cognisance are as vivid as any of his previous brilliance. As vivid and as haunting.

So, the ripping yarns about how he served his players a

glass of wine with lunch before their defiant European Cup display at Anfield in 1978 are fine but only to a point. The Chablis Supérieur is not the reason they held Liverpool, not the key to Brian Clough's breathtaking record of success. They won, he won, despite, not because of, those supposed aids to relaxation. He fortified his team in many other ways, uncorked the potential in frustrated talents by giving them a culture and a ball to pass.

Which brings me back to Martin O'Neill.

Cloughie was a tactile man. He threw a couple of infamous haymakers in his time but most of his body contacts were hugs and squeezes and even the occasional outrageous kiss. He wanted to be loved, he just went about it in a strange way with certain people. He never exchanged any cuddles with O'Neill but neither did he send him packing. Brian was proud and stubborn but he knew a player when he saw one.

He also knew that O'Neill could be every bit as proud and stubborn too. Here was a personality and an intellect that posed a threat to his authoritarian man-management approach. It was a threat that he took on to the lasting appreciation of both of them.

Their later meetings were cordial and friendly. Cloughie had always told O'Neill that he would make a good manager one day. The boss was right again. The biggest compliment Martin paid Brian was that some of his management techniques echoed Cloughie's own. Sincere flattery indeed.

But I must have a favourite Clough story, right? Oh yes.

It was 21 August 1976. My 22nd birthday, the opening day of the new league season. Forest's first fixture was at Fulham and I had been granted permission to travel with the club party by train to London. Departure was at 9.30. I was at Nottingham Midland station by 8.45.

It was a sun-kissed morning but I was formally dressed in a double-breasted blazer, grey pleated 'slacks' and shiny black shoes. The jacket was even a similar shade of blue to the club's own. My carefully-chosen wardrobe was set off by a Persil-white button-down shirt. I looked ready for a golf club prizegiving.

I was first to take my seat in one of the club's two allocated private coaches . . . by about 20 minutes.

When Brian arrived, he breezed past me with a boisterous 'good morning, young man' before checking his stride and returning to the table I was now sharing with a trusted friend, John Lawson of the *Evening Post*. The manager's two hands came to rest on the table as he leant over me and took an exasperated breath before delivering his sermon.

'Young man, you're very welcome to travel with the Nottingham Forest official party, but when you do, we expect you to wear a tie, understood?'

'I'm sorry, Mr Clough. I didn't know.'

First black mark of the day gathered in record time. I put on my stern, sad face and waited for the manager to move on to the more important matters of the day in the next coach. He didn't.

'Young man, you are very welcome to travel with the Nottingham Forest official party, but when you do, we do expect you to wear a tie,' he repeated pointedly without moving an inch.

'I'm really sorry. I've got money, I'll buy a tie as soon as we get to London. It won't happen again.'

I was now blushing, throbbing, sinking, gulping and a few other '-ings' besides. Brian wasn't going anywhere.

'Young man, as I've already said, you are most welcome to travel with the Nottingham Forest official party, but when you do, you . . . wear . . . a . . . tie.' And with the delivery of the final wailing word, a crumpled pound note suddenly appeared on the table and Brian turned and walked on.

'Train leaves in 15 minutes,' he added as if making a platform announcement.

I spent the next 13 of those 15 minutes, sprinting out of the station and rushing down towards Canal Street where, momentously, a gent's outfitters was just opening for business. An instant purchase was completed and I put on the burners back up the hill to the station entrance above which the giant clock was almost audibly ticking towards half past.

I was in my seat, tie in place, a good two minutes before the whistle blew for the train to roll south.

On 18 June 1994, Colombia faced Romania on the second day of the World Cup. The temperature inside the Pasadena Rose Bowl was over 35 degrees C. There was not a glimpse of shade. I sat in my commentary position in a short-sleeved shirt and chinos. I was wearing a tie. I had worn a tie to every game I worked on for the previous 18 years.

I was sweating even more profusely than I was after I'd slumped back into my train seat on that fateful morning in Nottingham in 1976, so I loosened the tie before the teams came out. Nothing terrible happened to me in the first half so, during the interval, I took it off completely.

If Brian ever appears to you as a ghostly spectre, promise me you won't tell him.

FIRST JOB:

Radio Trent

Independent Local Radio station, Nottingham

1975–77

The first break is always the biggest break.

If I had not been in Nottingham at the same time as Radio Trent was coming on air, I might not be writing this now. I was 20, I was enthusiastic, I was cheap and I was local. A brand new radio station has room for someone like that to grow.

Independent Local Radio had only been around for eighteen months or so. Capital, Clyde, Piccadilly and Metro were among the pioneers, Trent was part of the second tranche of pop-based commercial stations that were legally launched to replace the sound of the sunken pirate ships of the 1960s.

David 'Kid' Jensen, of considerable fame as a Radio Luxembourg DJ, was signed by Trent and hosted the Saturday afternoon sports show. The novel idea was to try to cut through some of the jargon of sporting vernacular by getting 'Kid' to question terms and phrases that his Canadian upbringing had never exposed him to before. The first lunchtime cricket scoreboard lasted about half an hour!

'At Trent Bridge, Nottinghamshire, 234 . . .'

'Is that 234 goals?'

'Nottinghamshire 234 runs for six wickets . . .'

'Six wickets? What are they?'

'234 runs with six men out, declared . . .'

'Declared what?!'

It was an idea we quickly had to revamp.

ILR did quickly become an established and trusted part of local and national sports coverage. It was the testing ground for the careers of Jeff Stelling, Steve Rider, Dougie Donnelly and many others. The likes of Tony Butler and Tom Tyrrell became synonymous with their regions. During my time in radio, I worked directly alongside both Elton Welsby and Richard Keys.

When I was driven past a trail of fleeing refugees to a hotel in beleaguered Belgrade in 1995 for some filming on a BBC documentary I was involved in, there were two television war correspondents eating in the hotel restaurant on arrival, Paul Davies of ITN and Ben Brown of the BBC. I'd shared a local radio newsroom in Liverpool with the pair of them. ILR stations were serious operations and also seriously good classrooms.

The news and sports output of the various stations was augmented by a network news service, IRN, that not only pooled content but provided opportunities for broadcasters like me to work on major national events as part of their team. I was IRN's man at the Open golf for five years. During the last three of those, I got to take part in the first radio interview with the champion immediately after he had spoken live on television at the completion of his final round.

The sharing arrangements stretched to features and music too. If it's possible to think of a greater contrast to my 'what did you hit at the last?' chats with Tom Watson and Jack Nicklaus by the 18th green, then chewing the rock music fat with Frank Zappa, Captain Beefheart and 10cc would be it. I lived a hundred dreams in those first heady months in broadcasting.

Any interview that I could talk Brian Clough into was soon airing on radio stations up and down the country. He was getting me noticed and turning professional heads just by speaking to me. Cloughie got me my next job. The ILR station on Merseyside liked what they heard. I was heading for Liverpool. And so was he.

Royal approval. 1983 Sony Radio Award winner.

4

SHANKS

'Some people believe football is a matter of life and death,
I can assure you it is much, much more important than that.'

It is Bill Shankly's epitaph. And it shouldn't be. That's not how
the man that I came to know during his last four years on earth
thought about life and death. He loved life above all else.

He loved life even more than he loved football. Just the
most human of human beings you can ever imagine. Of all
the people that I've met through my career, there is nobody
that I would like to have spent more time with than Shanks.

Ask his players and they will tell you that every morning –
rain or shine – Bill would eulogise about the joy of being and
feeling alive before a ball was kicked in training. The 'life and
death' epigram was always accompanied by one of his throaty
laughs. It was a joke. The joke of a very serious man.

When I landed on Merseyside in 1977, Bill was already
three years retired. He had his own Saturday lunchtime chat
show on Radio City, so I saw plenty of him. He was my co-
commentator for several games including the 1978 European
Cup final at Wembley.

He was alongside me four months later when Liverpool were beaten 2–0 at Nottingham Forest in the first round of the following season's competition. Garry Birtles scored the opening goal in what was his second senior appearance.

'Oh, can you believe it?!' I wailed to a despairing audience back on Merseyside. 'A week ago, we'd never even heard of him, Bill.'

Shanks thought for a second, placed the ribbon microphone onto his top lip and then opened his mouth and his heart.

'You've fuckin' heard of him now!' he roared.

We didn't receive one phone call of complaint. Not one. He had simply spoken for every listening Liverpool fan. I have often thought that commentators should be allowed one 'f-word' per season. Sometimes it's the only adjective that really works in football.

We would be trusted to use it wisely like a cricket captain manages his umpire challenges, but uttered at the right moment for the right incident, the occasional profane outburst would give football commentary some renewed street cred.

Bill's capacity to speak for Liverpool fans, to think as a Liverpool fan, to care like a Liverpool fan created the most holy of trinities between manager, team and supporters at Anfield. The perfect match. 'It was a kind of marriage. Liverpool was made for me and I was made for Liverpool,' he often said.

How does a football club know when they've got the right manager? Like marriage, like love itself, it can be a first glance across a crowded room thing. It is a transient and often capricious relationship with a terrible divorce rate but the manager is the focus of attention at almost every club in the world. Only one neck is ever on the line.

Players win and lose football matches. However close to the action the white lines of their technical areas allow the watching, waving managers to get, they don't kick a single ball. The responsibility for every swing of a foot is theirs but the passes, the shots, the acrobatic volleys and the hapless mis-kicks that decide the outcome of games are all executed by other people.

As Terry Venables' faithful assistant, Allan Harris, used to say ruefully, 'Players? . . . they'll get you the sack.'

Shanks had no more faithful servant during his time in charge of Liverpool than Chris Lawler. The manager had a particular blind spot about injured players. He hated them. Wouldn't talk to them or acknowledge them until they were fit. Chris was never injured, so Shanks loved him. A tall right-back with an eye for goal, he played over 300 consecutive games for Bill from 1965.

He was as quiet as he was reliable. So, when his remarkable unbroken run was brought to an end by a minor muscle strain in 1971, he wasn't exactly the ideal choice of referee for a training match that Bill had joined in. There was only one rule in these impromptu games. Shanks' team won. If they fell 3–1 behind, the match continued until it was 3–4.

The score in this particular match was a draw at the moment that Bill himself managed to propel the ball towards the goal that consisted of a couple of crumpled training tops. In time-honoured fashion, it rolled across the sweatshirt calling on the man with the whistle to decide whether a goal had been scored or not. The world stopped to look at Chris Lawler. Where is Stockley Park when you need it?

'Sorry, boss, I don't think I can give that,' he said timidly.

Now the world turned to look at Shanks for a response.

'How long have I known you, son? Since you were 16 years of age. How long is that, 10 maybe 12 years? And I've never heard you say a word in all that time. And when you do finally say something, it's a bloody lie!'

The goal stood.

Timing is the magic ingredient in any recipe for managerial success. Right place, right stroke of the clock. It can come down to a matter of days. The stories may be apocryphal but it's fair to assume that Sir Alex Ferguson and Howard Kendall both teetered on the cliff edge of getting the fatal push before overseeing the most successful eras in the history of Manchester United and Everton. At the very lowest ebb, most of the players that would lift the two teams and their managers to dizzy summits were already in place. The rocket ships were steaming on the launchpads but the astronauts were still to push the button.

Bill didn't win promotion to the top flight until his third season at Liverpool in 1962 but the timing could not have been better. Merseyside was about to move to the epicentre of the universe. The Beatles' music was probably not altogether to Bill's tastes – he once told Gerry Marsden that he preferred Mario Lanza's version of 'You'll Never Walk Alone' – but Shanks was quick to identify the perfect storm that John, Paul, George and Ringo were whipping up. He marched right into the very eye of it.

Shankly's Liverpool and the Merseybeat pop bands were shooting stars from the same galaxy. They were adored and screamed at by residents of the same households. Anfield and Goodison by day, the Cavern by night. Young scousers had it all.

Across Stanley Park, another Scot Alex 'the Golden Vision' Young, fired Everton to the title in 1963. Liverpool finished top of the league in two of the following three seasons. If the Beatles weren't top of the hit parade, Gerry and the Pacemakers or Cilla Black or Billy J Kramer or the Searchers were. All Merseyside acts.

Local pride was chorused on the swaying congregation that was the Spion Kop terracing at Anfield. Twenty-eight thousand hearts with one voice, one mind. There is a famous BBC *Panorama* report filmed in front of the baying Koppites on the day that the first of Bill's three Championships was sealed in 1964. It is extraordinary footage for so many reasons, not least that the songs being belted out by almost exclusively adult men were two love songs, 'She Loves You' and 'Anyone Who Had A Heart'. But they were their songs on their territory at their moment. Shankly seized that moment.

He felt at home on Merseyside from the day he arrived. Bill spotted similarities between his old backyard and his new one. There were common denominators in the pit villages of Ayrshire and dockland Liverpool in terms of humour, spirit and confidence. 'They've got life in them, just like me,' he told me in one of our many radio interviews. 'They're arrogant, cocky and proud. They are everything I want their team to be.'

It takes some front for an outsider to arrive on Merseyside and tell the locals what they're like. I have managed to recover precious copies of some of those Radio City interviews that I did with Bill and they make for hypnotic listening. Every time he says my name I break out in a silly smile.

Certain managers just seem born to take charge of certain clubs. Pep Guardiola and Barcelona. Diego Simeone and Atletico Madrid. Both Ferguson and Kendall shaped the whole character of their clubs in their own image once they silenced their doubters and got lift-off. Arsène Wenger likewise. Other managers have felt perfect fits for some jobs and not for others. Sam Allardyce, Unai Emery, Roy Hodgson. Horses for courses. If it were an exact science, none of them would ever fail.

An increasing number of forensic mathematics majors are graduating into high-profile positions. They pass job interviews with PowerPoint formulae and set about exploring their atom-splitting theories on their new club's tab. I've never quite worked out where words like 'ideology' and 'project' belong in a profession where the reality of the next result is so harsh and long-term planning relates to the following week at most. Philosophy is for Karl Marx, not Karl Robinson.

One of the defining statements of modern football was made by the German national coach Sepp Herberger in the 1950s. 'The ball is round and the game lasts 90 minutes. That's fact. Everything else is pure theory.' It was his way of saying that anything can happen during a match and no amount of tactical principles and hypotheses can truly prepare you for very much of it.

The touchline puppeteers like Guardiola and Rafa Benitez that seem to be trying to control the detail of every movement their marionettes make on stage will beg to differ. To them, the field is a giant chess board on which their pieces threaten and develop and sacrifice and check until their King's Gambit prevails and the opponent resigns. Bloodless coups. My overlapping centre-backs trump your underlapping full-backs.

That's not a game I've ever witnessed. You've got to get your knees dirty to win real matches. If VAR has taught us anything it is that twenty-first century football is played on the margins, on the cross hairs between the offside toenail and the defender's t-shirt line. It is won and lost by fractions that no coaching boffin can possibly calculate. Football is measured solely in goals, not counter presses or overloads.

Shanks hated new-fangled jargon. It was one of his recurring rants when I found my latest excuse to visit him at his unremarkable home in Bellefield Avenue adjacent to Everton's training ground. When he was Liverpool manager, he frequently mocked Everton – 'the only two teams in Liverpool are Liverpool and Liverpool Reserves', etc – but in his pensionable years he grew ever closer to the old foe on his doorstep and regularly crossed the blue line for a walk and a chat.

And Shanks could chat. I am not naïve enough to think that our chats were ever anything more than fillers for spare hours released by his unnecessary retirement. By the time I fell for his charms, the spell had maybe started to wear off with the seasoned reporters and associates that had heard his tales of yore a million times over. I couldn't get enough of them.

If Bill had been invited to speak at a charity sports forum in some smoky working men's club in Bootle, I volunteered to drive him there. If there was any vague pretext to seek his views on England's failure to qualify for the World Cup or Sir Alf Ramsey's return to management, I was making an appointment for another audience with Shanks. Press play and record and just listen.

My Uher tape recorder was barely portable. It was a bulky, cumbersome piece of apparatus that chipped a few door frames in famous homes as I pursued my cub reporter career. My right shoulder ached constantly from lugging it around. Occasionally, the two small spools of tape would clog and jam the tape head and the whole recording ground to an embarrassing halt . . . usually at the very moment that the interviewee was revealing all.

Because the operation of the machine was such a bloody palaver, it was difficult to lull a subject into forgetting it was there and simply relax and open up. A lot of the most memorable words that Bill spoke to me came during the first minutes that I spent settling into a chair in his front room while Nessie Shankly dutifully brewed tea and arranged some plain biscuits on an ornate plate for us. It was a particularly 'traditional' marriage but she was unfailingly welcoming, a favourite auntie's face forever smiling from beneath her bonnet of bouffant hair.

Bill was not a rambler. Once the interview began, he would pick his words thoughtfully. Some of his answers were short and brusque. From time to time, he plucked a mesmerising memory from his cloud and paused to let the words echo around him for a moment, adding only a pensive 'yes, yes' by way of affirmation that his latest comment was now official.

Roy Evans once said to me, 'Bill talked at you, like everything he said was a fact.' Spot on. There were never any 'in my opinions' or 'others may not agrees'. This was de facto. Legal and binding. The certainty jolted your head back like he had just landed a punch on your nose. Understood, son?

Certainty is a key weapon in every manager's armoury. Any doubts infect and spread through the decision-making that is a daily requirement in their occupation. The leading managers leave you in no doubt at all. It is a fine line between 'focused' and 'blinkered' but the captains of the ocean-going vessels that are major football clubs have to keep their eyes fixed on the lane ahead of them at all times.

Wenger was comically famous for not seeing debatable decisions that went Arsenal's way. Ferguson was clinically one-eyed too. They could both put up a very persuasive defence for the indefensible. If you can convince yourself, you might just be able to sway the undecided. But neither went out on a limb for the sake of their own interests. They always tried to protect their club, their team, the reputation of one of their players. Leading from the front like that has to be underpinned by serial certainty.

You didn't debate anything with Sir Alex or Shanks. They may occasionally have let you get enough of a word in to give the impression that you might be changing their minds, but the concrete had long since set around their standpoint.

I like debate. They didn't know the meaning of the word.

I don't like television debates where they sit Mr North and Mrs South in opposite chairs and allow them to rant at one another until they have to be pulled apart. Debates should not be won or lost. They should open minds not close them. Further investigation can never dilute an argument but it can shift it.

Following the evidence, following the science, is my kind of journey. About-turns can be some of the best and bravest moves we make in life if they steer us away from dogma and gospels. And yet U-turns by public figures are portrayed as signs of indecision and ineptitude. There is no future in being open-minded.

Shanks was never a fair-minded Liverpool manager. For all of his basic human decency, he was an impossibly bad loser. Hard on referees and grudging towards opponents, he could plead injustice close to José Mourinho levels. His certainty didn't entertain the idea of deserved defeats.

While Bill's team eventually won the UEFA Cup in 1973, his experiences of the European Cup were bitter ones. I have recordings of long, grumbling tirades about 'the queer decisions' in Milan by which Inter beat Liverpool in the semi-finals of 1964 and their fog-shrouded demise in Amsterdam at Ajax's hands two seasons later.

'I was on the pitch and the referee never saw me,' he insisted. 'The bloody press were reporting the game and I couldn't see it from the touchline. I only knew Ajax had scored because the linesman told me. So I went on to tell Geoff Strong and Willie Stevenson to stop trying to win the tie in the first leg. I was standing next to Willie talking to him. The game should never have been played. We were four-nil down at half-time. Some of the players weren't sure of the score. It was a disgrace.'

That hazy 5–1 hiding at the hands of Johann Cruyff and company left its mark on Bill. He could see enough of the match to know that Liverpool were being out-passed. While he was devout in the belief that there was nothing original in tactics dressed up with a new vocabulary or terms like 'total football', he could recognise teams that were moving 'his' football up a notch.

As with Cloughie, 'simplicity' was his byword. It is often the most complex of notions to grasp. Ronnie Moran told me that he learnt more in Bill's first three months at Liverpool than he'd absorbed in the previous seven years because the new manager's ideas were so clear and simple. Any player that couldn't grasp those ideas was gone in no time, though. He was as stubbornly committed as Guardiola in his way.

Here is another passage from my interview archives. 'When I bought Ian St John from Motherwell, he asked me what I wanted him to do. I said "I'm going to change your game. Change it completely. At Motherwell, you always passed to an amber shirt." Because that was their home kit, Clive. Claret and amber. I told him, "you're never going to do that again. Not with me. Now, you're going to pass to a red shirt. Always to a red shirt. Pass to any other shirt and you'll be hearing from me. Pass to a red shirt now. You don't need to change another thing. Nothing else."

'When we pass the ball, we pass it like a baton in a relay race. You know, like in an Olympic games. The baton goes round faster than any of the runners can carry it on their own. The baton is covering the most ground, not the runners. That's what we do with the ball here. We pass it because it can do the running for us. That's why it has to go to a red shirt. The ball is part of our team.'

Any embellishments to the dogmatic simplicity of Bill's possession-pinned doctrine were added by Bob Paisley. Ian Callaghan told me that Bob was always the tactician, Joe Fagan the adjutant-in-chief. The team behind the team is another recurring common factor in successful management.

Shanks inherited Bob, Joe and fellow Scot Reuben Bennett. He enlisted Moran and Evans from his dressing-room and brought in the wisest of owls, Tom Saunders, from a career in schooling. Talent spotter Geoff Twentyman was another vital member of the staff that gathered to put the world to rights in the cramped, windowless boot room that became the Anfield inner sanctum.

If the conversations were anything like Bill's radio show, he would have done most of the talking. Vaunted guests such as Harold Wilson and Ken Dodd agreed to come to chew the fat with Shanks at our studios and ended up being thrown the odd bone. He wasn't a great one for asking questions. If he did, it was usually a rhetorical one for him to go on and provide the answer to.

Bill was a showman. His roots, his assets, his lifestyle were all humble and grounded. But he had a strut and a swagger that belied that unassuming backdrop. One of the few things we ever discussed beyond football was gangsters. We shared a liking for a vintage television series, *The Untouchables*. It starred Robert Stack as an American prohibition agent, Eliot Ness, taking on the mobsters in 1930s Chicago. I liked the show but Bill thought he was in it.

He loved James Cagney, George Raft, Rod Steiger and Edward G Robinson, the celebrated Hollywood portrayers of Al Capone and friends. He loved Jack Dempsey, Rocky Marciano and Joe Louis, the timeless titans of the American boxing ring. Bill even adopted a bit of a fighter's stance – hands and arms often raised and loaded at waist height, head and torso slightly turned and tensed ready to duck a left jab.

Even on the day he announced his resignation in 1974, he looked a million dollars. No cigarette ever went close to his lips and the only alcoholic drink that anyone can recall him ordering was one stiff brandy before a perilous flight in stormy conditions. He took blooming pride in his good health and habits.

His shirt of choice was usually one of the darker tints beloved of the gang leaders and racketeers, the middle button of his jacket was ritually fastened. He was always primed and ready for Machine Gun Kelly if he happened to come calling.

The Liverpool squad toured the United States in the summer of 1964 and Bill made a point of visiting Dempsey's Broadway bar in Manhattan and even Capone's burial site at Mount Carmel, just outside Chicago. They were pilgrimages for him that he recalled for many years to come. What he didn't talk about quite so much were his problems with time zones. Ian St John – the master of Shankly stories – will tell you about the morning that Shanks demanded breakfast in a hotel restaurant at 3 am. 'I'm not having any yank telling me the time,' he protested pointing at his watch.

As football orators go, he is without rival in my lifetime. If Bill told you it was 8 am, he was persuasive enough to make even a hard-headed Manhattan waiter wonder if it might just be.

He was the original sports psychologist. The call of his preacher's zeal could lift ordinary mortals to extraordinary deeds. Shanks used his folk-hero status to make a believer out of every Liverpool fan. The energy of the collective conviction was piped directly into the veins of the players the moment they set foot on the pitch. A mass transfusion as they touched the 'This is Anfield' sign at the tunnel entrance. It was hung there to remind the foot-soldiers in red and intimidate the enemy in turn.

Bill liked a confidence trick. When Liverpool drew the Bucharest side Petrolul Ploiesti in the first round of the European Cup in 1966, Reuben Bennett was despatched on a spying mission to assess the mystery opponents. Nicolae Ceausescu had just come to power and the Iron Curtain was pulled tightly shut. Travelling to the Romanian capital was a moon shot back then but Petrolul's last fixture before coming to Anfield was in Arad, an eight-hour drive from Bucharest.

Reuben was away for three days, returning to Merseyside with tales of military road blocks and invasive body searches. He was the kind of guy who would always tell you he'd had worse. In Bob Paisley's words, 'still fighting the war'. Diligently, he compiled as detailed a dossier as he could on the strengths and weaknesses of Petrolul and proudly presented it to Bill on the morning of the first leg.

Another extract from my Shankly library . . . 'I got all the players sat down in the dressing-room before the game. I told them Reuben had been to Romania and seen this team play. I told them all about the journey he'd been on. Strip searched by soldiers. Down to his underpants. Terrible. Then I held up the book that Reuben had written about them. Twenty pages all about the players and what they do. And then I said to the players, "Do you know what we're going to do with Reuben's book? We're going to throw it in the bin." And I did. Threw it right there in the rubbish bin where Reuben was. He was standing right next to it. And I said to the players, "We are not going to worry about them, we are going to make them worry about us." Aye.'

Just to have seen Reuben Bennett's face as an entire week's work was tossed in among the used chewing gum wrappers and discarded strappings. Classic Shanks.

The story of Kevin Keegan's first encounter with the national hero that was Bobby Moore at West Ham in 1972 has been recounted many times. Of how Bill told Kevin that he'd seen bags under Moore's eyes and that the England captain was limping and even had dandruff on his shoulders. Kevin was assured that Moore now 'moved like a robot' and would not be able to live with his own youthful vim and vigour.

Liverpool won 2–0 and Kevin returned to the Upton Park dressing-room to feel his manager's firm grip on his shoulder accompanied by the words 'you've just given the run around to the greatest defender in the world.'

When Shanks persuaded an eighteen-year-old Ray Clemence to reject other advances and sign for Liverpool, he told him that his current first team goalkeeper, Tommy Lawrence, was approaching his mid-thirties and the end of the road. Lawrence was twenty-seven and Ray spent the next two seasons waiting in the reserves. You didn't check what Bill told you.

Some of the managerial immortals remain unsolved riddles even to their most devoted disciples. Many of Bill's former players reminisce about him with a bemusement in their voices. They laugh out loud when they think back. Almost as if they don't really know what he did to them or how. I've heard the same glazed mystery in the yarns that ex-Forest players tell about Brian Clough and the stories that Ipswich veterans recount of Sir Bobby Robson.

They talk like they've all been beautifully 'had' like Keegan and Clemence were, like their careers have been one long, extended Derren Brown show. An illusionist's act. Scented smoke and funhouse mirrors. The magic managers.

Bill's spellbinding verbal tone and his evangelical delivery lent a crashing weight to everything he said. He spoke in sermons. You felt indoctrinated just listening to him. He possessed an innate timing. He knew his audience. When he had them in the palm of his hand, he could make them wait and wonder about what was coming next. If he had gone into politics, he would have won landslide victory after landslide victory.

He was in his element when he got to address massed crowds after trophy parades from the balcony of St George's Hall in the heart of Liverpool. That was the venue for his epic 'bastion of invincibility' speech. Somehow Chairman Mao and Napoleon found their way into the intoxicating script before it climaxed with the rallying revelation that 'my idea was to build Liverpool up and up until eventually everyone would have to submit and give in.'

You just couldn't say that now. Not even in Liverpool.

The monument to Bill Shankly is not the bronze statue outside the Kop with his arms outstretched proclaiming all of the above and more. It's not the gilded Shankly Gates at the other end of Anfield. It is the all-red kit, the 'This is Anfield' sign, the pre-match observance of Gerry Marsden's hymn, all introduced on his watch. It is the culture, the stamp. It's that 'arrogant, cocky and proud' team that he fashioned back then and that all of his successors have been charged with trade-marking and replicating. Shanks started all of this.

People talk about football 'projects' and 'philosophies', but the Bill Shankly project is still going strong sixty years on, the philosophy has barely been tinkered with. He was one of football's founding fathers.

His influence stretched far beyond the playing careers of his players. They lived their lives to the tune he called.

Ray Clemence was a particularly close personal friend of mine. I feel privileged to have known him and I miss him.

However great a keeper he became, he was an even greater man. Twenty years of confronting illness never dimmed his spirit or the lust for making the most of life that he found between Shankly's Kop goalposts.

He was my mate and my hero. Just the most wonderful antidote to so much of the snide cynicism and judgmental reproval that infects contemporary life. Clem lit up every room he walked into with the warmth of his smile and the value he placed on making others smile.

He was as competitive and opinionated as Bill himself but never at the expense of others, never without a clear view of the bigger picture. That engaging naivety that Shanks took advantage of was soon replaced by a potent focus on seizing his opportunity and rewarding the trust that others placed in him. Rewarding it by returning their trust with interest.

Shanks would have been so proud of the man that Ray became. I spent his last afternoon with him and his wonderful wife and family last year. As humbling an experience as I've known. Clem left us all far too soon.

Bill's retirement from Liverpool remains an unsolved mystery. Apparently, he threatened to resign every year. I've never heard a definitive explanation as to why 1974 became that year. A few months after taking the decision he said it felt 'like walking to the electric chair'. He hated the word 'retirement'. 'You only retire when the flowers come out,' was another of his oft-recited mantras.

I was awoken late on the night of 29 September 1981 when Bill Shankly retired prematurely from all our lives. I drove into the radio station to compile tributes and memorials in a state of disbelief. He had always seemed and sounded invincible. At

68 years of age, he was still joining in five-a-sides right up to the day he passed.

Inevitably, during the endless hours of local radio mourning that followed, I was asked for my own dearly beloved Shankly story. I think it was a fitting one both for the day and forever.

In his final years, Shanks would take a daily constitutional around the perimeter of Everton's training pitches with the club physiotherapist, Jim McGregor. Another Scot, Jim was a very good friend and ally to me.

On this particular crisp, fresh, blue sky, autumn day, Bill was trotting alongside Jim deeply breathing in the clear air, deeply breathing in life itself.

'I feel good, Jim,' he said proudly. 'Good to be alive. Do you know what I wish?'

'What's that, Bill?'

'That when I die and I'm lying in the coffin asleep, that the people come by and look in and say, "Christ, Shanks looks well."'

Now, that's an epitaph.

My Mersey Beat. On the way home from Wembley with
Derek Mountfield and the FA Cup, 1984.

SECOND JOB:

Radio City

Independent Local Radio station, Liverpool

1977–89

The timing of my own arrival on Merseyside wasn't bad either.

Two months after I joined Radio City, Liverpool won their first European Cup. Anfield and Goodison ran out of silver polish during the 15 years that I lived there.

My ex-wife is a scouser, one of my children was born on the Wirral, the other became a Liverpool fan. I can nearly do the accent.

I was working for a local radio station but covering matches as big as any being played in Europe, so I was mixing with major network broadcasters and national newspaper football correspondents. No other city in the world could have provided a better grounding for the career I hankered after.

There is never a dull moment in Liverpool. I commentated on everything from Bill Shankly's funeral to the Pope's visit for Radio City. I was roped in to work on coverage of a General Election that Margaret Thatcher won and, four years later, on a local election at which the Militant Tendency took control of the city council.

I was on duty in the newsroom the afternoon that John Lennon was shot dead in New York. My ex-wife's parents owned a shop that was damaged during the Toxteth Riots. The news is never far away on Merseyside.

Through football, and the part it played in every Liverpudlian life, I came to know a medley of unique characters – Alan Bleasdale, John Conteh, Jimmy Tarbuck, Ginger McCain, Sue Johnston, John Peel, John Parrott and the Reverend David Sheppard to name but a famous few. No meeting with any of them passed off quietly.

It's a city where every bar, every office, every schoolyard is a pop-up comedy club or theatre. Every street corner is a stage where impromptu farces and follies are acted out in everyday natter. I really thought I could talk the talk until I arrived in Liverpool. I was an amateur.

No wonder Willy Russell and Elvis Costello can write like they do. No wonder Stephen Graham and Jodie Comer can act like they do.

If you want to open your mouth for a living, there is no harder school than Merseyside, and no better place to learn.

5

MOTTY

John Motson is a national treasure. I will never be that.

Sir Peter O'Sullevan, Bill McLaren, John Arlott, Dan Maskell, Peter Alliss, Murray Walker, Brian Johnston, Henry Longhurst, Eddie Waring, Ted Lowe . . . all national treasures.

That is not the full list. It is certainly not the official list. As Barry Davies once said to me, 'One man's commentator is another man's pain in the arse.' We are a matter of taste, a matter of opinion, but the place that Motty and the other household names above have won in the public's affections is a place in their hearts. It's for good.

They are totems of a halcyon age when sport was watched almost exclusively inside households on the family television, by a gathering of three or four generations. That age has passed to the point that Motty may well be the last gold doubloon to be lifted from the chest of British broadcasting treasures.

Multi-channel, multi-purpose commentators will never be able to forge the same intimate, trusting relationships with the audience. There are too many of us, too many games, too many platforms. Nobody knows or really cares who is behind the mic anymore.

I have been subjected to Twitter rants about live commentaries by other people on channels I've never worked for. I can be sat in front of the telly at home with a glass of wine in my hand, but viewers are still tapping out abusive reviews into my '@mentions'. Guilty of crimes a thousand miles from where I'm sitting. That couldn't happen to Motty or Murray or Bill. They are unmistakable. One-offs.

As a sixth former at school, I wanted to be John Motson. Or at least I wanted his job. I wanted it at that very moment. I was ready and very willing. Like Yosser Hughes in *Boys from the Blackstuff*, I was mentally stalking him thinking, 'I can do that. Giz a job.'

It is one of the many insecurities that go with a career in commentary that millions of onlookers believe they can do it better than you do. That's not the case with brain surgeons and scaffolders.

In my opinion, Motty did it better than anyone had done before him. There had been richer, more wine-stained voices than John's, there had been bards of broadcasting with more lyrical vocabularies, there had been chiming Celtic preachers and lilting rollers of 'r's but never a football man that told it exactly like it was.

Motty was the first broadcast journalist of football commentary. He has always been famously well-researched but he is also as well-connected as any football writer. Not only could he phone most managers for team information the day before a match, their trust and respect for John led them into off-the-record conversations that afforded him real insight into their tactics and approach.

Meticulous preparation is one thing. Journalism is as much about framing the story of an event and then finding the words that tell that story in the most accurate and digestible way. Motty has been a technician of commentary. He identifies players, he amplifies action, he captures consequences. No poetry, no prose. Just does what it says on the tin.

Swotty Motty may be remembered for the sheepskin coat and the trainspotter's anorak but that is a misrepresentation of his broadcasting breadth and I've told him so. I can think of several sports commentators that use facts and figures more routinely, more unnecessarily than John. I have never believed that he has done his image any favours by playing up to the 'statto' caricature. He's better than that.

In any heavyweight football debate, he has a major contribution to offer no matter the company. His opinions are strong and strongly qualified. He is authoritative and verifiable. A serious thinker on the game. Football correspondent material. When I wanted to be John Motson, that's what I wanted to be. He could keep the coat.

That list of commentating 'treasures' is interesting because all of them are very different in style and delivery. One of the few factors that binds them is that they all worked for the BBC during an era when part of its 'service' to the nation was to mop up all the major sports rights with the licence payers' money. Those silky tongues became the 'voices' of their sports.

Wimbledon wasn't Wimbledon without Maskell's 'Oh, I say'. Murrayfield wasn't Murrayfield unless McLaren spent a minute name-checking a family in some minor rugby club bar in the Borders. A grand prix wasn't a grand prix unless Walker christened it with several clips for the next edition of *It'll be Alright on the Night*. These men owned and authenticated their sports.

Another common denominator was the material they provided for Mike Yarwood and the other impressionists of the time. It is an odd contradiction that these eminently revered men were so brazenly parodied.

Their eccentricities and affectations were mercilessly mimicked and lampooned and yet the final furlongs of the Grand National could not be run until the team 'out in the country' had handed dutifully back to O'Sullevan, the last tee-shots of a Ryder Cup could not be struck unless Alliss had put down his crystal goblet and picked up the microphone. Their dulcet tones were part of the event and yet also comedy gold.

I like to think that I have a working sense of humour but I must confess that is severely challenged by people ridiculing my work. During my radio days on Merseyside, I was once summoned by a group of giggling Everton players to listen to one of the club apprentices that 'does you'. Try as I may, I could raise no more than a fabricated snigger at the teenager's impersonation attempt. It sounded nothing like me . . . except everyone else present thought it did and was in fits. Just maybe I was the odd one out.

I remember the legendary *Private Eye* column 'Colemanballs' including an entry from one of Motty's World Cup commentaries in 1982. 'The Argentine squad are numbered alphabetically' he was reported to have uttered hilariously. Except that is precisely how they were numbered. Ossie Ardiles was No 1. John's phrasing could hardly have been more concise. He was having the Michael ceremonially squeezed out of him because commentators' reputations for misusing words were already running at zero on the Make a Rick Scale.

The really hilarious thing is that whenever enthusiastic amateurs try to parrot commentators, they invariably descend into the same hackneyed phrases that we are placed in the public stocks for using. Most football clichés serve a perfectly practical purpose. A game of two halves is invariably just that. Get over it.

There is no 'Voice of Football'. Not now. No voice of cricket, no voice of reason, no voice of the people. No oracle we can consult, no leading authority we can trust. Only a clamorous babble of voices across a hundred platforms competing to be the loudest.

We have become slaves to the soundbite, mere browsers of the long read, occasional glancers at the big picture. We have no time for dialogue, just special effects.

Ask an avid football watcher what their very favourite piece of commentary is and the answer will usually be a totally extreme overblown example of our craft. I recently appeared in a podcast where a digital media editor selected Jonathan Pearce's cacophonous radio description of an Alan Shearer goal at Euro '96 as the best ever. The extract ended with JP uproariously chanting 'Super Al, Super Al, Super Alan Shearer'. Capital Radio, England winning, national celebrations. Bang on message. A tabloid radio gem.

Would the same listener want all radio commentary to be like that? No, I don't think so. Ask someone where their most memorable sexual episode took place and the reply will probably feature some bushes, an office broom cupboard or the back seat of a car. Does that mean the confessor wishes all of their adult love-making had been enjoyed in public places? Possibly not.

For me, the best commentators and the best commentaries are the broadcast equivalent of a warm duvet, a comfortable mattress, some fluffy pillows and closed curtains. Someone you want to share it with again and again over years and years, someone you really come to know and like and invest some faith in. You don't want to wake up next to somebody who's frothing at the mouth.

I took over from Motty as the main commentator on the *FIFA* computer game in 2001. The gameplay is created at EA's Vancouver studios and the script that I inherited was comically over the top. Phrases like 'bursts the onion bag' are worthy of a titter the first time you come across them, but if you spend a whole afternoon with a PlayStation controller in your hands, the joke wears a bit thin on the 43rd time of hearing.

I rewrote the entire audio script for *FIFA* to be more credible and authentic. My argument was that, like television, gaming is primarily a visual experience and that the soundtrack should be no more than an accompaniment, a reassuring background voice. All media consumption is changing but, as commentators, we are invited into millions of homes and lives. They can turn us down or turn us off if we abuse the invite.

More and more televised football has been watched communally in pubs and sports bars. My own children are all in their mid-twenties and are more likely to drink up their football with a few friends and pints than sit on the sofa with the old man. They never come home talking about the commentary, not least because they don't hear much of it.

Those broadcast royalty commentators of the BBC's golden age of sports coverage all built up their devoted followings by somehow striking personal chords with home-based viewers that hung on their every word. I was one of their followers, one of their most committed followers. I still try to commentate as though someone is listening. Because I listened.

I remember travelling down to watch United play at Queens Park Rangers in 1974 and just standing outside BBC Television Centre for half an hour envying people going into work there. I so wanted to be one of those people. Twenty years later, I was.

Vintage ITV commentators like Brian Moore and Reg Gutteridge belong on that list of 'treasures' but *World of Sport* was a very different beast to *Grandstand* on sporting Saturday afternoons on the box. Dickie Davies was as likely to be introducing stock car racing or cliff diving as the show's staples of wrestling, horse racing and snooker. None of them were my bag.

By contrast, I actually hosted *Grandstand* myself for a spell in the 1960s. You won't have seen me. Not unless you were looking through the windows of 1 St Peter's Road in Bury. That was where my two cousins lived and the venue for many editions of our recreation of the BBC programme via book cricket, balloon football and a horse racing board game called Totopoly. The Scalextric track was a bit of a faff, but, on nice days, we would take the cameras outside for path cycling and garden athletics.

It's not easy to run a 10,000-metre race and commentate at the same time, but maybe a little easier at the age of 10.

I was that kid you are imagining.

I was a trainspotter. My grandpa and I used to stand on a rickety old foot bridge at Hest Bank near Morecambe and watch the hissing, snorting wild monsters of the West Coast mainline race through the tiny station like creations from

Game of Thrones. The bridge would shudder and rattle as the plumes of white steam enveloped us . . . and I looked down to try to record the number of the Royal Scot or Britannia locomotive that was hauling a dozen clicking carriages down towards Preston after its travails on Shap Fell to the north. Damn it, one I already had.

I was a cricket scorer. When Lancashire beat Gloucestershire in the evening gloom to reach the Gillette Cup final of 1971, the dramatic climax sent more than 20,000 fans spilling onto the outfield to celebrate with the players. One teenage boy remained in his seat in the Old Trafford stands fastidiously completing the bowling analysis in his scorebook – in pencil, just in case I had made an error. I rarely did.

The meticulous charts that I compile before commentary matches are descendants from those days. They are also an aid stolen unashamedly from Motty, whose own crib-notes were primly written in three colours. We tend to be creatures of habit, slaves to our own routines. Peter Drury's writing is virtually illegible and the late Peter Brackley sketched sheets akin to the weirdest Spike Milligan cartoons, but most of the old school pre-tablet sports commentators get nine out of ten for neat and tidy when their homework is complete.

John's wife, Annie, has even played a hands-on role in keeping his records up-to-date and collating the information for his match charts. He does live the job a lot more than I do. His penchant for a statistic is bordering on a habit. Psychologists would convene conferences about him. Even though commentary is a performing art, a large and juicy slice of the personality of every commentator I know can be heard in our work. It is how it should be.

Paul Doherty, the television executive who handed me my first microphone, once chastised me for trying to sound like Motty. He heard me utter 'and I have to say' a couple of times during an early commentary and told me bluntly, 'If I'd wanted bloody Motson, I'd have hired him.' I'm not sure that he would have been able to lure John away from the top of his profession to voice highlights for Granada TV at the time, but the point was well made. If you get invited to the party, bring yourself along. It's only human.

My predecessor at ITV, Brian Moore, brought his human touch to every occasion he was invited to. I didn't realise it until he was gone but he taught me that the greatest single quality that any kind of communicator can hope to possess is warmth. Brian oozed warmth on and off duty.

When he retired and left the way clear for me in 1998, ITV threw a small, select bash to honour him. I was seated next to Brian at the dinner table. We both liked our wine and a couple of very decent bottles down the road at the late hour when people were reluctantly making their apologies and saying their goodbyes, he grabbed me by the arm and whispered, 'There are only two things you need to remember.'

Oh great! The Worshipful Master of commentary is about to impart the two biggest secrets of the art and I am pissed.

'Be warm enough and be on time,' Brian revealed gravely.

I was just about sober enough to stare blankly back at him with a 'is that it?' bubble coming out of my head, but I was grateful that I hadn't needed to take notes.

Less than a year later, Brian was sitting next to me in the back of a taxi en route to the biggest game of my career. He had been asked by UEFA to speak at a sponsors' event ahead of the Champions League final at Nou Camp. We had lunched together in the Barcelona sunshine and now I had the reassurance of having him alongside as I headed for my first major gig as his successor.

'Do you remember what I said to you at the dinner?' he suddenly enquired.

'At the end? The thing about being on time?' I replied understandably distracted.

'Do you know what I was really saying to you? I was telling you that I thought you were ready to do this, that you were certainly good enough as long as . . .' Brian paused like a teacher waiting for someone in the classroom to put their hand up, '. . . I was on time and warm enough.'

I'm not sure that I've ever been paid a greater compliment since. Not by a greater man anyway. If I'm honest, I didn't realise quite how great a man Brian was until I sat in a cold church in Kent in 2001 listening to the funeral eulogies about his charity work, his Christianity, his socialism and the two heart operations he underwent during his outstanding career. He died at 69. Way too soon. I needed a lot more time with him.

I spent far too many hours grumbling away to myself about his commentary style during the two years that I understudied him before his retirement. I thought my identifications were sharper, my language more contemporary, my reading of the game better informed. I wasn't in his class. I was just being a resentful bitch.

The truth is that I was more a disciple of Motty's economic, staccato rhythm than the sweeping rhapsodic air that Brian brought to commentary. John was tidier, tighter, a proponent of the slow build. More of Brian's words came from the heart, Motty was engaging that mad scientist's brain of his.

Brian possessed more of the broadcasting 'X factor' . . . the cordial geniality, the mellow grace, the natural warmth. Because that was the man. People he never met came to love him.

Better than him? Who was I kidding! Never was, never will be.

It's a curious thing about top-level sport that the great fast bowlers all have different actions, the best golfers have different swings, the fastest sprinters have different gaits and stride patterns. The variations don't keep any of them away from the medals and the trophies. John Motson, Brian Moore, Barry Davies . . . diverse styles and approaches, same connection with the audience. Same treasure chest.

I finally got to walk inside Television Centre and work alongside Motty and Barry for four years from 1992. It was a year of major upheaval in English football and British broadcasting. BSkyB came bearing gifts to the newly formed Premier League. I managed to escape the wreckage of ITV Sport and jump ship just in time to catch the tide. I was a Beeb man at last.

I used to have three rejection letters from BBC Radio framed on my office wall. They dated back to the mid-1980s when I was commentating on European Cup finals and Everton/Liverpool title shootouts for Radio City. My burning, bursting ambition was to work for BBC Radio Two and three times I went through their taxing interview process without success. I cried my eyes out when the third 'PFO' arrived through the post in a twee little BBC envelope. Cried my eyes out at 32.

Bob Burrows has been a highly regarded, highly respected head of sport at both BBC Radio and, later, ITV. A lot of people in my profession will tell you that he was a good operator. I won't. I don't really know him and can't really judge his career but he personally belittled me in two of those interview sessions held in drab meeting rooms across Portland Place from Broadcasting House.

He put obscure, obtuse questions to me then leant back in his chair, rolled his eyes, looked to the ceiling and sighed when I couldn't find the hidden answer to any of them. He leant so far back he couldn't see how much I wanted to work for the bugger.

Why? I can only think that, as an employee of a commercial radio station, I was somehow below his idea of a BBC broadcaster. All three of those posts were filled from within the Corporation. I was like a state school kid trying to get into Eton.

The BBC I finally joined in 1992 was a little different. But only a little.

Every Tuesday morning, the head of sport, Brian Barwick, held a debrief meeting in his office to review the weekend's television output. There would usually be 25 or so chairs arranged in a circle and occupied by anyone from Motty and Des Lynam to junior researchers and runners. It was a democracy. Everyone got their turn.

In January 1994, the BBC covered a third round FA Cup tie live from Bramall Lane. It was the first time that we had employed a super slow-motion camera as part of our coverage and it captured a vivid sequence of Peter Schmeichel saving bravely at the feet of a charging Sheffield United forward. They were breathtaking pictures.

The super slo-mo images were rightly praised by member after member of the assembled group. When my turn came to offer comment, I did point out that such resolution and detail had been a standard feature of Sky's live coverage for nearly eighteen months. They'd had super slo-mo cameras at all of their main live football and rugby league outside broadcasts from their launch.

Brian called me privately after the meeting broke up. He didn't quite accuse me of treachery but he called me the 'Sky man' and reprimanded me for siding with the damned opposition. Several years later, when he had succumbed to treason himself and become my boss at ITV, we reflected on the incident with a smile and a glass. He reckoned that no more than a handful of the twenty-five or thirty BBC employees in his meeting were Sky subscribers at the time. Most of them had no idea what I was talking about. It was an ivory tower that housed a misplaced arrogance.

It is definitely a different BBC now. The days when they could wade into rights negotiations and just think of a number without any reference to commercial value are gone along with Pan's People and *Little Britain*. I have spent all but those four years of my career in organisations that have had to pay their way in the market place. I look back on my time at the Beeb rather as I do my university years. They were wonderfully rewarding and enjoyable but I was ready to move back into the real world by the end. Most areas of the BBC have followed me since.

Joining a commentary team headed by Motson and Davies was like being a middle-distance runner in the era of Coe and Ovett. You were only ever competing for bronze. Commentator hierarchies are inevitable at every channel. I have been at both ends of the ladder and it's not easy to remain a nice person when you're peering up at the fat backside of someone you believe you are the equal of. In the BBC food chain of the mid-1990s there were only scraps on the menu for Tony Gubba and me.

The 1994 World Cup in the USA was the first I attended. Tony and I were each awarded two live games, Motty and Barry were to do the rest. Both of my matches were in the first three days of the tournament in Los Angeles. I spent the remainder of the month covering a few games here and there for highlights edits, learning to play beach volleyball at Santa Monica, driving down Highway 1 from San Francisco and following the O J Simpson story at first hand. All at the licence payers' expense. I got a great tan. Thank you, all of you.

The famous white Ford Bronco car chase actually happened on the opening night of that World Cup. Simpson and Al Cowlings managed to totally upstage the evening's sporting action with their tour of the LA freeways. I was sitting in my hotel room watching the police and news network helicopters criss-crossing the skyline like darting dragonflies as I tried to get my head around my prep for Colombia versus Romania the following day. Like the rest of America, my mind was wandering.

You may think of the final of that World Cup as being between Brazil and Italy, but really it was Motty versus Barry. Like OJ, they managed to upstage the match action.

They are two very different men. As with Brian Moore, they commentated in character.

By chance, Barry went to the same Kent private school as Brian but he is more outgoing and self-confident by nature. A little pompous and contrary at times, a footballer once asked me how many England caps he had by way of a dig at Barry's tendency to introduce his own bold opinions into match commentaries. John's personal views would always be voiced in a qualified, sympathetic manner.

Barry's talents as a wordsmith made him more of an occasion man, John's closeness to the corridors of football gave him more of a definitive authority in his chosen specialist subject. The former's versatility went against him. Barry called major ice skating and tennis events among many other sports for the Beeb. Like I said, very different men.

The divergence in their styles split the nation. It was a Marmite thing, a matter of choice. It left Brian Barwick with a choice to make every time he had to nominate a cup final commentator. There could be no right or wrong, just a decision to be taken. In 1994, that decision went Barry's way.

It was nearly as much of a surprise as when the BBC football editor Sam Leitch plumped for John ahead of Barry to replace David Coleman on the FA Cup final in 1977. That was where the rivalry had begun. Both will tell you it was a friendly rivalry. They have too much class and mutual respect to say or think otherwise. I don't believe it was quite so friendly between their respective agents and camps.

When the BBC rota was distributed for the finals of Euro '96, my own match allocation had fallen to one: Turkey versus Croatia on a Friday afternoon at the City Ground. I noticed the words 'Commentary Rota #7' at the top of the page as I went into the office of football editor, Niall Sloane, to register my disappointment. He gave me about six seconds of his time before barking, 'I'm up to there with bloody commentators.'

John commentated on six World Cup finals for the Beeb either side of 1994. Barry was entrusted with the next two FA Cup finals too. It was the height of that friendly-ish rivalry. When Barwick's decision was relayed to him in New York just before the semi-finals, Motty opted to fly home early for some treatment to a broken toe he'd suffered in America. I was given the third place play-off match on the eve of the final in Los Angeles as a result.

I was early to breakfast next morning having been up since silly o'clock to watch the conclusion of the British Open on television. Barwick joined me with a request to be on 'belt and braces standby' for the final in case 'anything happens to Barry'. The catch was that I was told to spend the match waiting in the media centre for 'anything' to happen. Apparently, an unexpectedly high number of BBC executives had flown in for the game and there were no spare tickets.

It is the only time in my career that I have told my direct boss where to go. I was being asked to watch the World Cup final from a tent 200 yards from the stadium. This bloody commentator watched the game in a bar on Sunset Boulevard with a couple of the local drivers. I didn't hear the BBC commentary.

Me? I have got no opinion as to whether Motty was a 'better' commentator than Barry or Brian or anyone else. There is no such thing as 'better', only a point of view. Commentators are the very worst judges of commentators. We referee by our own rules. If we are honest, we will probably be disingenuous.

The most famous commentary line in English football history – 'they think it's all over, it is now' – is surrounded by some right rubbish. I swear the goal is credited to Charlton as Hurst celebrates. Well, you did ask!

The danger of watching your most cherished childhood movie again or downloading the favourite album of your teenage years is that they might just seem a bit naff now. They were not made or meant to stand the test of time, they were deposited in your memory bank not to accrue interest with the passing of the years, but simply to represent the same priceless value they held at the time when you look back on them.

Kenneth Wolstenholme's World Cup final commentary was a masterpiece in 1966. It was live and in the moment. That is where it will always belong, as one of the treasures of British broadcasting. It was the brilliance of their dazzling radiance that caught my young eye and gave me the ambition to do what they do. I'm in the debt of every one of them.

Dining with three of my heroes: Mrs T, Sir Bobby Charlton
and fine red wine.

FIRST TELEVISION BREAK:

1 June 1986

ITV World Cup standby commentator

I blew my first big chance in television.

ITV gave me the opportunity to work on their network coverage of the 1986 World Cup finals for a month. I lasted a day.

Despite the daggers skewered into my heart by BBC Radio interview boards, my stock was rising on the back of Merseyside football triumphs. In 1983, I won the Sports Broadcaster of the Year prize at a Sony Radio Awards ceremony that saw the likes of Terry Wogan, Denis Norden and Brian Johnston follow me onto the stage.

Princess Michael of Kent did the honours. Sweet.

The Mexico World Cup was always likely to present technical challenges for broadcasters in an era when global telecommunications were still transmitted on a wing and a prayer. ITV decided to back up the likes of Martin Tyler, Peter Brackley and John Helm onsite with a standby commentator in London. I got the gig.

I made the mistake of telling everyone I knew that if the circuits between Mexico and London failed for a second, mine would be the next voice they would hear. ITV agreed to put me up in the hotel on Sloane Street that Clough, Keegan, Channon and the rest of their studio pundits were using. I had packed for a month in heaven.

ITV's opening game was Brazil versus Spain on the second night. I was prepped up to the eyeballs. When I checked into the studios four hours before kick-off, I was told there were big problems in Guadalajara. I was placed on twitchy alert.

Half an hour before the match was due to start, the programme editor came to see me with good, bad and indifferent news. Contact with Guadalajara was intermittent so an alternative was required. ITV's lead commentator, Brian Moore, had remained in London to present from the studio so he was the obvious alternative if the lines to Mexico died. I was to adjourn to a sound booth and lay down an audition commentary for future consideration if chaos across the airwaves became the norm for the tournament.

It was just me and a sound engineer. Thank God.

I sat in the bubble of the voiceover suite and watched the players file out. There were no captions of any description on my feed but no matter. I was not only getting the chance to show what I could do but with a field full of well-known names – Socrates, Michel, Careca, Zubizarreta, Branco – and the prospect of a match to make a reputation on, I certainly managed that.

With less than ten minutes played, the Spanish defender Antonio Maceda hit the underside of the Brazilian crossbar with a well-timed volley. The replays indicated that the ball had bounced down over the line. Spain were ahead.

Brazil forced a corner almost immediately. As the ball was swung into the box, Edinho beat the keeper to the punch and powered in a header to make it 1–1. What a start. I was enjoying myself.

At half-time, the sound engineer asked me if I wanted tea and coffee and then added his $64,000 question. 'What score are you saying it is?'

Shit.

In those far-off, pre-VAR days, Maceda's goal had been disallowed, albeit wrongly. Edinho's equaliser was then rightly disallowed for a Maradonaesque sleight of hand. Forty-five minutes into my network television life and I was two goals awry of the correct score. It was still 0–0.

I was quick to confess the next morning. The next afternoon, I was on a train home.

'We'd be stupid not to use Brian if the lines go down again, wouldn't we?' said my hanging judge. No further questions, your honour.

I managed to resist the temptation to jump off that speeding train and ITV managed to resist the temptation to condemn my commentary career there and then. My mistakes would have been quickly corrected if I had been live to the nation. Without screen graphics, they were easy ones to make.

Without an audience of millions, they were certainly easier to recover from.

6

KING KENNY

Sir Kenny Dalglish may have the most childish sense of humour of anyone I've ever met, adult or child.

And yet for a couple of months in the spring of 1989 he was the most adult of all the adults on earth.

He didn't want to be. He wanted to be pulling infantile pranks on colleagues and friends and trying to avoid and deflect all of the serious questions that people like me were continually asking him in his capacity as Liverpool manager.

That capacity changed forever on 15 April of that year. Kenny's capacity to cope with the change swelled to proportions that nobody could have expected of him or anyone. He was simply colossal.

I commentated on an FA Cup semi-final in Birmingham that day . . . or I commentated on about twenty minutes of it anyway. My career was in transition between local radio and regional television and I drove to Villa Park to cover the 'other semi' between Everton and Norwich City for Radio City.

What follows next is a confession that has shaped a small part of my life to this day. A confession about an event that ended 96 innocent lives and ruined many more.

I wasn't at Hillsborough but I was at Heysel. I had never

seen a corpse before that night in 1985 but I found myself counting dead bodies at one point during it. I cried a lot in the days afterwards. To this day, I believe Heysel was a tragedy caused by hooligan behaviour.

Four years on, we cut short the Everton–Norwich commentary as soon as the first fatalities were announced in Sheffield. From memory, Radio City aired sombre classical music between news updates. It was the convention back then.

Driving back up the M6 to my Wirral home, I was as angry as I was shocked or saddened. My first assumption was that this was exactly the same disaster I had been an eye witness to in Brussels. I have never jumped to a conclusion so readily in 30 years since.

I was so wrong.

The radio station controller, Tony Ingham, was one of my best friends at the time. He called me on my return home and told me to report at 7 o'clock the next morning to host a phone-in. I refused initially. I told him, 'It's happened again, I'm just glad I wasn't there to see it this time.'

Tony insisted. I arrived at our studios in Stanley Street shortly before 7. By 9 o'clock, I was crying again. Crying at the awful detail, crying that I personally had presumed so much, so misguidedly.

The first person to greet me as I walked through the studio doors that morning was a middle-aged man holding his match ticket up to show me. The perforation had not been torn by a turnstile operator. 'They just opened the gates, Clive,' he said mournfully. How in God's name did it take 30 years for him to be properly heard?

The phone-in began at 8 am. Most of the Taylor Report had

been effectively drafted by half-past. Every caller told a part of the same grim story. There were no inconsistencies, no doubts. Lambs to the slaughter.

When Kenny Dalglish resigned as Liverpool manager nearly three years later, that slaughter still hung heavy across his shoulders. They were broad enough to hold off Terry Butcher and Gordon McQueen when they clung onto handfuls of his red No 7 shirt but the strain of carrying so much communal grief and stress in the weeks and months after Hillsborough wore him down, wore him out.

Maybe I imagine it with hindsight but he seemed to be forever yawning, often scratching irritated skin, often irritated full stop. One of the most natural smiles in football had faded.

That infectious smile broke out across his famous features each time he conjured the ball into the opposition net. No goal mattered more than the last or the next to him. Every single one was treasured. Dalglish goal celebrations were unrehearsed, unfettered. Two wide arms, one wide grin.

That grin was every bit as wide if he caught you out with one of his kindergarten wheezes. 'Sorry, Kenny, I didn't catch what you said.' 'Pardon?' 'I said I didn't catch what . . .' 'Waaaaaah!' And there he was peeling away in triumph as if he'd just chipped you in the last minute at Goodison, rather than lured you tamely into some juvenile wind-up.

Some of those wind-ups were Alan Hansen collaborations and were rather more PG or X-rated in content, but they all bore the same puerile hallmarks. It was a bloody hard school.

Alan Irvine was a tall striker signed from Falkirk on a hunch and a prayer. His Liverpool career only totalled four substitute appearances but he was part of the squad for an FA Cup replay against Luton Town at the start of 1987. The players spent the afternoon before the game resting in a city centre hotel. They were wakened to the news that the match had been postponed because of heavy snow that prevented the Luton squad reaching Merseyside.

A coach ferried the players from the hotel back to Anfield to collect their cars. There were still a few hundred fans gathered around the stadium because news of the cancellation had travelled as slowly as the Luton squad. The news hadn't reached Irvine either. Hansen and Dalglish had seen to that.

So, as the 24-year-old Scot was preparing himself for another frustrating night as 14th man, Kenny came down the bus to tell him that he would be making his debut. Not just that, but the manager had decided to try him out as a centre-back. The horror on Irvine's face obviously touched Kenny . . . when he staged a mock team meeting inside the dressing-room a few minutes later, he named the forward in midfield instead. Ronnie Whelan even threw a fake tantrum in protest.

Irvine duly disappeared in the direction of the toilet to fully prepare himself in the time-honoured manner. When he returned to the changing area, all of the lights had been turned off and the other players had legged it. The sting was complete.

There are a lot of things that happened in football back then that don't happen now . . . a lot of things that happened on the planet that most of the world has since mercifully grown out of. Kenny is a serious, sensitive man. He would be the first Liverpool director to step in if the current manager thought about pulling a stunt like that on a vulnerable young charge in this age of Twitter and tabloid scrutiny. But it is the contradictions in his character that make him so relatable to so many.

You don't become a folk hero without possessing a common touch. Kenny connected with the local frequency the moment he arrived. Remember, he was replacing a famous son of the Shankly era. When Kevin Keegan announced his leaving of Liverpool for Hamburg in the spring of 1977, it was left to Bob Paisley to replace the irreplaceable.

Most things that mattered at Liverpool back then were controlled by the quiet competence of a man called Peter Robinson. His title was secretary but his sphere covered the modern-day duties of a host of chief executives, chief operating officers and and sporting, technical and football directors. Nothing ever happened at Anfield without his nod.

He not only fed the Merseyside media the news of Kevin's imminent departure when it suited the club, he gave us four names from which a replacement would be recruited for a club record fee. Peter Sayer of Cardiff City was one of them. I can't remember the others. They were literally red herrings. At another time of Robinson's choosing, Dalglish was identified as the main target. The deal was probably long done and dusted.

Paisley never possessed the eloquence to fully explain his innovative gut coaching instincts, but if he described Kenny as 'a passing player' once during the informal briefing that Robinson set up for us local hacks, he must have done it a dozen times. Paisley was set on developing Shankly's all-action passion play of a team into a possession-based thinking man's side. Keegan's perspiration would be replaced by Dalglish's perception. A new die was to be cast. Same mentality, different tactics.

But Kenny's innate intelligence worked far beyond the nooks and crannies of a crowded penalty area. He just 'got' Liverpool from the start. Got the club, got the city, got the people. He was little more of an orator than Paisley. No Shankly, no Klopp for that matter. But he could communicate his passion and commitment to his new fans with a soft sincerity that rang loud and clear with every one of them. They could see he meant everything he said . . . even if they couldn't always understand it!

And Robinson could see it too. Eight years later it was 'the secretary' 'PBR' that oversaw the surprise elevation of Dalglish from playmaker to decision-maker after Joe Fagan found the Heysel aftermath too much to absorb. Managing from within a dressing-room so stacked with strong characters and reputations was a challenge that Kenny met without breaking stride.

Maybe it's a Glasgow thing. All the evidence points to something in the water on Clydeside.

Bill Shankly was born in an Ayrshire mining community 40 miles away and both Jock Stein and Sir Matt Busby hailed from satellite towns on the edges of the Glasgow conurbation. Walter Smith too. But Dalglish, Sir Alex Ferguson, George Graham, David Moyes and Tommy Docherty . . . born and bred downtown Glaswegians. Sound like it, act like it.

If you'd had to choose one of the above to win an argument with, who would it have been? No, me neither.

I could listen to Sir Billy Connolly speak all night long. His arresting wit and street wisdom emanates from the same geographical source. He was a boilermaker at a Glasgow shipyard until he talked and sang his way out into a career better suited to his creative bent. Brilliant, brilliant man.

Many of his colourful monologues and tales of yore capture the character of the hard-headed, thick-skinned men that have gone on to represent the city's nature and values so successfully in football management.

You wouldn't want to tangle with a single one of them. They are front-foot scrappers, they don't back down from a position. Their boneheaded streaks run deeper and thicker than the seams in the Lanarkshire coalfields. For such an ingenious and inventive performer Kenny can be doggedly and perversely set in his ways.

I may not be stupid enough to pick an argument with him but I did manage to start a famous spat between Kenny and another Glaswegian knight of the realm. Inadvertently it should be said, it was me that got Dalglish and Ferguson in the ring together in 1988. Eddie Hearn eat your heart out.

In the aftermath of a stormy 3–3 draw between Liverpool and United, I happened to overhear Fergie spitting some venomous words into the microphone of my radio counterpart from Manchester in the corridor just outside the Boot Room. He was going to town on the referee, claiming that visiting managers left Anfield 'choking on their own vomit and afraid to tell the truth' about some of the decisions that went Liverpool's way there.

I thought Kenny should be briefed on the outburst ahead of his own press conference, so I tiptoed the 15 yards down to his office to alert him to the incoming artillery fire. As I made my way back to where the United manager's ire was still boiling over onto journalists' notepads, I heard a familiar voice behind me calling out angrily. Contrary Kenny had appeared at his office door cradling his baby daughter, Lauren.

'You'll get more sense out of her,' he shouted up to the scribbling press men surrounding Fergie. Their stories were written in that moment.

It was a side of Kenny that he didn't let you see very often. Maybe a bit of the East side coming out. His responses to a challenge were usually more measured, more defensive. But he could put you down all right. Like a heckler at a Connolly gig, you were given the full treatment if you momentarily got above yourself.

My reflections on that famous tartan dust-up are that I was way, way out of my depth. It was none of my business. I should have stayed out of it. I was Bambi riling two lions.

Quite apart from anything else, the relationships we build with managers and players are essentially professional relationships. They require and demand discretion and confidentiality. You only betray the trust of people like Dalglish and Ferguson once.

I suppose it's inevitable in a profession where I am called upon to report the extraordinary feats of pre-eminent achievers that I am frequently going to see actions and reactions that are beyond my comprehension. I can't do a lot of things that Kenny has done. I definitely couldn't have done that.

Dalglish and Ferguson must be, by definition, extraordinary people. And extraordinary people, by definition, must be capable of extreme behaviour.

We cannot marvel at their sustained success in such a transient profession and be taken aback when they do things that the rest of us do not or cannot. It just isn't logical to analyse them by the same criteria we apply to the mere mortals around us.

Their field has different boundaries and limits. It is revealingly public and relentlessly demanding. As commentators and sportswriters, we spout about the pressures of management as if we know what they are and can account for their impact. We have no idea really.

What is pressure? Pressure is expectation. The sum total of the outside world's expectations of you plus your own expectations of yourself.

With serial strivers like Dalglish and Ferguson, the latter is the larger number. They push themselves even harder than they push the players they are paid to push. They don't take kindly to anything that pushes back against them. Particularly each other.

All of that pushing has got to take it out of you. Nobody else does it for them. Managers are individuals in a team sport. They have their assistants, their families and their representatives, but football is a blame game and the fickle fingers soon start to point at one guy and one guy only.

The Ryder Cup is one of my very favourite sporting contests because it is a team event played by individuals. The changed parameters bring out the best in some of those individuals and confound the life out of others. It is a sports psychology major championship.

There were a few years at the start of the century when Tiger Woods was arguably the outstanding individual sportsman on earth, but he couldn't get his head around the team culture of a Ryder Cup.

When you are standing over a six-foot putt to save a match, the technique is still that of an individual competitor because there are only two hands wrapped around the putter grip. The difference is that you are no longer hoping to hole that putt for yourself and your bank balance, you are trying to make the ball disappear on behalf of eleven other players and thousands of committed fans. The responsibility has been multiplied many times over.

Football managers carry that responsibility 24/7. Worse still, like the non-playing Ryder Cup captains, they don't even get to swing a club in anger.

They are hostages to fortune, to the break of the ball. We make them walk the tightrope of the touchline without a safety net while we gawp at them through a 4K high-definition camera lens. Whatever their body language is saying to us at the time of maximum stress, we note down and pore over at length. We define them by their behaviour in their most difficult moments. At the extremes.

A big part of dealing with managerial pressure is actually looking like you are dealing with it. Unless you cast your dignity to the winds like Diego Simeone, that look of control takes a bottled nervous energy that has got to escape somewhere, sometime.

On the field, the team that the manager has selected is making a collective, combined effort. They are playing a team game, their responsibilities are shared. If they win or draw honourably, the manager may be handed a ration of the responsibility for the 'good result'. If they lose or fail to impress, the manager gets to carry the whole can full of liability home with him.

The sight of a manager swimming against the tide is a haunting one. They are as helpless as a fly caught in a spider's web, as desperate as someone trying to rescue a failing marriage. It happens to the best of them. It's rarely their fault. It happened to Kenny in circumstances that no manager in the world could have dealt with.

Three or four days on from the Hillsborough tragedy, I was standing in the car park at Anfield along with the rest of the press pack waiting for the next announcement. The stadium had become a catchment point for a city's outpourings of emotion. The Kop terraces and the hallowed turf in front of them were soon covered in heartfelt floral tributes. The club opened its doors to the bereaved families to meet and mourn together.

Without warning or explanation, I was summoned from the gathered media corps to meet Kenny in the Anfield reception area. He greeted me with a solemn hand-shake and two words: 'Ian Whelan.'

Ian was 19 when he set out from his Padgate home to support his team at a football match. He never returned. His ambition was to be a football commentator, the very same ambition I had fancifully entertained throughout my teens.

I couldn't recall him immediately but a few minutes in the company of his sister Kerry and his wonderful parents Wilf and Doris reminded me. I had shown Ian around the Radio City studios a few months earlier because he had written to me. He wanted to 'be me'.

I sat in the old Players' Lounge at Anfield remembering Ian with his closest family. To my left and to my right, young footballers without even the vaguest training at any level of counselling were deep in dire conversation with grieving relatives. It is easy to wax lyrical about the communion of football but I've never witnessed anything closer than that.

Jimmy McGovern made a TV drama about Hillsborough that breaks me into a million pieces every time I dare to watch it. There is an extraordinary drama still to be made about the caring aftermath. About Kenny, about those spoilt, confident, vaunted young talents getting the biggest reality check ever given to a footballer. 'My dead daughter idolised you.' Jesus fuckin' Christ.

Ian's hero was, inevitably, Ronnie Whelan. Ian's nickname was Ronnie. I found myself tentatively interrupting a conversation that Ronnie and his wife Elaine were having with another family in order to introduce him to Ian's parents and sister. He was 27, he was a bit of a lad. I'd been properly pissed with him on more than one occasion, and here we were attempting to comfort three strangers that had lost the most important person in their lives simply because Ian supported Liverpool with a passion.

An hour or so later, I was still in the same 'hospitality' room when I happened across a young woman who I knew from a nightclub in Birkenhead that we both frequented. 'Karen, what are you doing here?' I asked mindlessly. 'My dad,' came the abrupt reply. Ray Chapman, 50 years of age, left a wife, a son and a daughter I'd tried to chat up more than once.

Liverpool was a small town that week. Everyone knew someone that hadn't come home. Kenny came to know them all. He was everywhere. Listening, reassuring, absorbing. I kept hugging him. I wasn't the only one.

Liverpool didn't play again for eighteen days after Hillsborough . . . eighteen days of harrowing funerals. Kenny went to almost all of them. His wife, Marina, was every bit as dignified and strong as he was. They were unprecedented times and his determination not to resume playing until Liverpool FC and all of its extended family was ready to do so was respected by the football authorities.

Eventually, a date was set for the games to begin again. Fittingly – given the way that the tragedy had consumed all of Merseyside – the first competitive fixture was to be against Everton. Kenny took the players away from the eye of the storm to prepare in Blackpool. I received a message to go to the Norbreck Hydro Hotel to interview him ahead of the match.

During the drive up there, I did wonder if I'd been granted an 'exclusive' in return for all the difficult, reflective moments we had spent together in the wake of the tragedy. Kenny never did exclusives. There is an inherent fairness about the man that overrides all of his stubborn opinions and deep-seated obstinacy. The deal was a five-minute recorded match preview to be transcribed for use by all media sources.

As he walked towards me in the hotel foyer, I smiled affectionately and made to share another embrace with him. Kenny's arms remained by his side. That chapter was over. 'Turn your machine on, let's get this done'. The interview lasted about four minutes, 55 seconds. The content was almost Churchillian. I'm not saying he had rehearsed it but it was pretty evident when he'd finished. The manager had returned to work. There was a match to win.

Unlike Kenny, I didn't play in the 1985 European Cup final but I did work on it. I can't speak for those that had to perform out there in the middle, but I commentated on the match less than an hour after I'd counted those lifeless bodies piled one on top of another. Don't ask me why but I even contested the penalty award that settled the game. The force of football does strange things to us. I think he would tell you that he tried all he knew to beat Juventus that eerie night. The game takes us to places we don't readily recognise. It heightens certain senses and shuts down others.

One of the main defining differences between those that succeed in football and the rest of us that merely observe and wonder is that the professionals are able to separate the business from the pleasure. The Liverpool team of the 1970s and '80s were business experts. Their social habits and diet regimes may not have stood up to comparison with the science and scrutiny of the twenty-first-century game but they had a winning culture and collective ethos beyond the mantra of any contemporary sports psychologist.

If I ever needed to interview Terry McDermott, I knew exactly which working men's club in Kirkby to go to. He regularly spent his afternoons playing snooker with lifelong mates and enjoying a couple of quiet pints. Very quiet. There was always a stale glass of orange squash sitting on a table as an alibi if a stranger walked in. Terry Mc was not a model professional but he was also ready to run further and harder than any other player in just about every match he played. Kenny bought into deals like that. Management.

Liverpool won ten English titles in fifteen years and lifted the European Cup four times in that same period. Dalglish was central to most of that success as player, manager and player–manager. The only honour missing from his collection was the belated knighthood conferred upon him in 2018. If he could have shared that title with his team-mates, he would have done. He was an elite soldier with private's stripes. One of the guys.

Not that he lacked a sense of his own ability or importance. You don't get to score 360-odd senior goals without a strut in your personal stride or a productive selfish streak. It's just not the Liverpool way to point at the name on the back of the shirt when you score, only at the mythical bird on the front. You play for that badge and the other ten badges around you.

As a Radio City commentator, I was around that all-conquering team for the most impressionable decade of my working life. I was the same age as those players. When they beat Real Madrid in Paris in 1981, I sat among them in the Lido on the Champs Élysées with the European Cup on the table and more posh champagne than I could drink flowing onto the club tab. I was with my mates.

The previous September, my mates and I had flown most of the way to the Arctic Circle for them to play against the Finnish part-timers of Oulun Palloseura in the first round of the competition. I made a routine visit to the stadium on the eve of the game to check out the commentary position only to find a local track and field event in full swing complete with shot puts and hammers crashing into the sodden playing surface. It was a mess.

On my return to the team hotel, Ray Clemence and Phil Neal interrupted a card game in reception to ask me what the playing surface was like. I gave them a full report of the damage being done to the turf by flying objects and steady drizzle. They laughed off the news with a roll of the eyes and the confident air that comes from having been there, seen it, won it.

Before I could get to the lift back to my room, I was apprehended by Ronnie Moran. He was the sergeant-major of the coaching staff. A Liverpool loyalist from cot to grave, he served the club as player and coach with a determination and devotion that few have equalled. But when it came to water levels, Bugsy was strictly a glass half-empty man. He was dearly loved by every player that he ever demanded an extra yard of, but his feet were nailed firmly to terra firma. And so nobody else's were going anywhere different.

'Don't ever do that again,' he barked at me, holding the lift with an outstretched arm.

'What?'

'Don't tell them the pitch is crap.'

'It is, Ronnie. You'll see for yourself tomorrow,' I protested.

'Tell them it's like Wembley.'

'What?!'

'Tell them it's like Wembley. Never give them an excuse. We don't do that.'

Liverpool didn't accept excuses. Not before the game and rarely afterwards. From Bill Shankly to Bob Paisley to Joe Fagan via Ronnie Moran, Tom Saunders and Roy Evans, the formula was consistent. 'Match the opposition for effort and desire and your ability will take care of the rest.' That went for an opposition that was probably pulling the shutters down on their family cafe or hurrying home from a bank clerk's job at the moment Ronnie was lecturing me on the Liverpool way. Nobody and nothing was ever underestimated.

Kenny bought into that Liverpool mindset from day one. He was the ultimate team player, the definition of a players' manager. Google away and you won't find a single disparaging comment about any squad member he ever handed a jersey to. Not in public. You won't unearth a pompous boast or a granted taken.

His twinkling toes scored some of the best goals I've ever seen but – like Ronnie – his feet never left the ground. Interviewing him was like trying to transfuse blood from a particularly jagged stone. He could be difficult. Constrained and contrary answers to straightforward questions were standard. I once began a post-match radio interview following a 6–0 win with . . .

'Kenny, you must be absolutely delighted with that.'

'Must I?' came the abrupt retort. 'You asking me or telling me?'

I've refrained from starting another interview with a statement from that day to this. Open with a question. A lesson learnt the hard way, the Kenny way.

He could be secretive to the point that even the players seemed ill-prepared for some of his selections. I was privileged to stand in a spot right outside the dressing-room before home games with an eye to being first with the team news. Ceremonially, he would take a match programme from my hand shortly before 2 o'clock and silently begin correcting the published XI with a pen. As he carefully crossed out a famous name and wrote an unexpected one next to it, I might venture an occasional 'injured, Kenny?' He never once broke the silence. No explanations of the tactical set-up. No need for anyone else to know in advance. A private man who put the club and the team before all else.

Well, nearly all else, because if there was a practical joke to be played on someone that he thought could take it, he struggled to resist. The story of Steve Nicol being duped into believing that Kenny was dying dates back to 1984. It has been told and reworked a million times and only those present can tell you the definitive tale. I just like the version that ends with the tables being turned on Kenny for once.

Early in January of that year, he suffered a badly fractured cheekbone in a match against Manchester United. Kenny was sidelined for eight weeks. On his return, he found goals and form a little harder to come by than usual.

Enter Nicol – a universally popular member of the squad, by the way. When he was let in on the concocted 'secret' of a terminal disease that was supposedly threatening the life of a revered friend and mentor, Steve was distraught even before he was led mournfully to Dalglish's darkened hotel bedroom to visit his stricken manager for the mother of all wind-ups. It was the cruellest comedy.

But, so the story goes, when Kenny whispered, 'Did you have no inkling?' Nicol replied with typical honesty, 'Well, I could see you weren't playing very well, but . . .'

Cue uncontrolled burst of laughter from the watching Hansen, and the end of the ultimate prank. The biter bit.

A face for radio. *Sportsweek* presenter, 1989.

FIRST FULL-TIME JOB IN TELEVISION:

Granada Television

Manchester

1987–92

I always wanted to be on the telly.

Walking through the front door of Granada Television's studio complex in Manchester with my own security pass was in itself a kind of fantasy acted out. Sometimes, I even got to share a lift with Tony Wilson or Richard Madeley. Or saw Ken and Deirdre Barlow in the canteen. Our dreams are strange things, right?

The first steps you take onto the floor of a television studio are tiptoed ones. You are surrounded by large red letters shouting at you to be quiet. The hangar height of the ceiling forces your eyes to look up in wonder at rows of chunky spotlights hanging precariously from a grid of metal supports. It is the *Starship Enterprise* without the delights of Lieutenant Uhura.

Studios are oddly cold, airy and forbidding places in which to look into a small round camera lens and try to be warm, cosy and welcoming. I am in awe of the light entertainment headliners like Dermot O'Leary, Declan Donnelly and Bradley Walsh who can transmit their engaging personalities to a faceless audience of millions through a piece of grey cinematic kit. I was never a threat to Des Lynam.

Thankfully, my first stab at presentation came at

around 1 o'clock in the morning. To thousands not millions. My television debut was on a late-night chat show called *Sportsweek*. Elton Welsby was the host and had been instrumental in putting me forward for a role on the programme.

That role consisted of a two-minute comment piece that I delivered straight into the black hole of the lens without a safety net. Granada's glowering head of sport, Paul Doherty, was a firm believer in schooling his presenters without the aid of the rolling script of an autocue machine. I think it was probably a budget issue.

I was still overseeing the Radio City sports department by way of a day job, but every Monday night I had a gentle make-up brush applied to my fat cheeks and Paul's 'firm' editorial boot swung up my fat backside as I tried to write, learn and pithily deliver some comedic reflections on the weekend's big sports story. Clive James, I was not.

Throughout my career, I've enjoyed the luxury of being able to walk down any crowded shopping street without people pointing at me and trying to remember what part I play in *Holby City*.

Very occasionally, my voice rings a bell with someone behind me at a checkout and I might get a tentative, 'Are you Clive Tyldesley?' thrown my way. They all get the same terse answer from me. 'Depends if you like him or not.'

Life as a 'voice' is so much better than life as a 'face', and in so many ways.

7

SUMMERALL

Pat Summerall was my favourite sports commentator of all.
He was the voice of American Football when I became hooked
on Channel 4's coverage of the NFL in the mid-1980s era of
Theismann and Marino, of Allen and Riggins.

Pat was the straight man to the crazy colour commentary
of John Madden. He never wasted a word.

Tap 'Summerall's best commentary lines' into a search
engine and you will be lucky to find a single entry. No 'Remember the Name', no 'Agueroooo', certainly no 'Greek God in
Rome'. Pat's idea of picking his words was, 'Montana . . . to Rice
. . . Touchdown.' As unerring with his connections as the 49ers
quarter-back and wide receiver were with theirs.

You don't need a Thesaurus to become a true wordsmith.
The value of language is not measured in syllables. Adjectives
are embellishments, they are not always required.

It wasn't Pat's words so much as the way he delivered them.
The timing, the phrasing, the capture of the moment through
tone and texture rather than froth and hot air. The most
memorable sporting stories are dramas, not melodramas. They
don't need selling.

It helps when you've got a voice that can shake people out

of a coma. Pat was never a shouter, he didn't need to be. His timbre was commanding and captive. Pitch perfect. He came through loud and clear without ever having to raise his voice. As rich as Sinatra's.

He was also the ideal foil for the manic outpourings of Coach Madden. John sounded more like he was searching the dial for the right frequency as his voice wavered up and down and this way and that. He drew his scribbles and squiggles on the screen while painting wobbly lines of investigation across our minds. They were attracted opposites. Solid chalk and runny cheese.

Madden was the born entertainer. Pat deferentially created a stage on which his partner could best perform. He recognised his own strengths and played to them. In doing so, he promoted the unique brilliance of his team-mate. The definition of a double act.

One of the first things that you've got to get your head around in our line of work is that you are only as good as the person sitting next to you, be they a co-commentator, a sound engineer or a runner asking how you want your tea at half-time. This is a team game.

The nature of the sport may change the detail of the way in which you complement each other but the long chain of inter-relationships is the thread that holds outside broadcasts together.

American Football has a structured order that makes it easier to work the rhythm of play-by-play commentary than in a football or rugby match. There are natural breaks for the lead commentator to pause and for the analyst to reflect.

There are also a lot of numbers in the essential vocabulary of each action – the time, the down, the yardage. Pat used those numbers to carefully build the tension before each explosion of action. Like he was solemnly counting us down to a Cape Canaveral space launch. He kept control at all times, kept Madden on message.

Of course, the beauty of the business is that the commentator I've just described might not be your idea of a good commentator at all. You may want a little more cream in your coffee. Or four sugars.

If your fondness is for the microphone to be in the hand of a verbal contortionist or some flowery poet or a clownish court jester, then you are most welcome to some of the most famous names in British radio and television sport. We cater for all tastes.

There are no rights and wrongs, only light and shade. Summerall was my cup of tea but without Madden there would not have been the same blend.

One of the enduring delights of *Test Match Special* on BBC Radio is the range and variety in the cast list. With the right blend of personalities on duty, you get a little bit of everything. But if that mix is wrong for the moment they are capturing, I end up throwing things at the car radio.

I was driving to a football game one Saturday morning during the 2019 Ashes series when England were hanging in after a calamitous start to the third Test. Australia held a lead of close to 300 with four second innings wickets standing. It was going to be a tense, taut session. We were in danger of being batted out of the series. The summer was on the line.

Jonathan Agnew and Phil Tufnell opened for *TMS*. Michael Vaughan, Jim Maxwell, Ali Mitchell, Glenn McGrath and Simon Mann were all padded up and ready to talk cricket with their usual studied authority, but instead the duty producer opted for half an hour of Aggers and Tuffers talking rural Leicestershire churches and garden fetes. I must apologise for my driving that morning.

Somewhere, someone will have rated that half hour of rambling charm as the broadcast highlight of their year. I thought it was self-indulgent and trivial bilge. I don't mind a lemon drizzle cake arriving in the commentary box from time to time or the occasional discourse on bird species and tree types in the locality. They are at the heart of the strange brew of broadcast styles that is *TMS*. But please, not when Jofra Archer is bowling his heart out to try to save an Ashes series.

The perfect gent that was Graham Taylor once said to me that he didn't mind outsiders disagreeing with his team selections as long as they understood one thing. However much thought they had put into arriving at their opinion, he had already given ten times as much to his. As professionals, we may get it totally wrong at times but it's not usually for the want of trying to get it right. Not usually.

Graham's career will be forever characterised by the invasive close-ups of him trying to weather that wretched night in Rotterdam in 1993. It was his misjudgement to allow the documentary cameras to get so close, but his agitated chuntering on the England bench is not remotely representative of a wonderfully earnest man or his legacy.

We are in an age where public figures are portrayed by subliminal snapshots of their lives. So, we can't be surprised that, as public broadcasters, our reputations are filed under one headline remark.

Nearly every obituary I read of the broadcast icon that was Brian Moore featured a reference to the moment he unadvisedly put Kevin Keegan on the spot during an England penalty shootout. It was just about the only mistake of a marvellous thirty-seven-year career that anyone can remember. Were his family supposed to take the highlighting of it as a compliment?

That fleeting moment when he lost hold of his impeccable judgement and asked Keegan if he thought David Batty would score lived with Brian for ages. It tortured him. He re-ran it over and over in his mind. He felt worse for Kevin than he did for himself.

We know that we are only commentators. Nobody dies when we cock-up. If the nation guffaws then that is a tiny price to pay for doing a job that was once a magic castle in the air for most of us. Just try to refrain from asking us at a charity event what our worst mistake has been. Our charity might just run out there and then. It's our job. We take it seriously. We are haunted by our mistakes.

I don't know for sure that every commentator takes his or her job as seriously as Brian did or as I do. I may be totally wrong but I can't imagine Murray Walker spending quite so long beating himself up over a single faux pas. Or Henry Blofeld. Or Stuart Hall. Or David Lloyd. Or Sid Waddell. Or Aggers and Tuffers for that matter. And that's fine. There is room for the nutty caramel and the creamy fudge and the rum truffle in the same selection box.

Bill McLaren and Peter Alliss have a million times more

admirers than I can ever hope for but neither was wholly to my taste. For me, Nick Mullins finds a better resonance when he refers to a junior club that a current rugby international once played for. In my opinion, Andrew Cotter brings a sharper sense of dry humour to golf coverage. Both men would be embarrassed by any comparisons drawn with their famous predecessors at the mic but they would be my preferred choices. And choices that I have given thought to. Alliss went to entertain his maker last year with a cavalcade of tributes lining his path to making St Peter chuckle at the Pearly Gates. The mellifluous chords that his dulcet tones struck with millions will be replayed long after my name has been forgotten, but we are both a matter of personal opinion and endearment. That's just how our profession is.

When Brian Johnston passed away in 1994, a clip of radio commentary during which he descended into a fit of giggles was played endlessly. We were being asked to remember him for one jocular farce in a long and decorated career that spanned royal weddings and funerals as well as cricket commentary. Johnston was adept at striking the right balance between description, comment and hilarity. He was a masterful commentator, not a music hall act.

Johnners' most famous commentary line was, 'the bowler's Holding, the batsman's Willey'. Guess what? He never actually said it. It's a myth.

The danger when a commentator tries too hard to build a trademark caricature is that they become known as that fictional cartoon version of themselves. I am not precious. I dare say I can sound a bit like Alan Partridge at times. Calling out names is a strange way to make a living. A little self-parody can keep us just the right side of sanity. But I think we've got to be careful not to invite mockery. It will come our way without courting it.

Like Johnston, Pat Summerall could mix the light and conversational with the heavyweight calls in his commentaries. In order to fully indulge the quirky detours that John Madden took en route to nailing a play, Pat needed to gently prompt and prod his running mate in the right direction.

He was a lead commentator on major golf and tennis events too. Such was Summerall's mastery of the feel and execution of sports commentary that I assumed for many years that he was broadcast-trained, that Madden was the ex-coach and Pat was the ex-journalist. Not a bit of it.

Summerall's name appeared on NFL rosters in Detroit and New York in the late-1950s. He could handle himself out there in the middle. At six-foot-four and a recovered alcoholic, I dare say he could handle himself anywhere.

However, because he retired in 2002, he never had to handle trial by Twitter. Surveillance by social media has changed the temperature of our working conditions. I opened my Twitter account in 2008. When I had only a couple of thousand followers, it was a very productive outlet for exchanging views and seeking opinions on the direction that sports broadcasting was taking. A consultation platform to share with people interested enough in our trade to register that interest. Fun.

That was then, this is now. Twitter has become one long stretch of quicksand. You step onto it at your peril. It is shifting quicksand. My @mentions billow and blow during the minutes that I am live on air, then drift and settle again until the next match. Someone else's turn to be abused. It is today's fish 'n' chip paper. Disposable waste.

Or it is until it's recycled. When the weather sets in, you've got to batten down the hatches and hang on for dear life. You get no warning when a Twitter storm is brewing. No gathering clouds, no freshening breeze. The skies above you are blue one moment, then dark and threatening the next. You can get swept away by a tidal wave before you know it.

I was once describing how *FIFA* is recorded during a live chat on the Mumsnet website and referring to the bizarre daily routine of sitting in a sound booth for hours on end randomly shouting out hundreds and hundreds of player names. 'If a psychiatrist walked in, the men in white coats would be called to lead me away to the nearest padded cell,' I said with a smile in my voice.

I spent the next 24 hours explaining myself to mental health campaigners demanding my resignation on Twitter.

The most disturbing aspect of such a storm is the whirlwind speed at which it wells up. The original context for the allegations has soon disappeared onto another page on everybody's timelines. One moment you may have made an insensitive remark about 'padded cells', the next you have officially disrespected anyone touched by a mental illness. Charged and sentenced.

The problem is not Twitter but the weight and validity that we afford it. It is a forum for opinion but it is not an opinion poll. We create our own sampling because we invariably follow contributors that share our views. If we choose to live our lives by the outlook sketched on our Twitter feeds then we are effectively opting to join a kind of cult in which we surround ourselves with fellow-believers.

I may be as guilty as anyone in so much that I enjoy waking up to a page full of like minds but, as an inquiring broadcast journalist, I then dare to venture further afield into the *Daily Mail*'s parallel universe of a Boris Johnson government and a Brexited Britain. The world outside.

It is there that I find random and totally unqualified tweets being included in the same news threads and stories that quote the managers and players we most want to hear from.

'Interesting words from Jurgen Klopp there. Meanwhile Steve tweets "Liverpool must go to a back three. Need more defensive security". Another tweet here from Michael . . .'

Er, point of order Mr Speaker. Have Steve or Michael ever put on a coaching session in their Bot lives? Oh, you didn't think to ask. You just read their tweets out on national radio.

Vox pop clickbait.

I'm on Twitter myself. If I want to read bonkers tweets, I know which keys to press. I don't go to the cinema to see the latest stock prices. I've chosen national radio for informed and authenticated information. Any chance?

When people I respect start getting their medical and financial advice from Twitter, I'll listen. Deal?

I've never quite worked out why television news channels feel compelled to visit a shopping mall to find out what the impact of a fall in world oil prices will have on the nation's GDP. They never show the members of the public that say 'sorry, I don't know', only those that want to be on the telly. It is no more than lip service to some skewed notion of public opinion. It's about as reflective as Twitter.

If I wanted to appear in a reality show, I would take the fee and eat the critters. The thought of living in my personal version of *The Truman Show* does not appeal to me. I want to broaden my horizons, not pull the shutters down on a *Big Brother* house of my own making. Twitter is only ever what you want it to be.

You can buy tweets, you can block dissenters. It's not the actual world. Alfred Kinsey shocked America by reporting what Americans were doing, not what they liked to think they were doing. I am still naïve enough to seek a researched truth, not a version pumped out on reality TV or in social media trends.

Too many assumptions are made about me to fall into the same pre-conceived traps myself. I am not so vain nor pig-headed that I can't see any error in my ways. The language I used during the webchat on Mumsnet was glib and dated at best. I am not a PC denier. Most political correctness is just good manners, a show of due consideration to the feelings of our fellow human beings. I'm all for that.

It's the appetite for a witch hunt that leaves commentators increasingly frightened to open their mouths. I don't have a huge problem with haters. Everyone is entitled to their opinion. If you've got a pulse and a keyboard, you can now publish that opinion with a few taps of your index fingers. On you go.

I get some Twitter abuse from time to time. I take it. I'm on Twitter myself. If you can't ride two horses at once, don't join the circus.

My wife is savvy enough to monitor my Twitter traffic during the course of a live broadcast and alert me to any recurring gripes or trending. If my clumsy vocal chords have hit a wrong note with a section of the viewers, I'm certainly not too arrogant to consider how or why. It may be easier to cause offence than it used to be, but that doesn't make it right.

My issue is not with my detractors but rather with my stalkers. Everyone in my profession is being tailed by amateur detectives. A flock of buzzards that circle above us waiting and listening for one rogue word. 'Was that racist?' 'Could that be deemed sexist?' 'Did he just call Guardiola a liar?' 'What's the number for the *Sun* sports desk?'

At lunchtime on the day of the England–Croatia World Cup semi-final in 2018, the excellent producer on my case, Anne Barker, asked me if I felt excited at the prospect of broadcasting live to a viewing audience that I believe touched 28 million on the night. My reply was unacceptably flip.

'I can only fuck up tonight,' I told her. 'There is nothing whatsoever I can do to enhance my own personal reputation.'

It was a cynical, narky response that I apologised for promptly. I was very excited about the game, the broadcast and everything surrounding the occasion.

I am not an old cynic. I hate old cynics. The crotchety comment was aimed at the keyboard vultures that hover above you on the night of such a big match. You can tell yourself to ignore them but they are not going to ignore you. They can bring you down and rip you apart. But only if you let them.

Guy Mowbray was commentating to similar numbers with similar scrutiny all that summer on the BBC. Neither of us messed up. You can argue all you like about whether we were good, bad or indifferent but we shouted the right names at the right times and steered our respective ships to port through the biggest swells of the television year. A jury of millions and millions.

Towards the end of 2018, the six nominees for Football Commentator of the Year were announced for one of the most prestigious awards going. Neither Guy nor I made the shortlist. We had each served more customers in one night than the chosen nominees had spoken to all year. Fine, it's a free country.

But when you are commentating to half that country, you've got a lot more to lose. What's more, you know it too. In order to assess any performance, you've got to take the jeopardy level into account. Ours were the high tariff dives. We were on the top board. Try getting up there yourself and looking down.

Pat Summerall was lead commentator on sixteen Super Bowls. There are usually 100 million Americans watching any minute of a Super Bowl. He was charged with the impossible task of making them all feel like he was smooth-talking each of them. The bigger the audience, the wider the diversity, the greater the challenge, the harder the examination paper.

Pat never commentated to win awards, only to win attention for the next play he was calling. Advice to budding commentators? To myself? Write that on the back of your hand before every commentary.

What I've learnt from listening to his underplayed, understated approach to capturing the essence of an overblown event like Super Bowl is that you should always be speaking to your audience. Not to the quick-witted *Guardian* columnist ready to review you, not to the radical editor of a football website primed to pick holes in you, not to the gong-givers or your commentating peers.

Just talk to those millions. And with words and sentiments they understand. That's all there is to it. There are few rules and regulations. It works if it works for you. The hairs that stood up on the back of my neck when I heard Pat say 'and Marcus Allen could be gone' are the same hairs that the guy sitting next to me might have been pulling out with rage.

I just felt comfortable when I heard Pat's voice at the start of the game. Like everything was going to be okay. I don't think there is any greater compliment that can be paid to a sports commentator.

I do have a favourite Pat Summerall line. And he stole it from Prince. And maybe another sports broadcaster, Stuart Scott. Neither of them delivered it like my man, though.

I once heard Pat describe John Elway as being 'as cool as the other side of the pillow' during a Super Bowl. He could have been talking about himself.

MANCHESTER CITY v MANCHESTER UNITED
23/9/89 MAINE ROAD
DIVISION ONE

#	City		#	United	
1	PAUL COOPER		1	JIM LEIGHTON	
2	GARY FLEMING		2	VIV ANDERSON	
3	ANDY HINCHCLIFFE		3	MAL DONAGHY	
4	IAN BISHOP		7	RUSSELL BEARDSMORE	
5	BRIAN GAYLE		5	MIKE PHELAN	
6	STEVE REDMOND		6	GARY PALLISTER	
7	DAVID WHITE		4	MIKE DUXBURY	
8	TREVOR MORLEY		8	PAUL INCE	
9	DAVID OLDFIELD		9	BRIAN McCLAIR	
10	IAN BRIGHTWELL		10	MARK HUGHES	
11	PAUL LAKE		11	DANNY WALLACE	
12	GARY MEGSON		12	LEE SHARPE	
14	JASON BECKFORD		14	CLAYTON BLACKMORE	

Referee: Neil MIDGLEY

My first television commentary chart. TV debut 1989.

FIRST TELEVISION COMMENTARY:

23 September 1989

Manchester City 5 Manchester United 1

My fairy godmother must have had a Harry Potter wand.

The first match of my television commentary career was a classic. 'It's been an afternoon they'll talk about for years,' I predicted a little presumptuously at the final whistle. I wasn't wrong.

If any final confirmation were really required that I was 'over' Manchester United, the rousing pomp and circumstance with which I serenaded the procession of City goals that day was proof enough. All of the joy in my voice was for myself, though. A high television commentary gantry was the peak I'd always wanted to climb. My flag was at the summit at last.

Only the edited highlights of the match were ever screened. It was a regional outside broadcast for 'Granadaland' but it meant the world to me. So, you can imagine my horror when a scuffle in the crowd prompted the referee to lead the players off the field with five minutes played. Not quite how I'd dreamt it.

Fortunately, peace broke out and City defied all predictions to race into a three-goal half-time lead and go on to win 5–1. When David Oldfield tapped the fourth goal into an empty net, I ventured to say, 'and I could have scored that' over a replay. Some City fans remember that and other choice cuts of my commentary to this day.

It's flattering to be a part of people's memories. Or their good ones at least.

Looking back now on that commentary, the pitch of my voice was friskily coltish and lightweight. It was still relatively untouched by the array of guilty pleasures I have subsequently discovered. Short of a few thousand subsequent bottles of red wine. I was trying a little too hard to impress and so the tone was a bit *Boy's Own*, but six or seven out of ten for starters got me another booking.

I have tried to watch back every commentary I've done since that day. It is the only way to learn. I'd like to think that I am my own biggest critic. A peep at my @mentions on Twitter would tell you otherwise, but hopefully I'm my own biggest 'constructive' critic.

I cannot listen to any sports commentary without dissecting it. I am an absolute pain to watch all television with. I editorialise my way through news bulletins, I review every drama, every comedy, even every commercial.

If you were to push me to nominate the thirty seconds of popular television that best nail the brief of 'broad' broadcasting, I'd ask for days to think about it.

Like an irritatingly indecisive contestant on *Who Wants to Be a Millionaire*, I would talk out loud through the wondrous options – *Ozark*, *Fawlty Towers*, *Breaking Bad*, *Lost for Words*, *The Sopranos*, *The Singing Detective*, etc × 100 – before remembering what 'popular' television is, and how it best connects with the millions that make up its diverse audience.

BAFTA won't agree, but for me Peter Kay's 'Ave it' cameo in the John Smiths beer advert is the ultimate thirty seconds of popular television. I wouldn't change a single frame.

If there is a commentary equivalent, mine's a pint of that, please.

8

SOUEY

I can't think of a footballer I would rather have on my side than Graeme Souness.

It would mean that I wasn't playing against him for a start.

I've never seen a player exercise such a strong influence over the other twenty-one men on the field. Craig Johnston once said that 'it was like having your big brother in your team'.

I am happy to call Souey a friend of forty years. I'd hate to have him as an enemy.

Let's be clear, for the six years that he was at the nerve centre of a hugely successful Liverpool team, he was probably the best midfield player in Britain. He could do the lot. Pass long or short, shoot with either foot, carry the ball, tackle, win.

He was his own definition of a midfield player, an all-rounder. Souey doesn't care for the notion of specialist holding players or playmakers or box-to-box men. He doesn't think there is any room for either/or players at the nucleus of a team.

He was no racer. Quicker opponents could run away from him but they usually wished they hadn't when he finally caught up with them. And he invariably did.

And that's the problem with Graeme's playing legacy. How-ever many of his thumping goals and deft scoring passes you revisit, it's as the brutal enforcer that even team-mates like Johnston remember him.

I've spent a fair bit of time in Roy Keane's company in recent years. So often is he reminded of his merciless 'take no prisoners' reputation by fans that approach him in airports or hotels, that he occasionally feels moved to defend himself with a plaintive cry of 'Hey, I could play too, you know!'

It's not a boast, so much as a straightening of the record. A point of order.

But when you've topped the bill as Gladiator Maximus or Braveheart in a few epics, it's easy to get typecast.

Souey played up to the part. His forest of a chevron moustache was thicker and creepier than any of the many that sprouted in the 1970s. More Pablo Escobar than Tom Selleck. He could turn on the charm like Magnum when he was in his civvies, but as soon as he got into uniform he adopted the character of a cool-hand gunslinger.

There was always a brisk menace in his bustling stride as he drove through midfield, almost offering himself up for a challenge if anyone was feeling lucky. Make my day.

The game reserves a special place in its Hall of Fame for the rogues' gallery of hard men and hitmen. For some reason, their waist-high, shin-scraping assaults provoke chortles of laughter when fans recount them. It's decidedly nervous laughter if you've ever actually faced the likes of Keane or Souness. Even in an interview.

If I had ever been any good at football, I would have hated Roy and Graeme. Not just hated playing against them, I would have hated them for their blatant disregard for personal safety on a football field. Particularly my personal safety.

You won't find me on *I'm a Celebrity*. There is a boxset in the list of things I simply couldn't stomach. The most dangerous thing I've ever volunteered for is teaching my wonderful children to drive.

Roy has often told me he hardly slept for nights leading up to a match against Arsenal. I'd have been exactly the same before a game against him.

As a commentator I have an aversion to using the word 'ruthless' in relation to a striker's finishing or a team's ability to close out victories. Ruthlessness, to me, implies risk to life and limb. It's tyranny, it's cruelty, it's Genghis Khan or Ivan the Terrible. It's Graeme Souness or Roy Keane in the tackle.

I cannot tune in to a mentality that places winning so far ahead of anything else. Because I've never competed at the level they did, I can only equate it to the guy that tailgates me at ninety miles per hour in the outside lane of a motorway, the guy that chills me to my bones, the guy I pull over and let past because he really doesn't care if we live or die.

In the middle lane of a football pitch, Graeme and Roy were both that guy. And yet I consider each of them a good friend now.

I think that says something about me, something I probably don't care to admit too readily. Even though I have no concept at all of their single-minded, bloody minded will to win a tackle or a match, I can be every bit as forcefully adamant about the use of a word or the tone of a commentary. I'm not easily budged when I'm in my lane. We all have our standards.

Souey's professional standards echo as loudly in every word he speaks in a television studio as they did through the aftershock of every challenge he made on the pitch. He has a stubbornness that takes some moving when it comes to defending his corner in a debate about football. Roy is exactly the same. And so am I when it comes to squaring an argument about broadcasting. I think we all recognise and respect that in each other. I just hope I'm not quite so intimidating.

Football is a team sport but it's full of personal duels. These individual match-ups are contested differently in different parts of the combat zone. Wingers and full-backs jockey and joust down the flanks, strikers and centre-backs grapple and tussle in the box. It is in midfield when the ball runs free into no man's land that the defining tackles are won and lost.

There is no such thing as a 50/50 in football. The odds always lean one way or the other. I'm sure the betting companies would love to find a way of freezing the action as the ball spins loose and two opposing players gird their loins in readiness to physically dispute possession. In football parlance, 'Who wants it the most?' Place your bets now.

It's a poker game in which it is particularly dangerous to bluff. You've got to know who you're calling. Players like Souey and Keano just don't fold.

Midfield is the dangerous junction where these head-on collisions happen, where two players hold their breath and offer their prayers before leaping into a battle of wills that only one of them can win.

It's a battle that is joined and decided in less than a second, but during those fractions of time each player somehow gets the chance to change their mind, to hedge their own bets. To either pull out or to go through with it. To protect themselves by bailing out or to protect themselves by taking out the opponent. It's like time has stood still, like the slow-motion replay machine has turned itself on.

The outcome of these crunch meetings can lay down a marker for an entire match. I enjoyed two years as a rugby league commentator at the start of the 1990s and one of the first things I learnt was that I couldn't begin a game with a few gentle introductory thoughts because the first tackle was often the most telling of the match. It set the tone, set the temperature.

The Challenge Cup final was by far the most prestigious annual occasion in the sport. In 1992, an Australian called Darryl van der Velde guided Castleford to Wembley to take on the all-conquering Wigan. He called me the week before the final to ask if I thought he could send his 'B' team out for the pre-match parade and ceremonials.

His argument was that he would spend the countdown to kick-off priming and rousing his players to explode at 3 o'clock and channel their stirred aggression into knocking Wigan off their lofty perch. He didn't want them spending the previous ten minutes waving to smiling family members in the crowd or shaking the hand of some minor royal.

'I think I'll send the kids out for the walk in the sunshine and keep my guys locked up in the dressing-room where they can stay hungry and angry 'til it's time. What do you think?'

My advice to him was that the singing of the national anthem was still a kind of big thing in this corner of the Commonwealth and that he really should honour the protocol and respect the occasion. He took my counsel. Castleford lost 28–12.

The rules of engagement for all sporting dust-ups are decidedly sketchy. Rugby prop forwards play by a different code of conduct to everyone else on the field. The laws of the jungle apply on the last bend of a middle-distance track event, in the final furlong of a Cheltenham feature race or when a basketball rebounds off the rim.

Great sportsmen and women respond in those moments. All of those clichés about 'digging deep' and 'second is nowhere' are mere branding for the haunting fear of failure that lifts the cream to the top. Coaches talk the talk, players walk the walk. As Mike Tyson famously said, 'Everybody has a plan 'til they get punched on the nose.' That's when you find out what it takes.

In football, when the going gets tough, the tough can get naughty. There are the usual suspects that carry their reputations before them and into the referee's mental notes, but not all of the villains are 'known' to the law-enforcement officers.

Any poll of former players will put some of the finest forwards of the modern era near the top of the list that regularly 'left one on you.' Alan Shearer, Luis Suarez, Diego Costa, Ian Wright, Mark Hughes, Dennis Bergkamp, Kevin Davies, Alan Smith (Leeds, that is). All named and far from ashamed. Self-defence, your honour. Get your retaliation in first.

'It's still a contact sport' is the standard defence for a stray elbow or toe stamp. Giving as good as you get is just part of that sport.

Only if there is a suspicion that a player has gone to ground without much contact does the moral outrage get operatic. Simulation is a far more heinous crime than mutilation. And if someone should dare to spit in the direction of an opponent, the indignation rises to biblical levels. Eternal damnation and hell's fury await. Not to mention a six-game ban. As opposed to the three matches for four studs down the inside of your thigh.

I am not about to condone any of the above but I know which of them I would rather be the victim of. Gob away, just don't hurt me. Maybe that's why I'm not a footballer.

Theirs is a life of organised crime. They're all at it. If they are not diving, they are standing over decapitated bodies accusing them of diving. I like footballers but they don't half tell fibs. They obey the laws of the game like I stick to the speed limit. When they think someone is watching.

We each draw our own red lines across the game's rule book. It's no more than a rough guide, a paper for discussion. I've seen players tugging at their own team-mates' shirts in a bid to fool a referee. They are all cheats. Ex-footballers sound off about how referees don't 'know' the game because they've never played it. Like you've got to do a stretch in E Wing to know you've been mugged.

There is a kind of communion between footballers that probably does more to prevent really serious injuries than any of the laws of the game, but it's not the holiest of communions when the result of an important match is on the line.

To Graeme Souness, the result of every match was important. More important than anything else happening on the planet during the ninety minutes that he was playing that match.

In 1984, he infamously broke the jaw of the Dinamo Bucharest captain in a European Cup semi-final at Anfield. There were 37,000 people inside the stadium that night but I've never met anyone who actually saw the knockdown punch thrown. Lica Movila clearly didn't see it coming.

Souey did what he felt he needed to do. That was the standard he set for himself and for anyone that ever chose to share a football pitch with him. His own standard.

I spent quite a few Saturday evenings in his company during his playing prime. Along with Liverpool team-mate Michael Robinson and our wives, we often shared a post-match dinner table. Nobody would have given more of himself to the game than Souey. But at dinner, he didn't want to speak about football.

'Put the ball away,' he'd moan if Michael and I began to chew over the match. Win, lose or draw, his work there was done. It was like we were out with someone who had never been to a game. His personality was wholly split between business and pleasure.

Pleasure in the 1980s could get pretty Roman around famous footballers. Graeme's nickname in the dressing-room was 'Champagne Charlie'. He didn't get it from the colour of his lounge curtains. His standards were a little different back then.

Everything was. My first 'bachelor' house in Saughall Massie, Wirral was a good party house. I was no Hugh Hefner but bringing together a few young football friends with some female acquaintances was a popular Sunday cocktail for innocent fun and frolics. Nobody died.

Alcohol was a staple constituent of a player's post-match warm-down. A few swift pints in the players' lounge were as much a part of the matchday routine as liniment rub and shin pads. Thirsts had to be quenched, sorrows needed drowning. It was the accepted norm.

When Bob Paisley launched a crackdown on golf among the Liverpool players, he told them, 'I can train you for drinking and sex but not for golf.' The logic was that he could sweat the lager out of their athletic bodies but couldn't protect them from the muscle fatigue of eighteen holes through the dunes of Southport.

Howard Kendall's answer to any dip in Everton's form was to convene a team meeting at a Chinese restaurant in Sefton Park, then ply the players with drink, loosen their tongues until they had aired any gathering grievances and finally bond them back together as a group over a night cap or four.

Nobody had a camera phone to record any of the above for posterity or the *Mail Online*. Maybe I imagined it all.

Liverpool, in particular, placed a religious faith in keeping both football and life plain and simple. There was a kind of perversity in the club's determination to try to keep everybody grounded, keep everything real. Play with a strut, win with humility.

The daily routine involved the players reporting to Anfield and changing in the matchday dressing-room before taking a coach to the training ground three-and-a-half miles away. That coach was usually a chugging charabanc of a vehicle into which many of Europe's most valuable players were squeezed with standing room only. Some of the training kit was as old as the bus.

At the end of the morning's session, the whole sweaty squad were loaded back on board for the return journey and, belatedly, a hot shower and lunch.

I heard various explanations for the practice. Bill Shankly was a firm believer that the players should not only think of

Anfield as their spiritual home, but feel part of the 'family' of the club and get to know and be among the ticket sellers, administrative staff and cleaners. There was also a theory that the coach transfer stopped players rushing off on personal business before they had recovered from their morning exertions.

A more revealing example of Liverpool's quaint customs was the cargo carried aboard the (more modern) team coach for away matches. One of the driver's tasks was to source a fish 'n' chip shop a few miles away from the stadium where they were playing. En route back to the motorway, a bus load of the most famous faces in British sport would roll up outside the chippie to collect their fish suppers. They were washed down with premium strength lager.

If there was a clear message to these champion international footballers amid the stodge and starch of the salted chips and malted beer, it was that they weren't too good to eat like the fans do out of the wrappings of a newspaper. That same newspaper would report their sporting brilliance the next morning. It was ground-breaking reverse psychology. Diet-breaking too.

When Souey returned to Merseyside as manager in the spring of 1991, he found that neither the club's approach nor the team's habits had changed during his seven years away in Genoa and Glasgow. So he put a stop to all of it. Almost overnight.

I remember driving Graeme and his assistant Phil Boersma around the picturesque lanes of the Wirral Peninsular on a house-hunting trip. Two things struck me straightaway.

Souey was talking football. Even though we were looking at estuary views and gated mansions, he was talking about the young right-back at Crewe Alexandra. And every other right-back for hundreds of miles. He was speaking in tongues I'd never heard from him before. Graeme had become a football nut.

Another change came over him on the Damascus Road he trod in Italy and Scotland. His basic thoughts on football underwent some time travel. At Anfield, what was good enough for Shanks had been good enough for Bob and Joe and even Kenny to a large degree. The upturned kit box in the Boot Room was still the seat of Liverpool learning. Souey was going to pull the whole thing down.

As a strict matter of fact, it wasn't his idea to knock through the walls of the old sanctuary where the saucy calendars hung next to the fixture list. Liverpool's head of operations, Peter Robinson, was proposing a remodelling of the bowels of the Main Stand to incorporate a new media suite. Graeme wasn't about to oppose the plans on nostalgic grounds, though. This was no sentimental journey.

The old school bus, the Cobra beers and the mushy peas were being thrown out with the chip paper. Liverpool were to develop their Melwood Training Centre to fit the age and to become the players' second home. A calorie-conscious chef was hired to come on board the refitted team coach and rewrite the menu. The Boot Room was condemned and consigned to history.

This was not the same as Howard Wilkinson walking into Leeds United and taking down all the photographs of Don Revie's silver-plated legacy. Graeme was not looking to deny the past but rather to renovate it. By his own admission he was a poacher turning gamekeeper. Champagne Charlie had gone on the wagon. He had converted to a new testament.

It is remarkable to think that the grizzly bear of a man that rampaged around English midfields in his playing days went hunting on a diet of sugared tea. After his familiar Friday evening plate of steak and chips, he consumed nothing but sweet tea until the final whistle had blown on Saturday afternoon. Sports science was not part of the curriculum back then.

It was only when he sat down for the Friday team supper with Roberto Mancini and Gianluca Vialli at Sampdoria that it dawned on him that there might be another way. They were tucking into a plate of mixed cheeses. Everything that Italian players did to their bodies was monitored and regulated. Why wouldn't it be? Those bodies belonged to the club.

The same was of course true of the bodies inside the Liverpool dressing-room. When Tommy Smith told Bill Shankly that his knee felt sore, the story goes that Shanks replied curtly, 'That's not your knee, it's Liverpool's knee.' It was probably the cue for another dose of painkiller to be fired into the joint. The game had a drug problem in the 1960s and 70s. A drug called Cortisone.

Liverpool, like many clubs, patched their players up to stand on their own two feet and find their own recipes for success. Nobody from the coaching staff appeared every five minutes peeling back pages on a flipchart containing diagrams of every free-kick routine known to man.

When Souey was handed his debut by the club in 1978, he made the mistake of asking assistant manager Joe Fagan how he wanted him to play. Joe, a truly lovely and gentle man, told him to 'fuck off'. The gist of the message was that Liverpool had bought him to play the way he did. Just do it.

If there was a Liverpool 'way', it was to place the responsibility on their players' shoulders. The club had no issue with the PG Tips diet as long as Graeme delivered a hungry performance every time they sent him out in one of their shirts. No questions were asked as long as answers were provided between minute one and ninety. The job description was as stark and brutally simple as that.

The hefty onus placed on the players produced distinctive personalities like Smith, like Dalglish, like Souness. It was character-building or else. There was little or nothing in the way of counselling or support for anyone who struggled with the silent demands. Any show of mental fragility was as likely to be treated with cutting sarcasm from team-mates as it was an expression of sympathy. Any weak links in the team culture were swiftly severed.

If you want to know where old school football thinking comes from, see the above.

Souey still lives by many of the old standards that Liverpool first gave him. He has picked the team at eight different clubs, one of only a dozen managers to have overseen 300 Premier League games. And yet when you hear him analysing football in a twenty-first-century television studio, his core values come from Anfield circa 1980.

To this day, he can hear Ronnie Moran yelling at him to pass the ball forward, so we hear it too.

There were still gramophone records in those days and the danger of harking back too far is that you can sound like a broken one. But wasn't this the man who bulldozed that old school? Wasn't this the moderniser who dragged the club kicking and screaming towards the future? Aren't there contradictory states at play here? Not at all.

Don't think for one moment that Graeme liked everything he saw in his playing days at Liverpool. And when Graeme doesn't like something, we all get to know about it.

This was a captain who didn't think twice about lecturing the rest of the dressing-room if he thought their standards were slipping. He delivered some of the loudest bollockings that team ever got. This was an intelligent man who could take an unintelligible dislike to even a team-mate if he didn't feel he was pulling his weight. He didn't and doesn't suffer fools.

He often talks about the value of leaders in the dressing-room. That's because he was one. Self-appointed, self-important, self-assured.

His first five years in management at Rangers were made easier by the presence of like-minded standard-bearers such as Terry Butcher, Richard Gough and Ray Wilkins to rally the troops. It had been nine years since Ibrox had celebrated a title success. Everyone bought into the new deal that Souey put on the table.

That kind of deal became an increasingly difficult sell with the changing of the times.

When he returned to Liverpool as manager, he found that the voice of the senior players no longer carried the same weight with younger ears. The dilution of the standing of Ian Rush, John Barnes and Ronnie Whelan was not helped by their own injury problems but a new wave had washed over that and every other dressing-room. Player power was gathering force.

You won't get very far into a conversation with Graeme

about modern football before he tells you that the tail is wagging the dog now. He found man-management increasingly difficult because his definition of a 'man' was being steadily revised.

Nothing whatsoever to do with misogyny or muscle. Not even the telephone number salaries that he found himself negotiating with players barely fit to lace his boots. That's a generation wage gap that every footballer has had to swallow when the time comes to cash in their chips.

The only old idea of 'a man' that Souey clings to is his notion of professionalism, of today's football professionals earning their place in his estimations through their dedication and commitment. Of facing consequences if they don't. I can see nothing outdated about that.

What we hear when he holds court with Jamie Carragher, Gary Neville and company under the Sky lights is not any breed of dinosaur. He is too smart to believe that you can manage a football team now like you managed one in the days when nobody could name a player's agent. Authority is bought with a different currency in 2021.

You can't parent now like you did a generation ago. He has children, so do I. We both get that. But when you are as strong-minded and strong-willed as either of us, we are entitled to think that there are still contemporary lessons to be learnt from the footballers and broadcasters that we learnt from.

Souey's inherent mindset demands more of the burden of responsibility be borne by the individual. If you are quick to point at the name on the back of your shirt when you score, you should also be around when that same name makes mistakes that need to be accounted for.

Mistakes are a daily occurrence in football. It's not a perfect science. Everybody makes them but not everybody pays for them. Souey is not frightened to admit his mistakes. They beat him up a lot more than he shows. They always did.

The big problem with making changes at a football club is that the success or failure of even the most rational reforms is determined by the irrational bounce of a ball. You've got to win games. If you don't, those changes automatically become mistakes. Particularly if it's Liverpool and you are used to winning games.

Graeme's Liverpool didn't win enough games. Not enough to challenge for the league title, not enough for a run at a European trophy. Not nearly enough for him and his precious standards. The whys and wherefores are almost incidental to how deeply the relative failure tortured him. He was a perfectionist in an imperfect world.

When Wimbledon came to town, one of their players defaced the sacramental sign above the steps to the pitch. Under 'This is Anfield' was scrawled 'So Fucking What'. Souey caught a couple of his own players sniggering at the joke. He went mental. He couldn't forgive them.

There is no light and shade when your vision is tunnel vision, no room for discussion, no margin for even occasional error. Having standards is one thing. Imposing them on everybody around you is a different matter. On the field, he could force his will upon most. Off the field, nobody can.

Not only does Graeme know now that he tried to change too much too quickly, he sensed it at the time and couldn't stop his insatiable urge to make Liverpool contenders in his image. The more he wrestled with the conundrum of piecing together a winning jigsaw, the more he tried to demand of himself and those that played for him.

He found it impossible to understand anyone that wasn't prepared to pursue success with the same blinkered focus that he had. It made him intolerant. Maybe intolerable. His arteries certainly found it so.

He celebrated Liverpool's 1992 FA Cup semi-final victory over Portsmouth with triple heart by-pass surgery. He was 38 and already grieving the passing of his father and dealing with a bitter divorce. He was about to make the biggest mistake of his life. He told the *Sun* all about it. It was an error compounded by the publication of the story on the third anniversary of the Hillsborough disaster that the same paper had mis-reported unforgivably. It made Graeme's mistake difficult to forgive too.

I can only tell you that he regrets that mistake more deeply than the rest put together. His apologies are full of sincerity and contrition. He believes now that he should have resigned as manager there and then. Only his desire to somehow right the wrong stopped him.

It's not my place or intention to speak up for him, not least because it is impossible to separate that thoughtless, heedless lapse of judgement from all the other calls he made. By his own confessional admissions, it wasn't all that he got wrong at Liverpool. The tough guy is especially tough on himself.

Those rigid personal standards clouded his own view of the club that he still loves with all of the heart that scared him half to death. He took the job at the wrong time. Showing the door to friends and former team-mates was a task too far.

Souey was less than halfway through his managerial career when he did resign. He took charge of three other Premier

League teams and coached in three further countries. The Liverpool experience neither stopped him in his tracks nor changed him significantly. When a club owner hires a manager with the distinctive personality profile of a Souness or a Mourinho or a Conte, they know what they are getting. They are not looking for a watered-down version. There is no Souness Lite.

Away from football, he is a surprisingly mellow and sensitive soul. One thing we definitely don't share in common is that he actually likes gardening.

On football duty, he can be an industrial digger. Can now, always could. I can promise Paul Pogba that he has never really been any different.

I commentated on a relegation battle that his Blackburn Rovers side lost at home to Leeds United in 2004. After the match, Souey invited me into his office where he was already making plans for the next game with assistants Dean Saunders and Tony Parkes. It was only forty-eight hours away at Fulham.

Player-by-player, he testily dissected the performances of the men he himself had selected. Player-by-player, Dean loyally agreed with Graeme's scathing, damning character assassinations. No heart, no pride, no way that A, B, C or D was going to be in the team at Craven Cottage on Monday night.

Tony and I listened on looking deep into our coffee cups. Our mute buttons were on. The fine wine wasn't coming out any time soon.

After ten minutes or so, Tony seized upon a short adjournment in the hard-line post-mortem to ask a question. 'What time do you want the minibus to leave here on Monday morning, boss?'

Souey didn't really hear what had been said. Tony was a part of the furniture at Ewood Park. A stoic and steadfast rock of a club servant who stepped up to take caretaker control at Blackburn on half-a-dozen occasions. Nothing ever phased him. He waited his moment to enquire again. 'What time do you want me to book the minibus down to Fulham?'

This time, the curious question found a way through Graeme's tense, taut outer skin and registered.

'What do you mean, minibus?'

'Well, boss, you've bombed out Cole and Stead. Said Emerton won't be playing. Reid, Gray. I think you said Flitcroft's not going. By my reckoning that leaves us with eight players. No point in taking the big coach.'

Even after forty years, I've learnt to hold my breath after tossing a little piss-take Souey's way. You just never know how it's going to land.

Tony knew what he was doing. A big and rather bashful smile broke out across the stern face of a hard man with nothing much to smile about at that moment . . . except his own demanding standards.

He made only three changes on the Monday night and Blackburn won 4–3 at Fulham. Just a big softie really.

SECOND JOB IN TELEVISION:

BBC Sport

London

1992–96

I nearly missed the call I had been waiting for all of my young life.

I was sleeping off a hangover in a Stockholm hotel room when the BBC finally came knocking on my door in the summer of 1992. A month earlier, BSkyB had jumped into bed with the newly-formed Premier League to shaft ITV and most of my immediate career plans to boot. No wonder I was drinking.

Live top-flight football in England was being fronted by Elton Welsby on ITV at the time, but Richard Keys was on the way. The Murdoch money blew us into the football backwaters as Super Duper Sundays appeared behind a pay wall and the BBC won the rights to show highlights on *Match of the Day*.

Alan Hansen, a good friend from my time on Merseyside, rang me just before the start of Euro '92 in Sweden to suggest I put a call into his boss at the Beeb, Brian Barwick. I didn't think I stood much of a chance and never quite plucked up the courage to get another BBC rejection.

It was all going so well, too.

Some of my regional Granada commentaries had started to get a network airing, I was spending every week filming features for *Saint and Greavsie* and then commentating on rugby league matches most Saturdays.

BSkyB went and bought up live exclusive rights to rugby league. ITV had only athletics and boxing. I didn't know a jab from a javelin.

To cap it all, having won a place on ITV's team for the European Championships and flown out to Stockholm, I was told that I would merely be the standby commentator on call if anything happened to Brian Moore or Alan Parry. Nothing did.

Every evening, I sat in a small studio with Gabriel Clarke, the standby presenter. Every night, the two of us joined the rest of the production team to drink and dance until dawn at Café Opera. It was great fun but not something I could really do for the rest of my life.

That life was on hold until the phone in my hotel room rang that bleary Thursday morning. It was Brian Barwick wanting to know why I hadn't called him. The editor of *Match of the Day* had primed Alan Hansen to sound me out three weeks earlier. Wires had got crossed and Brian thought I was playing hard to get.

I said 'yes' in the next breath. I was heading to London and my dream job. The hangover was gone.

9

REG

Reg Gutteridge OBE wasn't even my favourite boxing commentator when we first met, but he taught me most of what I know.

I didn't ask him to mentor me. We were total opposites. For some reason best known to himself, he took a shine to me and slipped me under his spell. I'm still there twelve years after his passing.

Every student that has asked me for advice in the last twenty years has been read a lesson from the Reg Gutteridge book of broadcasting. It should be on every media studies syllabus.

He was ITV's man at ringside for three decades. He was close to the action in every sense. Most of the legendary fighters that trod the canvas boards just above him in pursuit of the most difficult dollars in sport knew Reg personally. He was one of their own, a former boxer from a boxing family.

I most certainly wasn't. I've never been in a fight in my life. I wince and gasp when the dental hygienist goes to work on my plaque with her scaler. I've lived that life of mine by a strict mantra of 'no pain, no pain'.

Reg lived most of his life with a prosthetic leg. He could have given me a good hiding just standing on that. He was as redoubtable as Monty Python's Black Knight.

Boxing was a sport I followed rather than loved. As with Formula One and horse racing, I was never likely to 'try' it, so I watched from a safe distance when Ali or Tyson were fighting or if a Brit was bidding for a world title.

I actually commentated on a couple of fight nights at the atmospheric old Liverpool Stadium for Radio City. My abiding memory was of the showers of blood, sweat and snot that sprayed my front row seat and of the paralysed look of deep dread in the eyes of any boxer that knew in his sore bones that he was imprisoned inside the ropes with a better man.

It was only when I climbed through those ropes to interview the victors that I realised how small a boxing ring is. Not for me.

I actually preferred Harry Carpenter as a boxing commentator. To my untrained, unpunched ears, he was a better broadcast technician. More concise, more clipped, more BBC. I don't think anyone inside boxing would have agreed because Reg was the one that knew the game inside out. He was the boxer's commentator.

Ron Pickering was an athletics insider. He coached Lynn Davies to Olympic gold. David Coleman was a decent club runner. He had no true track and field pedigree. But when Coleman roared, 'The Bell!' with a lap of a major final to go, he lengthened his stride to an Olympian level that not Pickering nor any other athletics commentator could ever get near. That was his job.

I have always tended to champion the media-schooled skills of career broadcasters over ex-players that make a move into the lead commentator's chair from the one next to it. Maybe it's because I could never kick a ball hard enough to beat even Loris Karius myself. Maybe it's because I always wanted to be a commentator more than a player and I still think that's a good reference.

It's vocational and there is a trade to be learnt. The art of communication is journalism by any other name. The man who has taught me more about that art than anyone else was not just an ex-boxer, he was an ex-journalist too. Reg Gutteridge.

He first worked for the *London Evening News* as a 14-year-old office boy. Because his dad's idea of coming home from work was running back from the gymnasium, his boxing contacts were second to none. Reg was a breaker of stories rather than a crafter of prose but he knew what the readers wanted.

He knew what the viewers wanted too. His co-commentator of fifteen years, the affable Jim Watt, once said, 'I never felt nervous because I only ever felt like I was talking to Reg, and there's nobody I'd rather talk boxing with.'

That easy, enthusiastic conversational style that Jim and Reg perfected was probably the very thing that pushed me in the direction of the drama-building meter of Carpenter. It's just a matter of taste.

Reg duly changed my tastes over the years that he dropped his pearls of broadcasting wisdom all around me. Or rather he widened and sharpened my tastes. He loosened my stuffy opinions about clear, controlled correctness in commentary. He coached me to talk to viewers like they talk to one another, like Jim Watt talked to him.

In November 1999, I commentated on a live England international for the first time. It was a big one. A play-off against Scotland at Wembley to qualify for the European finals the following year. I may be my own biggest critic but I thought I'd done a good job. Until Reg called me the next morning. He had his gum shield in.

'The England manager was in the stadium, you know,' he informed me by way of some early sparring. 'Keegan was actually there.'

'Yes, I know, Reg. We got quite a lot of close-ups of him during the coverage.'

'So why were you commentating to him?' he asked with a quick jab to my head.

'Sorry, Reg, I'm not with you.'

'Was your grandma watching?' He was going to work on my body now.

'Yes, she always watches. You know that.'

'Well, commentate to her. Don't commentate to the managers, don't commentate to the dressing-room. Commentate to your grandma. She counts as one viewer just like anyone else. Commentate to her and the rest of us.'

It was knockout stuff. It went to the very heart of broadcasting. Talk to the breadth of your audience. Speak to them like they speak to each other, like Reg spoke to them.

When I get to speak directly to any of that audience at sports forums or charity nights, people tend to ask me questions about how I'm able to recognise all the players or learn the right pronunciations or stop myself from swearing. Nobody ever says, 'What exactly is it that you're trying to achieve?'

That's where Reg came in. He asked me little else.

He was a universally popular man but it wasn't as if he went out of his way to be liked. Not only was he never short of an opinion, but he didn't think twice about voicing it.

I had first come across him at his personable storytelling best in wine-fuelled late-night postscript meetings to those *Sportsweek* shows at Granada in Manchester. He was a wonderful raconteur with a vault of captivating material on every fighter that had ever pulled on a pair of gloves. When Reg fell ill with a particularly nasty bout of blood poisoning in the late-1980s, Muhammad Ali was among his visitors at Hammersmith Hospital. The most famous man in the world prayed at his bedside. Reg got better.

To say that his own fight career was cut short by injury would be a bit like saying King Harold's was curtailed by an eye problem. Reg stepped out of his British Army tank and onto a landmine during the invasion of Normandy in 1944. He lost a leg. His response to that awful tragedy was simply to build it into his comedy routine. Maybe laughing it off was his only way of dealing with it. Reg insisted that everyone else saw the funny side of his disability.

When he packed a spare prosthetic limb for three weeks at the Seoul Olympics, his suitcase ended up in Hong Kong and Reg told a hundred gags about his legs never having been so far apart. When he went swimming in the sea, he took great joy in emerging from the waves holding his artificial leg aloft shouting 'Shark! Shark!' to crowded beaches of bathers. It was the way he told 'em.

His show-stopping anecdote was an encounter with former world heavyweight champion Sonny Liston at a boxing dinner. Liston was holding court to the rest of the table about his hard upbringing. Reg began to tire of the tales of how tough and unflinching the ex-champion was and suddenly took an ice pick off the table and thrust it into his own leg so that it stuck upright through the pleated suit material.

Liston reeled back in horror as Reg eyeballed him without so much as a whimper of pain and then pulled the steel implement from his leg and calmly placed it back on the table. The story goes that the boxer subsequently asked if he could repeat the trick and stab the leg himself. He was just about to plunge a sharp fork into Reg's good leg before our hero managed to stop him.

'My wooden leg looked like a pepper pot when I took it back to the hospital, so they asked me to stop doing that trick,' Reg used to say with a twinkling grin.

The laughs kept on coming in his sparkling company but the moment that the conversation turned at all serious, he was fighting his corner with bruising opinions on his sport, his profession and the people in them. I never actually asked him for his opinions on me or my output but he called me every morning after a televised game to avail me of them. He wasn't backward at coming forward.

'Do you know how many times you said "of course" last night?' he began one audit session.

'No, but I've a feeling you're going to tell me, Reg.'

'I don't know. I stopped counting at six.'

Like Lieutenant Columbo moving in on an arrest, the findings of the post-mortem were theatrically revealed one by one until the case for the prosecution was watertight and an admission of guilt was my only choice.

'Every time you said "of course" you were talking down to half your audience. "Of course, he missed the last international because of injury." "Of course, he played here for his club side in the cup final." You're splitting your audience in two. Can't you see that?'

'Not really, Reg. It's just information. I was just underlining a point.'

'But it's information that some of your audience know already, correct? So, you're saying to them, "look you probably know this because you follow football like I do, but I'm just going to say it for the benefit of the other numbskulls that don't, OK?" You can't do that. It's condescending. If a piece of information is worth giving, then give it. Don't qualify it. Don't talk down to people. Good broadcasting is inclusive. It welcomes everybody in. Do you understand?'

'Yes, Reg. Sorry.'

It was tough love. And sometimes I didn't understand it. Or I didn't understand why Reg thought it was so important. But whenever I sat down and watched a recording of the game in question, the keynotes began to chime and echo around my head. 'Good broadcasting is inclusive, it welcomes everyone in.' Of course!

Reg certainly welcomed everyone into the 1985 world title contest between Marvin Hagler and Thomas Hearns in Las Vegas. A lot of fight fans will tell you it was the greatest opening round of all time. It got the commentary it deserved. The fighters were on a war footing from the first bell but Reg ducked and weaved with the force of every one of the fusillade of punches thrown and captured the sustained mayhem of it with a suitably colloquial air.

'They're not making any scouting reports, these two.'

'Not trying to baffle each other with science.'

It was a three-minute masterclass in delivering intense sporting drama directly to its targeted audience. No hype, no highbrow, just a salvo of phrases that reflected the sheer shock and awe of the hostile exchanges.

Reg was on the money with his reading of it – 'It's going to be a question of who can take the best punch' – but it was cool analysis with a buzz of excitement thrown in. He went along with the runaway pace of the skirmish, and took everybody watching with him. Everybody.

He once told me to 'commentate to white van man'. Out of context, that may sound a disdainful, almost insulting piece of advice. But the context that needs to be added is that Reg not only had a lovely common touch with his language and arid humour, but he was also proud and protective of the roots that gave him that empathy with 'the man in the street'. He was an extraordinary ordinary guy. He wasn't having anyone feeling left out of any work he did with microphone or typewriter.

'We've all been in that maths class at school where you don't understand a bloody word of what the teacher is going on about,' he once said to me. 'You sit in the back row with your head down just hoping he doesn't look at you. Not learning a damned thing about anything. Don't let that happen in any of your classes. Take everybody along with you.'

I used to get a bit of Twitter grief for explaining how the away goals rule worked at vital moments of Champions League knockout ties on ITV. Choruses of contempt in 140 characters for my stating of the bleeding obvious. Except that when you are broadcasting to 10 million viewers, it is not always that obvious to all of them.

At an England World Cup game when the figure is twice that number, there is an argument for going over the offside law at some point. It's no longer a football match, it's a national event. The *Strictly* final with shin pads. Your Uncle Jimmy and Auntie Sandra are making their annual visit to football. They've got to be made to feel welcome. Be inclusive.

It is a different brief if you're calling a Europa League game on a subscription channel. Not only is the audience much smaller but they are far more informed and invested. When you have actually made a financial commitment to watching football on television, you probably don't need the VAR protocol spelling it out to you. You know your clear and obvious.

The bigger picture that Reg was always trying to paint with a billboard brush is about serving your audience, not yourself. You need a healthy slice of vanity just to take up a career in television but the people on the other side of the screen are the most important ones in the industry. The viewers, the listeners, the followers. They invite us into their homes, their cars, their train carriage. Pushing past them and starting to communicate in a foreign language is plain rude.

I feel for commentators in more technical sports. I couldn't tell you how many Formula One races I've watched over the last ten years but I still don't really understand DRS. I'm certain the excellent Martin Brundle has walked the uninitiated through the theory and the practice of Drag Reduction Systems several times over. I just happen to have missed the tutorials.

The petrol heads would lynch any commentator that was continually trying to bring the rest of us up to speed. It's a dilemma for commentators of various sports to wrestle with. As viewers, we all have our own blind spots. I do still feel like the guy at the back of the maths class whenever the F1 cars enter the DRS zone or if a nightwatchman comes into bat in cricket or with the award of any kind of scrum infringement in rugby union. I love a mystery but they all remain unexplained to me.

It sometimes needs an alien to land from another planet before a sport and its correspondents can see how they look to the outside world. In 1994, I was a reporter on a BBC film about the Irish national hunt jockey, Adrian Maguire. At 22, he had emerged to challenge the elegant poise and polish of Richard Dunwoody with a style of riding that took a thin racing line between daring and reckless.

Maguire was whipping up a storm with his blinkered will to win. A few fines, a few falls, but a lot more visits to the winner's enclosure than to the stewards' room. He was a great sporting story.

We filmed him driving his hard bargains in the final furlong at a couple of 'three men and a dog' midweek meetings before sitting him down for a set-piece interview at the offices of his agent, Dave Roberts, on the outskirts of London.

My line of questioning was different from anything Maguire had faced from any racing journalist. Not that I was anybody's idea of a searching investigative reporter but I simply wasn't interested in his owners, trainers or horses. I didn't know whether he rode long or short. His controversial use of the whip was only a sub-plot in the tale that I was trying to tell.

I wanted to know why he was so fearless. In a sport where the protagonists are routinely followed by a couple of ambulances as they go about their work, I was looking to get under the thick skin and chipped bones of the jockey that appeared to care least what happened to him. I asked what on earth was going through his plucky mind when the horse's neck dipped on landing, and he and his own neck began the perilous fall between the thundering hooves.

About three minutes into the interview, agent Roberts called a timeout. He said he wasn't happy with the framing of the shot and wanted a quiet word with me in the kitchen.

'You can't ask him what you're asking him,' he said from the midst of a mild panic.

'He's brilliant,' I protested. 'Just no understanding of fear at all.'

'And that's the way I want to keep it.'

Most 22-year-olds with an innate flair for a sporting pas- time have delightfully little idea as to why or how they've been blessed. There was nothing that I could say to Maguire that would dilute his red-blooded approach to racing. Only the first fall that left a lasting mark could do that. He didn't stop riding until a Jockey Club neurological surgeon told him to.

During my time on Merseyside, I interviewed a popular local boxer called Robbie Davies on the day that he announced his retirement in 1980. Robbie was an outgoing character with a dauntless front-foot style. He had a good amateur pedigree and a big, boisterous following in his native Birkenhead. In victory or defeat, I'd never seen him anything less than proudly sure of himself.

That afternoon in the modest living room of his terraced house, he cried his eyes out into a local radio microphone. His speech was stumbling and slurred, partly through raw emo- tion, partly through the concussive hits he'd taken the night before. He was at the end of a Rocky road.

When I listened back to the tape in the edit suite, I spooled much of the interview onto the floor. It wasn't Robbie I was hearing. It was a beaten and broken shadow of him. I couldn't justify putting that sad imitation of him on air. He was too noble to deserve that.

Robbie died of dementia at the age of 67. His son, Robbie Jr, is a successful professional boxer. Adrian Maguire's nephew, Jason, is a Grand National winning jockey.

It is not easy to take a step back from sporting communities as tight and insular as racing and boxing. The family saddles and gloves are ceremonially passed on from generation to generation. By his own admission, Reg Gutteridge was never a starry-eyed fan of the fight game. Never an autograph hunter at the gym door. He was inside boxing from day one. And vice versa.

Communicating that inside knowledge of his sport to the wider audience he was always looking to reach was a product of his days at the *London Evening News*. Reg may have been a promising boxer once upon a time, but he was a much punchier journalist.

He saw any sports commentary as a piece of journalism. He insisted that the whole process from the very start of the research through to the delivery of the pay-off line at the final whistle or bell was a test of the same skill set that a good sportswriter required. It was storytelling. Reg used the word 'story' a lot.

I was commentating at Selhurst Park on the night in 1995 that Eric Cantona leapt over the perimeter wall and into football folklore, feet first. It was quite a story. And I missed it.

The match was not shown live. My commentary was for a highlights edit on BBC's *Sportsnight*, so the production back-up was basic. Cantona was shown a red card for kicking out at an opponent. His martial arts display happened forty-five seconds later as he took his leave on the far side of the pitch from my position. The incident was captured by only one television camera and, as the main protagonists were quickly engulfed by onlookers, it was over as soon as it began.

The camera followed Cantona to the mouth of the tunnel at the corner of the pitch. I knew that I'd seen something I'd never seen before, I just wasn't entirely sure what. As my eyes darted between pitch and monitor, I only caught the very end of his infamous tangle with Matthew Simmons.

My commentary words were, 'He's got involved in a scuffle with supporters. This is outrageous. It's all got wildly out of hand and once more Eric Cantona is at the centre of a dramatic controversy.' They were no more than fillers to buy time while I waited for a couple of replays to appear and show exactly what had escaped me.

I'm still waiting for them to this day. The match director felt that the one available camera shot was not clear enough to run again. I commentated on the remainder of the game with no more than a passing reference to Cantona. A ten-man Manchester United were chasing the victory they needed to go top of the table. Gareth Southgate actually denied them that victory with a late equaliser.

But that wasn't the story, was it?

I had only just become the proud owner of a cell phone in 1995. It lived mainly in my car. It was there that the *Sportsnight* editor tracked me down to suggest that I return to Selhurst Park to re-record my closing remarks. I was already two miles away.

The final words of that commentary were, 'Crystal Palace 1 Manchester United 1, but nothing will keep the name of Eric Cantona out of the morning headlines.' Not bad in the circumstances. It was too late to go back anyway.

Des Lynam opened the show with a gallery of the indelible still images of Cantona's flying assault. They were accompanied by Jon Champion's typically descriptive BBC Radio account of the incident from the side of the ground on which it happened. No replay of the attack appeared even in the television edit of the match on *Sportsnight* but it was discussed at length with the youthful studio guest Gary Lineker afterwards.

If there had been a full live outside broadcast unit in operation, I'd have had the back-up of a floor manager reporting in from the touchline and the director would have found many more camera angles of the extraordinary events of that evening. If it had all happened twenty years later, social media would have been heaving with eye-witness accounts and videos. I don't beat myself up about it but I was present at an unforgettable football moment and I didn't see it.

Football commentators can get a bit macho over how quickly we call the name of a goal scorer but I would rather miss an identification than miss a story. The most satisfied I feel after a game is when my summing up of a match is on the same page as the views of the studio experts or the opening paragraph of a report by one of my favourite football writers. I'm happy if I've told the same story as them.

I wonder who I got that from?

Reg was a great advocate of allowing the pictures to tell the story where possible. It is often said that sports commentators talk too much but he added his own qualification to that.

'Commentators talk to themselves too much' was his contribution to the debate. No names, but he was of the opinion some of his peers 'liked the sound of their own voice a bit too much'. He would have hated the direction that football commentary seems to be heading at the moment.

Streams of consciousness gush over too much of the action. Some of those currents meander off in a totally different direction to the flow of the match we are watching. It's like we needn't follow the action until it reaches either penalty-area. That's called basketball. Commentaries that are laced with continual digressions are not fit for purpose in a sport of captivating continuity like football. You've got to follow the action, go with the flow of the match.

If I could only offer one piece of advice to my successors, it would be 'watch and commentate the game'.

Reg had a particular bone to pick with 'television commentators that think out loud'. He didn't believe in 'silences for silences sake' but rather in hitting your own personal pause button occasionally in order to take a time out to choose the words for your next contribution. A pause had to be for thought, not for a rest.

He had a big thing about the difference between a conversation and a discussion. 'The pictures give us the luxury of some thinking time. You can have a conversation with your co-commentator about the way the game is taking shape because the viewers can hopefully see exactly what you're talking about. What you can't have is a discussion about something else. The pictures have got to lead the conversation. It's a visual medium.'

Ah, if I had a pound for every time Reg said 'it's a visual medium'. He would never let me forget it. 'The match director is the most important person on the OB. They call the shots. We are just the rhythm section.'

I have developed those thoughts into a lecture that I've given to hundreds of undergraduates. Not always the same script or text but always from the same source, and still as relevant today as when Reg was guiding prime-time audiences of 15 million through the rumbles that Chris Eubank, Nigel Benn and Barry McGuigan served up on Saturday nights in the 1980s and '90s.

The notion of a 'rhythm section' is perhaps a bit too Rolling Stones for twenty-first-century students, but what television commentators are is the soundtrack to the movies that the match directors cut up onto your screens. There have been some memorably evocative and rousing film soundtracks in motion picture history but nobody ever went to a cinema to see one. 'It's a visual medium.'

If you are eating at an Italian restaurant, you don't listen intently to the ambient accordion strains that are providing the accompaniment to your penne all'arrabbiata. If you are eating at the same restaurant and the background music is being provided by a traditional Japanese harp, you call the waiter over. It doesn't sound right. It's distracting.

Commentary is lift music. Our first priority is to make sure you don't all want to jump out.

It's often said that a good referee is one that you don't notice. I'm not sure that's quite true. For me, the best referees are the ones you don't notice until there is a big call to make and they get it right. That is a better analogy for authoritative commentary.

Referees and commentators tend to get on pretty well. Maybe we share the same failed ambitions to be players, perhaps we are all just a little anal about rules and regulations, facts and figures. Good referees not only know their stuff, they know how to apply it. Good referees let a game breathe but don't lose control. Good referees buy themselves thinking time at critical moments. Good referees don't run around waving their arms saying 'look at me'.

Good commentators say ditto to all that. Or they should do.

Radio commentary is different gravy. It's a lot more fun for one thing. In radio, you just plug in and go. You are far more important to the whole production so you can indulge yourself more and call the game from the heart. The television commentator has to use the head, has to concentrate not only on what to say but also when. You have to bow to the power of the pictures. Most of us take an audio feed of the director's instructions to the camera operators. We are talking and listening at the same time.

The best directors do likewise. They are choosing the most relevant pictures for you to see while at the same time trying to tune in to that commentary soundtrack and visually illustrate a point that we may be making. Like all the closest relationships, it gets tested and frayed at times but usually only because both parties really care about what they are doing. It's not easy to care calmly.

Calmness is everything when you are at the wheel of a live outside broadcast. Rants are for later. As a commentator, you drop a big lump of your reputation into a director's lap every time the red light comes on.

If you are true to Reg's motto of following their lead, you call most of the match looking at their tail-lights. You just hope they know where they're going, you trust them not to take any sudden turns down blind alleys, you rely on them not to hit either pedal too hard. Because if there's a prang, you are the one that the public prosecutors will come after. No match director ever gets Twitter abuse.

As a commentator, you grow a greater appreciation of a director's talents when you call a live game from hundreds of miles away in a small sound booth. 'Off-tube' commentary assignments are more and more routine as more and more matches are screened simultaneously to live audiences.

On a Champions League night at a studio hub in west London, there is a long corridor of these sound-proofed compartments where a row of commentary teams are shouting out to huts and hovels all around the globe. It's called the 'English language world feed'. Cheat commentaries from the San Siro and Nou Camp live to South Africa and North America via a building in Ealing.

When your tunnel view of the game is wholly dependent on the pictures that the Italian or Spanish director is selecting for broadcast on site, you are in the lap of the gods never mind theirs. I actually believe that 'off-tube' commentating has refocused my attention on addressing what the viewer can see on the screen. That discipline has tightened and tidied up my commentaries and made me less of a rambler. Concentration is our greatest skill.

A lot of that ramble in sports commentary is created by a fixation with statistics. Gone are the days when Motty was ridiculed for trotting out some obscure fact about the most consecutive games without a foul throw. Instead, the viewer is besieged by information as a matter of course. Graphics containing data with little or no relevance to the narrative of the game are flashed up like neon signs and billboard lights. You've got a sofa in the middle of Piccadilly Circus.

How many times do we need to see a half-time 'pass completion' caption before we work out that the two centre-backs are spending a lot of their time successfully rolling the ball unopposed to one another? There is nothing cool or contemporary about number crunching. That famous saying about 'lies, damned lies and statistics' dates back to the nineteenth century.

I compile copious notes for each and every game I commentate on. I collate data of all kinds and lay it out for display on hand-written charts. They are disturbingly neat and uniform. So collectable that I've started a business selling prints of some of them. But if I use more than ten per cent of the information that I've prepared, I run the risk of sending the viewers to sleep. If you don't like the idea of losing huge chunks of your life to late-night research that will never get used, don't become a commentator.

Preparation is just that. It's covering bases, building safety nets. You owe it to your professionalism and to your audience to know more about the circumstances of that particular match than any of them. Any of that audience with the time and the will could replicate your research but it is your job to do it on their behalf. If there is an art to that job, it is using the research well.

As Reg would say, 'Some commentators should have a crawler running across the bottom of the screen reading, "I've bloody well done this prep, so you're bloody well going to hear it." The only numbers that really matter in football are on the scoreline. Any other numbers that you use should tell us something about why that is the scoreline.'

That sense of journalism that he tried to infuse me with was all about editorialising the material you gather and dropping it into the commentary where it belongs, where it clarifies, where it adds to, where it emphasises. Too many of the information graphics that appear on screen now do none of the above. They are wallpaper. Decorations. You may as well put up horoscopes or train times.

Those dapper, prim charts in four colours that I slavishly write out are psychological props as much as reference books. They are my comfort blankets, my night lights. I take time and care over them because that process gives me a feeling that I've prepared well.

Brian Moore was an apostle of the 'fail to prepare and you prepare to fail' maxim, but his own preparation for a commentary game was as much about travel planning, warm clothing, parking arrangements and accreditation as it was about killer stats. If it is a pressured job, you can ease much of that pressure with forward planning.

There is more to be gleaned about the 'story' surrounding a game from visiting a couple of popular news sites than there is from trawling through stats packs and press releases. It is easy to become dismissive of tabloid speculation and gossip, sexed-up beneath rabble-rousing headlines and stood up by only anonymous sources. They are the papers that our viewers read. We must read them too.

Reg Gutteridge loved a nod and a wink. He was the lord of spiel. His compendium of scandals and sagas was full of memories that could only be recalled after the kids had gone to bed. *Jackanory* with an 18-certificate. The most wonderful company. You could give your voice a rest when Reg was in the room but your face ached from smiling.

It was almost difficult to reconcile the scurrilous tale-teller with the earnest journalist that took it upon himself to make me a better communicator. The highest common factor between Reg's twin personalities was a mission to include everybody in his conversations. To make sure that, even in something as incidental as a sports commentary, the average guy wasn't lost or talked down to.

I was a bit of a broadcasting snob when he first got on my case. I think he knocked that out of me.

He wanted the same people that laughed at his stories to enjoy his commentaries. His audience. They were the king and queen when Reg was on air. He served them royally.

We must never be apologetic for what football is. Its appeal is a public appeal and that public frames what the game is and how we should portray it. Warts and all.

Football is a populist sport. If a political party or religious movement could mobilise that great British public as actively and devotedly as the national game does, it would be an irresistible force. Perhaps a dangerous one.

It is headline news every minute of every day because there is an appetite for football news. Demand shapes supply.

So many Twitter trends are football trends but the hashtags usually relate to the players or clubs in the headlines, not to the topics with deeper social or moral contexts that we charge the game with a responsibility for. The most compulsive ongoing narratives in football don't care much for right or wrong. They are about moments and memories.

Reg caught those almost without looking, without trying. He served them to his audience gutted, filleted and with all the fat cut off. There were no decorative garnishes, no sides, no pretty petals sprinkled over the main dish that you had to scrape away before you could tuck in. He wasn't looking for Michelin stars.

Spectator sport is fast food. It is mass entertainment. It is played in huge arenas so that thousands can gather in a kind of fellowship. It's not staged for the suited, booted CEOs and VIPs behind the smoked glass of the executive boxes. Reg didn't teach me to commentate to them.

Season ticket holders may not pay the players' wages anymore but their loyalty is the beating heart of club football. It not only drives the business model but also creates the theatre. Hopefully, we've all heard enough fake crowd noise in the last year to remember the vitality of the live audience for the rest of our days.

But let's not try to deify that core football audience with broadsheet prose. I don't think they wish for any of that. Most of the fans that I meet want their ventricles stirring as opposed to their temporal lobes. Supporting your team is a rush of blood rather than a study of human behaviour. Football is a saloon bar argument, not a *Newsnight* debate.

Its public is indeed inspirationally public spirited, but take a good look at the television they watch, the newspapers they read, the websites they visit before you attempt to elevate football to a force for the nation to promote a greater *Guardian* good. It is where millions of people look to escape all of that.

Yes, the national game can set examples and raise awareness of that unique meritocracy I referred to earlier but don't burden the young performers with such grave responsibilities, don't demand that the administrators create a perfect world to hold up as an example to the real one and certainly don't expect the television commentators to protect the historical purity of every word in the dictionary.

If football is actually 'the people's game', then let its stories be told in a language that all of those people can understand and enjoy. Reg's language.

Asking the right questions. With John Francome
at Aintree, 1983.

THIRD JOB IN TELEVISION:

ITV Sport

London

1996–present day

1996 was a summer of love in English football but it was the end of the affair for me.

With Messrs Motson and Davies vying for the number one spot at the BBC, I was little more than a backing vocalist during Euro '96. So, when ITV asked me back to understudy Brian Moore, I was very happy to return to my commercial roots.

Four years of being tied to Auntie's apron strings had served a boyhood ambition and I completed my time at the Beeb by working on my one and only Olympic Games as the basketball commentator in Atlanta. Shaq, Barkley, Reggie, Scottie, Olajuwon and me. My last dance. I came home with neck ache.

My career was being driven at the time by a charismatic television executive called Mike Murphy. He was a true force of nature. Murph sounded like Michael Caine and could charm people like him too. So, when he appointed himself my agent for the deal with ITV, I knew he'd get me a good one. I just didn't know he was taking twenty per cent. He was worth every penny. Wonderful company. Much missed.

In all my years in broadcasting, I've had representation for a matter of months only. Just never found my Jerry Maguire.

Brian Moore put down the microphone for the last time after the 1998 World Cup final, leaving me to take over as ITV's senior commentator. We have survived the Tactics Truck, a couple of spooky technical calamities and an unfortunate knack of knocking England out of major tournaments to bring Solskjaer's winner, Gerrard's header, Drogba's equaliser and Pickford's penalty save to yours and millions of screens since then.

When head of sport, Niall Sloane, told me he was replacing me as ITV's lead voice in the summer of 2020, I was as shocked as I was upset. I felt like I had been robbed. Maybe I should have got myself an agent after all.

Close on twenty-five years of calling all of the above, working closely with Lynam, Rosenthal, Logan, Rider and other doyens of sports broadcasting, and having the time of my life. Nobody lives forever. I haven't regretted the decision I took in 1996 for even a day. Still don't. I would never have appeared on *Through the Keyhole* otherwise!

In the mid-noughties, Loyd Grossman's successor, Catherine Gee, came to my old home near Maidenhead to ask, 'Who lives in a house like this?' She filmed the reference books in my office, she took shots of the awards I'd carefully left lying around and she played football with the children in the garden.

A couple of weeks later, I travelled to Leeds to see how long Sir David Frost's star-studded studio panel would take to uncover my identity. If one of them hadn't been an ITV Sport colleague of mine, I swear we would all still be waiting for their answer.

Jean Rook and Bonnie Langford were none the wiser

when Sir David finally spilled the beans and ushered me onto the set. Fortunately, Angus Scott had been sitting between them on the panel and had clocked me straightaway. He spent the next five minutes pretending not to know before theatrically solving the riddle.

Sir David then confirmed it to the world of daytime television. 'Yes, it's football commentator, Clive Tillsdale.'

Fame is not all it's cracked up to be.

Minor celebrity. Fifteen minutes of fame. *The Chase*, 2019.

10

SIR BOBBY

Sir Bobby Robson was the DNA of English football. Still is.

Proud, passionate, brave, committed and just a tiny bit bonkers, Bobby coached and managed some of the finest players of the modern era. And mispronounced the rest.

I have never known better company and I've never worked with a worse co-commentator. I loved him for both.

Following Ron Atkinson's forced resignation from ITV in the spring of 2004, Bobby was asked to take the seat next to me for England's opening game of the European Championship finals against France in Lisbon. I could hardly have wished for a more qualified or respected wing man for such a mouth-watering match.

It was his first ever game as a co-commentator, though. And his last.

Brian Barwick and I spent two long lunches talking him through the job description. We told him that this game was as important to us as any of his ninety-five internationals as England manager had felt to him. He liked that idea. He was keen and enthusiastic in a way only Bobby could be.

During the game, he hardly said a word.

Frank Lampard headed England in front and David Beckham missed a penalty before Zinedine Zidane stole the most
dramatic of French victories with two very late goals. It was a
heart-wrenching and ultimately heart-breaking game. And yet,
the biggest heart inside the stadium never found its voice.

I managed to extract a few syllables of agreement out of
Bobby from time to time but little more. Despite a half-time
talking-to, he just couldn't catch the flow of live commentary.
It left him virtually speechless.

After the match, we took the ten-minute walk back to
the broadcast compound together. Bobby never shut up. He
was lucid, animated and insightful. He talked me through the
match from A to Z. Or he would have done had I not stopped
him abruptly around about 'T' with a curt 'it's no fuckin' good
now, Bobby'.

I think it's the only time I've ever sworn at a legend. It was
a rebuke quickly followed by a hug. Sir Bobby Robson was the
most huggable man I've ever met in football.

I wanted to hug him the last time I was with him but it
would have hurt him even more than he was hurting already.

He was sitting in the same Portuguese sunshine on the
terrace overlooking the eighteenth green at Vila Sol Golf Club
on the Algarve. He was hosting the sixth annual Sir Bobby
Robson charity golf weekend on behalf of a children's refuge
in Faro.

Bobby had about a month to live. His 76-year-old body
was fighting its fifth battle with cancer. You would never have
known it. He was defiantly cheerful and serenely philosophi-
cal. Just a class act to the very end.

Popularity in modern football is relative. Nobody commands unanimous support. The game is too tribal, too embittered to have universally admired Olympian figures like Jessica Ennis or Chris Hoy. Bobby would be about as close as you'll get. He'd be up there with Frank Bruno and Freddie Flintoff as the kind of sporting personalities anyone would find difficult to dislike.

He might not have been much of a co-commentator but he was a sparkling studio panellist. That big heart of his was always worn on the sleeve. He talked about football like he was witnessing a solar eclipse. A man that must have watched a million games somehow always found a sense of rarity and wonder in the next one. Like every match was his first.

I sat next to him in the stands on a night off during the 1998 World Cup. He took me to the Parc des Princes to watch his protégée Ronaldo score twice for Brazil in a 4–1 victory over Chile. I was nursing sore ribs for days afterwards. Watching football with Bobby was a physical experience. His restless enthusiasm spilled over into a salvo of digs and prods as he repeatedly drew my bruised attention to Ronaldo's latest run or surge.

'Look, look, look!'

'I am looking, Bobby!'

I wasn't being taught so much as man-marked. If the Chilean defence had got half as close to Ronaldo as Bobby got to me, they'd have stood a better chance of reaching the quarter-finals.

That eternal flame for football was what melted the viewers when Bobby was holding court on a World Cup television panel. If football were a religion, he was the missionary you would have sent out to convert the masses. He was such a devout disciple of the game and his sincerity would have turned even the most deep-seated agnostic.

How many football people can you truly believe? Sir Bobby Robson, for one.

Bobby's fervour for football was not that of some public school games teacher trying to chivvy up the boys for a cross-country run. He was spirited but he wasn't doe-eyed. He retained much of the athletic pride and self-regard of his playing days. Bobby liked to look good, liked to be able to cut the mustard with the players in his charge. He did fancy himself as a bit of a smooth talker.

The constant fever that he ran for the game transmitted itself to everybody around him. It was too virulent to resist or to shake off. He was a one-man contagion, arresting your attention with his hands-on, full-on lectures about any and every detail of football. He was in your face, asking you questions and answering them in the same eager breath.

That yen to make an impression did get the better of him sometimes.

In Mexico during the 1986 World Cup, he cadged a pair of new boots off Glenn Hoddle in order to join in an impromptu training game with his squad. They hurt him, really hurt him, as new boots can. Bobby's discomfort was obvious but he wasn't about to bail out in front of the players. At the end of the match, he kicked the boots off and complained to Glenn about the tightness of them. Only then did he realise that they both still had the paper padding stuffed into the toes.

That earnest lust for football life did leave him open to starring in a few comic interludes but Bobby's book always seemed open, you always felt you could see what he was feeling, hear what he was thinking. You might occasionally query his stance but you knew that he was already sold on it. His conviction was gospel. There was none of the flannel and spin of the modern designer manager.

What you saw was what you got with Bobby. Not many football managers take that chance.

Ten or a dozen years ago, I was introduced to Mick McCarthy at a drinks reception on the eve of Bobby's charity golf event in Portugal. I had interviewed him on a number of occasions and so I held out a hand with a polite, 'yes, we already know each other'. Mick being Mick shook my hand firmly and countered, 'no, we don't'.

The denial was made with a wicked grin. He went on to qualify it by saying that, although we had met on a number of occasions under the harsh lights of the post-match interview area, the person I spoke to there was not the one I was with now. Manager Mick McCarthy was a different beast from Mick McCarthy, husband of the lovely Fiona and father of three.

Those previous professional encounters were between Mick and the very first outsider he'd met in the wake of a disconcerting defeat. An outsider that was about to start asking him difficult questions about a situation he was finding difficult enough already. Me.

If I asked the same questions again now among friends over a glass of wine I would get different answers to the ones he gave me when the camera was rolling.

Football managers cannot usually afford to be themselves

when they are on the record. Like contestants in the *Master-mind* chair, they know that only their first answer will be accepted. Unlike contestants on *Mastermind*, they cannot pass. Every answer counts until the show is over and they can go back to their real lives.

Believe me, seeing Tony Pulis playing with his grandchildren is a disorientating experience. It's difficult to equate the coochy-coos with the way his Stoke team blocked and barged at corner-kicks. It's the same guy, though.

Bobby appeared much the same guy on and off stage but he didn't get to win major trophies in four different countries without being able to work the room, without being slippery enough to keep a secret. That essential Englishness of his travelled as well as it did because he was light on his feet and knew most of the tricks of his trade. He usually had a cunning plan on the go.

His reputation as a genial gentleman of the game was well-earned, but his honourable air was a bit of a front for his competitiveness. Bobby may have appeared quaintly absent-minded at times but his was a mind that usually had a bit too much running through it, rather than too little. He was cute all right.

Football managers can set out as principled and deferential leaders by example at the start of a career, but the codes of conduct get scrambled when battle is joined. In a dog-eat-dog world, not everyone can have their day. The moral standards are up for constant revision.

When Derby County called for an investigation after catching a member of Leeds United's coaching staff loitering outside their training centre in 2019, Leeds manager Marcelo

Bielsa promptly helped that investigation by freely admitting to spying on all opponents. You had to admire his honesty as much as his dishonesty.

He didn't know he'd done anything wrong. He said he believed he hadn't 'violated the norm'. And yet his secret agent had been equipped with pliers, binoculars and a heavy disguise. Only a stash of poisoned darts to fire at Derby's best players was missing from his rucksack. Some norm.

Secrets don't keep very well in football. It's one big gossip circle, a game of Chinese whispers. My profession muddies its waters with daily rumours and speculation but football takes a lot of its own dirty linen down to the public launderette for a wash and spin. Managers can only manage so much. I have frequently engaged in a spot of espionage of my own.

In November 1992, I commentated on a Premier League match between Leeds and Arsenal at Elland Road for *Match of the Day*. Before heading north on the Friday afternoon, I called George Graham on several occasions in a bid to seek out some team news. On a five-minute loop, his secretary repeatedly told me that he was busy and to phone back, then at my last attempt she informed me that he had now left for Yorkshire but had told her that the squad was unchanged from Arsenal's previous match.

I found Howard Wilkinson a bit of a verbal bully in my early broadcast years, so I didn't bother calling him. Fortunately, I had a snout in the Leeds dressing-room. David Rocastle gave me confidential chapter and verse on Howard's selection before adding, 'Do you know Smudge is injured?'

'Smudge' was the man whose goals had carried Arsenal to the top of the league that November. Alan Smith had picked up an injury during training and was out of the game. Who knew? Nobody except for the opposition. David had obviously been in conversation with one of his former Highbury team-mates and been told that George Graham's 'unchanged squad' was, in fact, missing its most lethal name.

By chance, when I pulled into the car park of the Leeds Holiday Inn that Friday evening, the first thing I saw was the Arsenal team bus. Not only was I sharing a roof with George and his not quite unchanged squad, our night's slumbers were interrupted by a fire alarm shortly after midnight.

Dutifully, I trudged down the back stairs of the hotel in t-shirt and shorts to share a cold car park with Ian Wright, Lee Dixon, David Seaman and company, all in a similar state of undress to me. George then appeared as immaculate as ever in club suit and tie, apparently from the bar. He caught my eye and came over to warmly apologise for his unavailability at lunchtime. Forever the charmer.

I couldn't resist.

'I don't want to worry you, George, but I can't see Alan Smith anywhere.'

My observation was met with the most knowing of grins. A rare defeat for Gorgeous George.

The Saturday morning newspapers didn't have so much as a sniff of George's secret. No report of Smith's injury anywhere. The only other people that had been let in on it were the very people he was trying to keep it from.

Undressing football's secrets is part of the brief of the hack with the sharpened pencil or the roving microphone. An 'exclusive' is still a notch on the gun of a hungry reporter. It can come at a price – either a hefty fee to a paid informant or divorce papers served on a trusting relationship. But there is still an antique cachet in claiming first dibs on a story.

'The BBC has learnt that' usually translates into 'the BBC read in this morning's *Mirror* that', but editors from the days of newspaper barons and broadcast tycoons can't resist claiming territorial rights to slivers of the public domain. Modern media departments spend more time trying to kill and conceal stories than they do trying to create publicity.

Football and its media is a fixture, not a partnership. The silly season runs all year long.

Every story that I have ever broken, I have stumbled over quite accidentally. In 1984, I travelled back from the League Cup final at Wembley with the official Liverpool party. My ex-wife shared a table on the train home with a couple of the players' better halves and a couple of bottles of wine. As we walked to our car on arrival at Lime Street station, she blankly said, 'It's a shame about Graeme and Danielle going to live in Italy, isn't it?'

I knew about the Souness transfer to Sampdoria about two months before I was supposed to. I chose a quiet moment to mention it to Peter Robinson. He asked me to keep it under wraps on the understanding that I could be first with the news when Liverpool were ready to release it. Deal.

I think Michael Robinson's wife was probably the innocent source of that lead and it was her husband, the late lamented ex-Liverpool forward, who accidentally let slip to me that Howard Kendall was following him to northern Spain in 1987.

Michael left Anfield for Osasuna a few months before Howard's surprise move to Bilbao and had been offering the Everton manager some secret counsel on settling in the region.

Michael and I often spoke on the phone. He didn't know that I didn't know about Kendall.

When I calmly confronted Howard with the story alone in his office a couple of days later, he looked me straight in the eye and said, 'Don't make me lie to you, Clive.' I took that as a confirmation. He promised me the first interview.

I was commentating on a Manchester derby in the FA Cup for ITV at the start of 2012. I happened to make a call to the Football Association on the Friday before in order to check on potential replay dates. To my surprise, my contact at the FA volunteered the information that they had just received an application from Manchester United to re-register Paul Scholes, who had retired at the end of the previous season.

I didn't think anything of it until I checked into the Lowry Hotel the following evening and bumped into Scholesy. He was an elusive player in his pomp but I've never seen him move so fast as he did up the stairs and out of sight that night. Two and two suddenly added up. I knew about Paul's second coming before any of his United team-mates. Right place, right time.

The one career assignment that actually charged me to try to be a newshound was as the BBC's reporter in a cup final hotel.

For those of you under the age of 70, you might be surprised to hear that the FA Cup final was once the biggest game in town. Not only was it one of the few football matches broadcast live on national television until the late 1980s, it was live from dawn 'til dusk. No 'exclusives' here, BBC and ITV locked aerials from the moment Saint cheerily said good morning to Greavsie on one side and Stuart Hall guffawed at Eddie Waring ahead of *Cup Final It's a Knockout* on the other.

And, as sure as the weather follows the news, once the nation's comedians, soap stars, magicians and astrologers had made way for Des Lynam and Dickie Davies at lunchtime, the first guess at the team news followed from the reporter hiding in the foliage at each team's leafy country retreat. For three years from 1994, I was that man in the Home Counties rhododendron bushes.

I dropped lucky with Everton in '95 because not only did my radio background on Merseyside mean that I knew half of the squad personally, I enjoyed a firm friendship with manager Joe Royle too. When I say 'enjoyed', I'm not exaggerating. Joe is one of the warmest, funniest, brightest buttons I've ever been lucky enough to press for an opinion on football. He was never short of one either. Until I checked into their Hertfordshire cup-final base.

Joe knew exactly what I was after. And he told me so. He knew that I knew his players. The sum total of what Joe Royle didn't know could be written on a match head. The very qualities that endeared him to me were the very qualities that were going to defeat me before my date with the nation on Saturday lunchtime. I may have been a friend, but I wasn't getting his team.

One of my very favourite pieces of journalism was delivered by an embedded reporter. During the Falklands War, Brian Hanrahan was the BBC's man aboard the Royal Navy aircraft carrier, HMS *Hermes*. He was working under clearly defined restrictions as to what he could reveal about the detail of operational activities. Not least because so many of the friends and families of serving airmen were tuning into the nightly bulletins. And then there was wartime morale back home.

One film report that he recorded against a backdrop of Harrier jets landing on the deck of the carrier belongs in broadcast legend. Mindful of his remit, Hanrahan looked down the camera and said, 'I'm not allowed to say how many planes joined the raid, but I counted them all out and I counted them all back.' Twenty-three words, a million messages. Truly brilliant broadcasting.

The flying machine that I was trying to pick out in the skies above Sopwell House hotel that May Saturday morning was Duncan Ferguson. He was in recovery from a double hernia operation and was scheduled to undergo the gripping suspense of a late fitness test. The result of it was bound to impact on how the whole game would be played. Bielsa would have had George Smiley on the case.

My waiting world needed to know the outcome when *Cup Final Grandstand* came on air, but I was working under Joe Royle wartime restrictions. I scoured the hotel grounds for signs of activity, I looked deep into the eyes of the Everton players as they filed into the breakfast room, I struck up idle conversations with those I knew best in the hope that one of the least suspecting might let a 'great news about Big Dunc' slip out.

My manoeuvres were so badly concealed that some of the senior players began to take the piss out of me. Now I was surrounded by a whispering campaign full of false leads and diversionary tactics designed to throw me even further off the scent.

'Have you heard about Stuart Barlow?' said David Unsworth.

'Has John Ebbrell ever played up front before?' asked Dave Watson as he walked past me.

'Fancy him dropping me,' chanced Gary Ablett (who was far too nice a man to pull off such a stunt convincingly).

I had become a laughing stock in my own serious assignment. Time only for one last roll of the dice. Nearly high noon. Do not forsake me, Big Nev.

I went back fourteen years with Neville Southall. Never at any time in those fourteen years had I known what he was going to do next. Even by the zany standards of goalkeepers, he was madcap. As consistently contrary off the field as he was consistently brilliant on it.

I had been to Neville's home near Llandudno and interviewed him at length, I had known him walk right past me with no more than a grunted expletive. If anyone was going to drag me by the ear to the door of the manager's room and report my frantic digging, it was Nev. But if anybody was likely to break rank and break silence . . .

Five hours later, I was standing outside the door of the Everton dressing-room at Wembley. Paul Rideout's goal had defeated Manchester United and I had been granted tacit permission to take a camera into the cavernous changing area to film the joyous celebrations. I just needed a final nod from the boss.

Joe came skipping down the old Wembley tunnel with a rascal of a smile from ear to ear. I held out a microphone, he held out both arms. I disappeared into a Baloo of a bear hug.

'Congratulations,' I shouted out from a patch of sweat somewhere between Joe's broad shoulders. Still he squeezed me. Tighter and tighter. Then I felt his breath warm against my right ear. Surely not a kiss too.

'Who the fuck told you my team?' he wheezed menacingly.

Five hours. Five hours in which Joe Royle had selected that team (with a half-fit Big Dunc only on the bench), roused that team before kick-off, coached and cajoled that team to play as they did, counted that team down to the final whistle that crowned the greatest success in the careers of most of that team and then lapped Wembley in triumph with that team.

And still he hadn't forgotten my words to the nation five hours earlier. 'My information is that Joe Royle won't risk Duncan Ferguson from the start and will kick-off the final with the same eleven that beat Tottenham at Elland Road in the semi-final.'

Well, Joe, now you know who fuckin' told me. It was Nev.

Bobby was every bit as guarded about classified information. I would call him at a pre-agreed time specifically to be let into the secret of his latest selection, but he still spent the first twenty minutes of the conversation agonising over whether to tell me or not.

Would it be unkind to suggest that Bobby's capacity to conceal team news was curtailed by the fact that he couldn't always remember the name of half his team? Maybe, but when he was pressed for his line-up ahead of the World Cup semi-final against Germany in 1990, he famously told the assembled media, 'Hitler didn't tell us when he was going to send over those doodlebugs, did he?'

The hand of the football manager is always kept tight to the chest. It's the way they play. Or try to.

The League Managers Association is football's best-run trade union. It is fronted by the excellent Richard Bevan and well-supported by the dons of the profession – Ferguson, McMenemy, Wilkinson, Hughton, Curbishley, Hodgson, Pleat, Allardyce, Moyes et al. Active board members all.

Bobby was a vice-president of the LMA. He was a mentor to many. José Mourinho took copious notes during the Robson sessions he watched at Barcelona and translated them into a coaching career of his own. Borrowing material is how you get on. There can be no true union.

Football management is a profession in which you are being perpetually stalked. Statistically, bomb disposal officers probably have safer jobs but it's not just the inevitability of the sack race catching up with you that follows the manager around like a shadow. It's the shallow sense of communion in a congregation in which everyone is after your job.

Protective gear for a manager consists of blinkers and ear plugs to block out not only the sound of a preying, prying media but also of those from within your own ranks who are touting themselves for the embattled post you are defending. 'I'm flattered to be linked with my mate's primary source of income, but I can't say any more at this stage.' It's a predatory profession.

The various vultures that constantly circle above managers force them to circle their wagons on the ground. They become distrusting and disingenuous by nature. Attitudes harden in pace with their arteries. Men like Mourinho and Guardiola are vaunted coaches but they are routinely rude and dismissive in interview situations. Unnecessarily so.

Don't you just love it when a manager begins his post-match interview by saying, 'it was never going to be an attractive game'? Where did it say that on the ticket? Next to

£60? Imagine buying a ticket for a West End musical and being told afterwards, 'the singing was never going to be very tuneful'. But that's where the results-driven obsession drives them. Deeper and deeper into themselves and their survival.

Media interrogation is often adversarial but a manager's true enemies are usually much closer than the press are allowed to get. They probably invited them into their office for a post-match drink earlier in the season. Journalists may boast pompously about the power to get managers the sack but it's other managers that take their jobs. There are only so many horses on the carousel.

Bobby was sacked within a year of first becoming a manager. He learnt of his dismissal by Fulham from a headline displayed on an *Evening Standard* news stand outside Putney station. Sporting Lisbon got rid of him when they were sitting top of the Portuguese League. Barcelona took Bobby's job away from him a couple of days after his team had lifted their third trophy of the season. He didn't even have his own office at Nou Camp for the year after he was brusquely ushered upstairs to make way for Louis van Gaal, who has since denounced the club's treatment of Bobby.

Freddy Shepherd was the last chairman to sack Bobby at Newcastle in 2004. He truly hated doing it. The decision was taken as much to spare Bobby the indignity of senior players turning against him as anything else. A couple of them had made it their business to tell the chairman that his manager had 'lost the dressing-room'. They should be ashamed of themselves to this day.

A couple of years later, Freddy and his family were in Portugal supporting Bobby's charity golf event when he told me how he had paid several thousand pounds of his own money to buy and destroy a photograph of a player putting two fingers up behind the manager's back at the training ground. Freddy wasn't having Bobby being exposed to such an embarrassment.

I can understand how the inspiration and influence of even a figure of Bobby's standing might wear a little thin after year on year of the same voice making the same demands with the same intensity that football brings with it to those operating at the highest level. Perhaps players need a change every three or four years. In fairness to Freddy and every other chairman, it is cheaper to change the manager than the playing staff if that is the case.

But the notion that a man of Bobby's integrity and fervour can 'lose' a group of twenty young adults with the world at their feet and a wedge in their bank accounts is a damning indictment of the players, not the manager. The decency that Sir Bobby Robson epitomises in this or any other era deserves better than that. It was with a very heavy heart that Freddy Shepherd opted to replace the manager rather than the shower of players that forced him out.

It must be difficult to believe in the fellowship of football with parishioners like that, but Bobby always kept the faith. He was as avid a touchline ranter as any manager, as devastated by defeat as any of his peers. But he soon found some perspective, soon rekindled his optimism, soon recharged his glass to at very least half-full. Bobby treated football's two imposters the same.

His engaging smile was a given. Sometimes it was rueful, other times it was reflective, oftentimes it was forced in the aftermath of a setback or an injustice. But the smile was never far away. Bobby wanted to make people around him feel good, wanted to take them with him to a better place, to the next victory, the next smile.

The very fact that Freddy Shepherd was there on the Algarve as a committed friend and protector of the Robson reputation spoke volumes for Bobby's ability to see football for what it is. The most important of the less important things.

Perhaps his Herculean fight against cancer gave Bobby that context and that sense of proportion. It certainly gives him a legendary status over and above anything that he achieved professionally.

For seventeen years, he took on the most terrifying of opponents and gave it a game. In 1995, he had a palatal obturator fitted into the roof of his mouth that kept his face in shape. Without it, he couldn't so much as speak. He went on to take charge of another 400 matches and win another five trophies. Bobby was as tough as they come and as lovely as they come.

To quote the title of the beautifully-crafted and evocative Gabriel Clarke film, *Bobby Robson, More Than a Manager.*

I sat next to Bobby in the back of a fast car from Lisbon down to the Algarve on the Friday before the European Championship final of 2004. Vila Sol was hosting the first playing of his charity golf event in aid of the children's hostel in Faro. I've hosted the gala dinner there every year since.

His sons – Andrew, Paul and Mark – all have a bit of the look of him. It's eerie but warming. You get tiny glimpses of the great man and hear little echoes of his voice when you reminisce with them. Lady Elsie was determined to keep the event going in Bobby's memory after he left us all in 2009. We hold the most uplifting wake for him each summer.

His good friend, Roger Eastoe, raised the money for a bronze statue of Bobby to be unveiled by the eighteenth green at Vila Sol. It is one of the most heart-warming memorials I've ever seen. The smiling figure of Bobby sits typically upright on a plain bench watching the golfers play the final hole. You can park yourself alongside him and even rest back against his outstretched arm. It's a delightful thing to do.

In *More Than a Manager*, José Mourinho says 'a person only dies when the last person that loves him dies'. Sir Bobby Robson's unique DNA is still going strong.

COMPUTER GAMES:

Championship Manager 2 (1995)

FIFA (2001–15)

Recording *FIFA* is the hardest I have ever worked as a broadcaster.

When EA Sports first employed me to work on their flagship football game, the contract was for five eight-hour studio sessions. That's a lot of shouting. It was like being in a stormy marriage for a week.

My son, Paddy, was just getting into gaming when I began to record the commentary track for *FIFA*, so I was soon aware of its reach and impact. For years, I was cursed by every parent at his school. 'I've had to listen to your voice all bloody weekend.'

Not only was I that 'voice of *FIFA*' for a decade or so, I rewrote the script for the game too. EA flew me to Vancouver to deliver a couple of seminars to the team that developed and programmed *FIFA* out there. I went on to present a Video Games conference as part of the Edinburgh Festival.

I am absolutely hopeless with a games controller in my hands but the one thing my anal commentator's mind could do was work out the sequencing of the game's soundtrack. Every corner-kick is a corner-kick but the script requires ten different versions in order to avoid repetition.

So 'it's a corner' . . . 'corner then' . . . 'going to be a corner' . . . 'corner given', etc, etc.

Then 'taken short' . . . 'it's a deep one' . . . 'delivered low' . . . 'floated high' . . . so that each starting point leads to a variety of alternatives spreading out from the one source like a family tree. Each branch, twig and leaf of that tree requires ten different phrases to describe it. Somehow – and don't ask me how – the programmers sync the sound to the movements. Artificial high intelligence.

In 2012, my wife and I enjoyed a wonderful holiday in the Middle East. One of the highlights was a couple of nights under the stars in the awesome setting of a sandstone desert called Wadi Rum in southern Jordan. It is so 'out of this world' that the virgin landscape has been used to depict the surface of far-off planets in Hollywood movies.

We were driven to our canvas retreat from earthly life by a Bedouin man in a rickety jeep. His two young sons joined us for the fifteen-minute journey. The vehicle's engine was too noisy for much in the way of conversation but I managed to shout loudly enough over the din to inform the nomadic Arab at the wheel that we were from the UK.

His children began to laugh and he engaged in animated conversation with them for a moment or two, then said to me, 'They say you sound like the man on FIFA.' I turned to look into the wide eyes of the boys on the back seat and then delivered a line or two in my theatrical commentator's voice. They whooped and giggled like I had suddenly produced a dove from up my sleeve.

'Ooh Fee-far! Fee-far!' they shrieked in delirium, pointing at me like an alien being.

If football is the world's game, the commentary track of FIFA is its universal language.

11

BIG RON

Ron Atkinson was always someone I considered a friend.

Some of you may have a problem with that already.

He was sat adjacent to me when he said the 'n word' on the 20th April 2004 in the commentary position at Monaco's Stade Louis II Stadium. I didn't hear it at the time, I was listening to a rehearsal for a post-match studio discussion.

I'd never heard him use that word before and I never heard him utter it again. Not in any context.

He has said that he was muttering to himself in the wake of Chelsea's semi-final exit from the Champions League. ITV were on a commercial break at the time. The offensive words were picked up accidentally and only on sister channels in the Middle East.

Or they were initially.

Ron apologised for saying them, both publicly and privately. He has expressed his regret many times over.

The comment he made about Marcel Desailly that night was inexcusable. It was overtly racist. In career terms, it was deemed unforgivable. Ron offered his resignation the following morning and never worked for ITV again.

There is no lining to the cloud he left under but if the headlines and the discussion that accompanied them took that word out of the psyche and the vocabulary of even one single person, then some purpose was served by the depressing fall-out. There can be no debate about such gross abuse.

As yet, there is no known cure for the disease of racism in football either.

•

Some very serious alleged crimes have been pardoned in the interests of peace and reconciliation in recent years. Some relatively minor mistakes and ill-judgements have not. Who decides?

The closest thing to a popular adjudicator on moral standards in the UK appears to be the *Daily Mail*. It would be funny if it weren't so true.

We are an opinionated species. We all draw our lines in the sand on every topic large and small. Matters of opinion are not matters of record, though. Not mine, not yours, not anyone's. They are opening remarks in a trial by a jury drawn from all sides of the issue.

Sand shifts. Experiences and circumstances can bring about changes in position. Can and should.

Only change can bring entrenched warfare to an end. Something has got to change to stop racism. Something has got to change in the way we all set about combating it. That is surely clear.

What though?

I was ITV's commentator for England's international game in Sofia in October 2019. It is remembered not for the 6–0

England win but for the mindless, moronic abuse of several black players by an organised posse of young Bulgarian men.

Not all racist abuse is mindless. Far from it. Abuse can be used as a weapon to coerce and control in order to orchestrate and enforce the most oppressive persecution. Right now, there is a young child shivering aboard a refugee boat in the English Channel who is an awful reminder of that.

The abuse of the England players in Sofia was orchestrated in so much that the ultras turned up as a group, but it carried no obvious purpose or threat. It felt like a ritual, a demonstration.

Or it did to me.

My commentary from Sofia won some plaudits. I managed to find a few chosen, considered words of suitable condemnation and I had done my homework. I knew the published UEFA protocol and I had researched all of Bulgaria's previous convictions. Sadly, the Nazi salutes weren't exactly a surprise development.

But if I was pleased with anything I said as Gareth Southgate firmly took charge of a situation that seemed to be escaping the officials on duty, then it was an observation that came straight off the top of my head.

The television director cut up a camera shot of Raheem Sterling. He looked rather bemused by the sad inevitability of the temporary halting of the game.

'What must he be thinking?' I asked out loud. And then, 'I can never know. This will never happen to me.'

It will never happen to me. I hope I never forget that.

It will never happen to Adrian Chiles either. My former colleague at ITV was sufficiently motivated to get to the bottom of what Ron said in 2004 to make an hour-long television programme for the BBC called *What Ron Said*. It was well-meaning but probably about fifty-nine minutes and fifty seconds too long.

The grounds for the commission were to follow Ron on a journey of re-education. All the way to Birmingham, Alabama at one point. It was an uncomfortable journey. Uncomfortable for Ron as he took the stand before a variety of accusers and character witnesses, uncomfortable for me as I saw him sinking into the morass on which his age, his upbringing and his culture had drawn their own lines.

There is a big difference between apology and contrition. The more fingers, the more cameras that were pointed at Ron, the less contrite he became. It was a show trial, complete with continuity shots set to atmospheric musical soundtracks and pithy voice-overs. Watching him take a guided tour of a 'museum of racist memorabilia' was like watching Canute at high tide.

The defining moment in the programme, for me, was when Ron admitted, 'I didn't even know I'd said it.' It was a remark as casual and yet as worrying as the one that condemned him in Monaco.

We all say things we wish we hadn't but they may just be the things that define us in the eyes of others. They are possibly the most important of all the things we say. We cannot simply dismiss them with an apology or a retraction. Our failings in life are often what characterise us.

If we allow our standards to slip to the point that we don't realise how routinely we swear, how fast we drive, how much we drink, how we stare at anything different from us, then we are lost in ourselves. If we don't look deep into the mirror, we are in danger of disappearing onto our own lonely planet.

The lines we draw on behavioural issues are camouflaged battle lines. Like Ron, we defend them without realising we are doing it, without asking ourselves how they impact on others, without ever trying to know what it's like to be Raheem Sterling.

Empathy is a walk in the shoes of others. It can help us challenge the conviction that our view of the world is the right one. It can help all of us do that.

It's easy for me to write that the Bulgarian ultras' abuse carried 'no obvious purpose or threat'. It may not have looked quite as mindless from Raheem's side of the line. We have got to view racism, sexism, homophobia, ageism from the other side in order to have any chance of understanding them and knocking down the walls that segregate the sides. If it is an uncomfortable watch, so be it.

I can get angry and vocal about racism without being a victim of it. Can and must.

Incidences of racist or any other abuse deserve individual analysis and judgement like any crime but they are all examples of something appearing at the surface that is still in existence deep down below. That something is the disease that infects opportunity and respect and has done for generation after generation. That's what's got to change.

It is one thing me declaring myself a supporter of an anti-racism group like Kick It Out, but anti-racism is not a default position. It's not a hashtag, not a taking of a knee, not even a few hundred words said or spoken in public like these. Words are not nearly enough. Anti-racism is a proactive attempt to change the status quo.

Ron could not see the value of the museum tour through bygone racism. He couldn't recognise the need to see or change the status quo of his white privilege.

That privilege is our wrongful inheritance. There is in existence an ingrained, systemic racism that he and I have grown up with and must accept and process. It's not necessarily our fault. There need not be any guilt trip attached, but it is our responsibility to acknowledge it. We can't simply consign it to history as a problem that is not ours or a problem slowly solving itself.

And, by the way, it is a privilege that comes with challenges and uncertainties of its own and there are questions we may need help with because we will 'never know what it's like to be Raheem Sterling'. Never.

Dealing with a minority lifestyle as a black person, a homosexual or a female in sport is not a situation I will encounter. At the same time, neither is the sense of cause and belonging that comes with all of them. As part of my largely favourable deal with fate, I don't have the same kind of identity. I don't have white, male, middle-aged movements, music or culture to relate to.

Or if I do, they are not movements I would ever join, not a music or culture I like.

That's not a complaint, certainly not a hardship. It is just another point of separation, another potential point of difference. Difference is beautiful as long as it is not discriminatory, not weaponised, not armed to be divisive.

No performer in any field has pulled on my heart strings more powerfully than the black singer Ella Fitzgerald. Her voice melts me to mush. Her career encountered routine prejudice and sanction in 1950s America. Her manager, Norman Granz, fought the entrenched establishment and released her song-book for all to be enchanted by.

Tony Bennett, a famous Italian–American singer of the era, often recalled Ella's simple soliloquy to tolerance. 'We're all here.'

The argument for fellowship in difference is that straight-forward. It is that inescapable, that rightful. Colour fades under the searching light of human justice, but we have got to keep pointing that light at the past in order to redress the future. Study 'then' to learn about 'now'.

In my field of television, *Till Death Us Do Part* was a satir-ical ground-breaker in the 1970s. It was a situation comedy with a one-eyed central character, Alf Garnett, that challenged so many Britons to take a long hard look at him and ask if they could see anything of themselves. It was a challenge repeatedly voiced in the scripts by the mocking comments of his daughter and son-in-law. The show had bigotry but it had balance.

Comedy is critical by nature. Alf was continually made to look stupid. The power of persuasion is much stronger than the sledgehammer of censorship.

There are only so many things that I would march on Parliament in support of but the defence of comedy is one of them. Laughing at something we don't think we should be laughing at is a revelatory act. An involuntary act. It tells us so much about ourselves.

Not only that but it gives us a peep at how others see us. It's enlightening and so kind of healthy. As long as we find answers to the questions it asks.

Till Death Us Do Part would not be screened publicly today because so much of it was deliberately offensive. But it could be shown to students of social history to give them a screen-shot of where attitudes, and even comedy, were then compared to now.

Revising history is tricky but the importance of what Ella Fitzgerald, Nat King Cole and other black performers went through in the 1950s is that they provide further evidence of how we need to reassess the way in which we depict past events. These were not romantic tales with happy endings, they were real-life stories full of unhappiness.

It's not a rewriting of history that is required but a re-telling of the same history in the light of fresh evidence. A refreshing of the syllabus we teach and learn at school and at home.

I can't change the circumstances in which I grew up. The only black faces on my radar during the first twenty-five years of my life were a handful of brilliant musical vocalists that I rarely heard speak. I would be different if I were a kid today. The majority of my 26-year-old son's favourite performers just happen to be black. Singers, rappers, actors, basketball players, footballers.

He hasn't chosen them by skin colour, he has chosen them by the connection they have made with him. His affection for them is natural. For him, it is bigotry and abuse that are unnatural. Whether by legislation, debate, protest or satire that must be the key message. Racism is plain wrong. You shouldn't have to campaign for equality or to 'matter'.

Football's problems in this area do reflect society's issues, only bigger and uglier. The hateful image is blown up in our national game. Everything is. Football is discussed through a megaphone.

Mindless abuse is part of the language of football. It is central to the lyrics and themes of half of the game's most chanted anthems. Most of it is beyond any reasoned com- prehension, but then none of us are at our most reasonable when we have squeezed through the turnstile of a football stadium.

We pay our money and we make our choices. Us versus them. For no good reason, we take an instant dislike to 'them'. For ninety minutes, they are the enemy. The rivalry possesses us.

Human prejudice and enmity invariably have a source. A source, rather than a justification. Identifying 'the festering sore', as Nelson Mandela famously referred to past divisions, has surely got to be part of any attempt to treat it, to finding real solutions to racism and all of the other 'isms' that blight our sport and our world. Their mindlessness needs exposing to the minds they have infected.

They are not logical, they are not right. They are, quite literally, indefensible. These are arguments we should be able to win. But how?

The historic speeches with which Mandela and Martin Luther King inspired many millions were mainly concilia- tory in tone. The 'dream' that King shared on the steps of the Lincoln Memorial was 'deeply rooted in the American dream' and pictured black and white children joining hands. Look at the footage and you will see a lot of white faces in the crowd that day in 1963. The text of his sermon was already irresistible to many of all colours. It's a 'word' that should be simple to spread.

I can't begin to guess at the origins of the hatred that induced a few dozen young Bulgarians to aim anachronous salutes and monkey noises at total strangers of a similar age simply because their skin was a different colour to theirs. Whatever the sorry spur was, we need to find out. They may not seem worth spending time on or with, but they are the people we've got to change.

They were breaking the law and a handful were identified and hopefully charged and punished, but will that punishment have 'knocked some sense' into them? I doubt it. Any more than visiting the 'schoolhouse door' where the Governor of Alabama had stood to block the entry of two black students forty years earlier was going to 're-educate' Ron.

Unlike the Bulgarian youths, most racists don't think they are racist. Ron didn't.

He thought he was embarking on the equivalent of a speed awareness course. We have all been on them. They are revealing but not altogether reforming. Not in themselves. Their appeal is the three points we are dodging.

I think Ron was persuaded that his best chance of dodging the bullet from his pundit's job was to volunteer for the racism road trip. It was all a bit of a performance and one that he soon tired of. 'I've overpaid the price for what I did. I know it was politically incorrect but who isn't?' he protested halfway through the programme.

His protest was occasionally backed up by friends and for-mer players like Cyrille Regis and Brendan Batson highlighting

Ron's record of recruiting black football talent at West Brom. The case for the defence. But, as one of his American interrogators observed, 'his mistake is trying to rationalise it'.

If there was an attempt to explain 'it' away as some kind of momentary lapse, the attempt was as damning as the original outburst. The word was there in his dictionary. The thoughts around it were embedded beside it. This was not about someone dropping their guard for a second and letting a naughty word slip out. This was not a goof, this was a bad accident that had been waiting to happen.

The bigger problem is that it was an accident that happened to someone with a flair for saying exactly what the great British football public were usually thinking. Big Ron, the co-commentator, was the personification of the bloke in the pub. He was a very qualified bloke in the pub because he'd managed three clubs to major trophies, but his delivery and his connection were those of someone we all knew and liked the company of. A popular and populist communicator.

Not just Big Ron, but Our Ron too.

I've been asked about that night in Monaco by people whose attempt at a sympathetic conclusion is something like 'you've got to be careful what you say these days, haven't you?' That's really not the point. This is not a question of accidentally swearing in front of the vicar, this is corrosive, hurtful language. That is why it is a delicate matter.

In March 2019, six months before Sofia, I commentated on England's game in Montenegro. A radio colleague referred to what he believed to be audible abuse of black players during the first half. I was not made aware of it. By the time I returned home from Podgorica, the awful treatment of Danny Rose and others was the biggest trend on Twitter and my failure to denounce it was the second biggest.

I had a defence. I couldn't report what I didn't know. I speculated during the commentary about the possibility of abuse when Sterling pointedly celebrated a goal with hands cupped to his ears. As soon as I put the microphone down at the final whistle, I sought out FA officials and was able to confirm that Rose had been verbally abused close to the end of the game. ITV could then pursue the story with Southgate and others in the remaining minutes of the broadcast.

The following day I was asked to explain my own silence on the matter by TalkSport. The radio presenters, Paul Hawksbee and Andy Jacobs, were joined in the studio by respected anti-racism campaigner Troy Townsend. All three men are personal friends. Paul began the live interview by referring to my work alongside Troy with Kick It Out. Immediately, I interrupted him. Any previous 'good deeds' were inadmissible evidence.

I didn't need testimonials or mitigation. I knew that I simply wasn't guilty of the specific charges made by the social media hanging party. I couldn't have condemned on air something I hadn't heard during the match. That's just sound journalism. I would have liked to but I couldn't because I was as unaware of any abuse as I had been of Ron's dire words in 2004. You really do have to be careful what you say when you are live to millions. These days, all days.

Condemning racism publicly is not a ticked box, it's a message that has got to be as accurate as it is forthright if it is to carry any force. Getting that message across is, like any journalism, an exercise in gathering and assessing information from as many sources as you can before relaying it. It's no good preaching to the converted, the message has got to travel beyond them.

I have been told by black colleagues that they simply have a different awareness of the sounds of abuse. A higher frequency on their radios. Like I said of Sterling, 'I can never know', but I certainly listened more intently in Bulgaria. Ron had stopped listening long before the end of his trip to the States. Stopped listening, stopped understanding.

One Saturday back in 2012, I was playing golf at a private club in leafy Berkshire a world away from the difficult debate about racism in British culture. When I walked into the bar, a couple of dozen golfers were watching a television report about the refusal of Rio Ferdinand, Jason Roberts and others to wear Kick It Out t-shirts on a designated 'action day'.

'What do they want now?' asked a disgruntled voice from behind me.

'Probably not to be called "they",' I countered without thinking.

The bar went very quiet. I didn't hang around for long. I don't know who the voice in the shadows belonged to but whoever it was, we can't just silence him. He may actually have a contribution to make.

His point was amplified by Lord Ouseley, then the chair of Kick It Out, when he countered Ferdinand's protest at a lack of action by publicly asking if Rio would 'tell Manchester United where to stick their shirt and their £150,000 a week?' Questions are allowed.

It's not a crime to seek clarification and we must not consider it a chore to provide it.

Racism is, and should be, a matter for impassioned and spiky debate. It needs to be examined from all angles and standpoints. If there are 'what do they want now' questions that are left unanswered because they are deemed too sensitive or too stupid, the 'stupid' will never become any the wiser, any more sensitive. They will become Alf Garnett.

In *What Ron Said*, there was an incongruous moment when Ron looked to challenge the use of the re-spelt 'n word' in hip-hop culture and music. I'm not aware that he ever had a lot of Kanye West or Snoop Dogg on his own playlist, but was he wrong to question it?

No question should be off limits in the interests of understanding. Understanding is so dangerously missing around racism.

Back in the summer of 2007 when Monty Panesar was spinning the England cricket team to a series victory over the West Indies, I dropped in on my ageing father one day.

'This Pakistani is good that plays for us,' he said disarmingly.

'He's from Luton, Dad,' I corrected him. 'Half our team is from South Africa but Monty's from Luton.'

Misapprehensions soon become misrepresentations without correction. You have got to listen to doubters and dissenters in order to win any argument. If your crusade moves beyond them without addressing their qualms and questions, you leave pockets of resistance behind you. Grumblings and mumblings that will gather and grow. You've got to convince the unconvinced. That was Mandela's greatest victory, King's greatest quest. True change.

You can change by tyranny or you can change by debate, and it was tyranny that got us into this mess.

I was commentating for Radio City on the day in 1988 that John Barnes backheeled a banana that had been thrown into his path during a Merseyside derby match. I broadcast my disgust at the racial abuse he suffered that day. I received three or four letters asking whose side I was on. A couple of men even made a bee line for me in a nightclub one night and advised me to watch my tongue.

John would be the first to say that life for a black footballer in England is different now than it was then. He has been the first to say a lot of things about Liam Neeson and other headline issues that have divided opinions. If someone as iconic and as thoughtful as John Barnes can attract strong criticism from people of the same ethnicity, it makes it clear to me that this issue is not simply about black and white. And nor should it be.

Difference is a different issue in Belfast or Jerusalem. It is not black and white but still potentially toxic without integration. Diversity just works. It always has. Listen to anything that Quincy Jones made with Rod Temperton. Brilliant people have crossed boundaries in search of fusion in music, food and art. It can't be that difficult in football.

One of the many sad side-effects of the Covid lockdowns was a suspension of the kind of social interaction that broadens minds and mixes ideas. The restrictions corralled us back behind our own doors into our own camps and cultures and closed them behind us.

The moment that dividing lines are daubed across the minefield of prejudice and discrimination, the debate is over and the tyrannical war is ready to be fought to a bloody end. Not all racists are white, not all sexists are male.

We cannot afford to close our minds because we will simply be closing the file on an unsolved crime. We all sing in harmony from the same hymn sheet when there are official statements to be drafted and read, but we can't all possibly be on the same page. There would be no racism if we were.

There has got to be a more open platform for discussion. One that makes us all look outwards to listen carefully to testimony that we will never experience ourselves, and one that also makes us look inwards at our own conditioning and habitat.

There has been a lot of recent advice and research into stereotyping in football commentary, but the moment we trust historians and philology professors to draw up lists of unsuitable words we are heading into *Handmaid's Tale* territory. Like everything, meanings change too. There are already more than enough words in the dictionary from which to choose the right ones to get this message across.

Nothing will ever dissuade me from marvelling at the exceptional speed and strength of Adama Traore. I would not be doing my job if I hid from praising his most eye-catching qualities. Nor would I be doing it fully if I didn't add that he has made himself so fast and so strong through his own hard work and dedication. The athleticism didn't come free with his birth certificate or his genes.

I am old enough to remember an era when there were murmured questions about the ability of black players to 'do it on a wet Tuesday night at Hull'. Laughable now, but only because a couple of generations of black footballers have repeatedly kicked that myth into the North Sea and changed minds, changed perceptions.

Change. We used to think the earth was flat.

I keep hearing the word 'conversation'. How many of these 'conversations' are conducted in echo chambers? Party rallies. There needs to be more range and less fear in our conversation. We can only change when we are all open to change and being changed. Or, like Ron, we will become barricaded into our own 'schools'.

The most hurtful and harmful part of *What Ron Said* was maybe not even the 'n-word' itself. It was the two words that preceded and accompanied it. 'Lazy' and 'thick'. There was the racism. There was the proof beyond doubt.

It was the association between skin colour and character traits that condemned Ron in my mind. The fact that he prefaced the outrageous insult with the phrase, 'he is what's known in some schools as a lazy, thick, etc'.

The 'n-word' is abhorrent. It represents so much that is so shocking to so many. But using it in the context that Ron did was what really shocked me. The roots of his suspicions about even an iconic black player such as Desailly were uncovered. Bad habits never quite outgrown. The wrong 'schools'.

Ron made me laugh many, many times. I won't defend his words or their connotation on that far-off night on the French Riviera. I have no compulsion to even try.

I haven't had any contact with him since the last funeral we both attended a year and more ago. No reason, no need. Ron Atkinson has no apology to make to me. I didn't even hear what he said at the time.

He owed Marcel Desailly a huge apology and I believe he has made it. Only Desailly can choose to draw a line under what Ron said.

For me, there are already far too many lines drawn across the racism canvas for us to see a clear route to change. We need a new and wider pathway. One that we can all tread.

MOVIES:

Will (2011)

The Class of '92 (2013)

Grimsby (2016)

Do please tell me if I start to name-drop but I have starred in movies with Damian Lewis, Sacha Baron Cohen, Bob Hoskins, Penelope Cruz and Eric Cantona.

Well, 'starred in' may be stretching it. 'Appeared in'. Actually, 'movies' is probably pushing it a bit too. *Will* was bland, *Grimsby* was gross, *The Class of '92* was good but my dubbed commentaries were the worst thing in it.

Those of you that don't rate me as a commentator probably think that most of my earnings border on 'immoral'. The fees I picked up for my contributions to the above were downright prostitution.

My net worth has been periodically boosted by film-makers and ad-makers looking for a caricature commentator to add some stereotypical nonsense to attempts to sell their story or their washing powder. I say 'no' more often than 'yes', but working with the man that created comedic super-heroes like Ali G and Borat was too tempting to resist. It was a mistake.

At least it was a mistake that I shared with Raheem Sterling and Adam Lallana. Both also appeared in *Grimsby*.

Andy Townsend and I were contracted for a day's filming at Warner Brothers' Leavesden Studios near Watford. Thank goodness I'd managed to secure a power of veto over the content of our scripts. Even by Sacha standards, it was an outrageous movie.

Not only did it feature a scene set in the womb of an elephant and references to Donald Trump contracting HIV, it crudely trashed the image of the fine title town and portrayed football fans in general as boorish losers. Redeeming features were few and far between and it bombed at the box office.

Andy and I played ourselves and did nothing worse than commentate on some make-believe World Cup games. It was a fun session with some skilled and affable people on set. Cohen monitored the recording via video link from Los Angeles and was constantly trying to persuade us to add some lewd and smutty asides.

I convinced him that the comedic value was in us delivering a straight commentary.

It is one of the great movie mysteries that football has rarely been well observed by cinema. Some evocative documentaries have appeared but few original stories that have captured the game's true wonder. In football, truth is better than fiction.

12

GLENN

Glenn Hoddle was a football magician. That's not an opinion, that's a fact.

Not only could he make a football float and balance and spin and dip and then disappear before your very eyes, he also knew how he was doing it. Magicians do.

Many of the most gifted footballers play by instinct, by feel, by memory of the days when they ruled the school yard or local park with their untouchable talent. They have no idea how. They don't need to.

Only when age wearies their muscles, and their legs won't do what they're told anymore do they have to ask themselves how and why they were once the best.

How and why are the province of co-commentators. They are the two questions they must address and answer. Glenn Hoddle knows the how and the why. He sat next to me because I don't. And, most probably, neither do you.

The co-commentator is the man or woman that has been down there on the floor of the Colosseum, where the rest of us will never go. Been down there with the wild beasts and the wilder gladiators and then come back to let the watching spectators know what it's like to be in the arena. How you survive, why you succeed.

In 1989, I recorded a film feature with two young Third Division forwards for Granada Television's *Kick Off* programme. David Reeves and Tony Philliskirk were striking up a potent partnership in the Bolton Wanderers attack and my idea was to invite Burnden Park legend Frank Worthington to run the rule over them and offer some advice.

Ten years earlier, Frank had scored perhaps the most iconic goal in Bolton's history against Ipswich, juggling the ball twice before lifting it over his shoulder and Terry Butcher, and then turning to volley it home first time. It was the kind of thing Frank did regularly between seducing beauty queens and quaffing vintage champagne. He belonged magnificently to the 1970s.

Frank was 40 when I introduced him to Reeves and Philliskirk. He dusted off an old pair of boots for the shoot and tried to teach them all he knew. Lesson one was to control the ball with your back to goal by scooping it skywards with the outside of your foot before pirouetting smartly to lash it into the roof of the net. Now, you try.

I stopped the camera roll for a moment to try to explain to Frank that he needed to walk the two eager youngsters through the precise technique of the miracle he had just effortlessly performed. He simply performed it again. And again. The two most confident strikers in the lower divisions were visibly wilting in awe of the superior skills of a man nearly old enough to be their father.

Frank couldn't teach them anything because he didn't have a clue why or how he was so blessed.

Glenn Hoddle was a player–manager at the last two clubs he turned out for. I've heard that he was still the best player in the five-a-sides at the next two clubs he managed. It's even been suggested that he intimidated players half his age with his skill levels. What was he supposed to do? Mis-control the ball to make them feel better?

The art of good co-commentary is not for Glenn to bring his understanding of the game down to the level of the rest of us, but rather to raise ours up a bit closer to his. To tell us what we can't see for ourselves. To add, not to echo.

You may remember the 1999 Champions League final. I certainly do. One of the unsung highlights of ITV's coverage of Manchester United's epic win was Terry Venables' analysis of Teddy Sheringham's late equaliser. As Bayern Munich cleared the initial corner, the ball found its way to Ryan Giggs on the edge of their penalty area. Sheringham loitered in the six-yard box with intent.

By the time Giggs scuffed a hurried shot through the goal mouth mayhem, everyone else in the box had followed the ball's path and turned to face him. Everyone except for Teddy. What Venables noticed was that Sheringham's body remained side-on to the action, so that when Giggs' shot bounced towards him, he was able to help it on its way and sweep it home. Any other striker would have turned his back to goal and been unable to score from that position.

That's how Sheringham equalised. That's analysis.

Venables' dissection of the goal was carried out with the luxury of time to consider everything from the comfort of a studio chair. Glenn is comfortable in that seat too, but he prefers the challenge of trying to read a game minute-by-minute from the commentary position outside.

Constantly adapting to the changing face and balance of a match is what Glenn had to do as a manager and player. It's what the co-commentator is charged to do. You've got to think on your feet. You need to work out the 'how' and the 'why' on the hoof.

Anyone can tell you what went wrong once the black box has been recovered.

So much football analysis is delivered with that benefit of hindsight. Experts assess performances from the final whistle back to kick-off. Football matches are actually played in the opposite direction. They start at the start, not at the end. A game is a sequence of events. Each of those events impacts on the next one, and then the next one.

If a team loses 1–0, their manager cannot hark back to a penalty they were denied in the first minute and claim some kind of moral draw. It doesn't work like that. If his team had been awarded that penalty and taken the lead, the remainder of the game might have been totally different. One wrong turn can mean you have got to find a whole new route to get to where you want to go.

A studio pundit that tries to explain away the outcome of an entire match by repeatedly revisiting one replayed incident is wise only after the event. And where is the wisdom in that?

Football events happen in a long succession of moments. When you choose to appraise one of those moments separately from the others that happened around it, your verdict only relates to that one incident. You can't read any more into it.

If you draw your lines on the screen and change the way that moment could have worked out, you change the basis for the way the rest of the game is played too. There is no way of knowing what may have happened next. Peter Schmeichel would not have gone forward for that corner from which Sheringham scored if it had still been 0–0.

The curse of the commentator wouldn't exist if we all knew in advance that we were about to put the mockers on a player by praising him. The future in football is never more than a second away. The co-commentator is trying to read the tea leaves of the game and predict that future, based on their past experiences. Glenn has plenty of those.

The notion that he was born to play football overlooks how hard he practised in order to play as well as he did. It's strange how human nature can make us grudging and green-eyed when someone sits down to play a piano well or begins to dance like Britney. As if we couldn't have learnt the same notes or steps ourselves if we'd only put the hours in. Envy is the laziest of the deadly sins.

I dare say that Glenn's divine skills taunted and goaded jealous opponents when he turned it on in a Friday lunchtime training game, but I've never seen any vainglory in him. There's a fine line between teasing and grandstanding on a football field. Between confidence and arrogance. For some reason, matadors are not welcome in this ring.

It's not disrespectful to run faster than your adversary. Or jump higher. Or tackle more ferociously. But if you knock the ball through his legs a couple of times and give the paying public a memory to take away with them, you are in breach of football's code of ethics. Deemed out of line, out of order. Sorry?

Football is an entertainment industry in which showmen are oddly unwelcome. The only time I've known Glenn show off at anyone else's expense was during the high bits in 'Diamond Lights'. Chris Waddle just couldn't get up there.

I first got to know Glenn while compiling a film profile for BBC *Sportsnight* ahead of the 1994 FA Cup final. He was Chelsea's player–manager at the time.

I interviewed his parents, Derek and Teresa, in the back garden of the family home in Harlow. There were no silver spoons in the house when Glenn came into the world. His football may have become aristocratic but his was a blue-collar, not a blue-blooded background.

The magician's spell he put on a football was diligently learnt. He taught himself to juggle, to levitate the ball and saw defences in half. The wizardry was not God-given.

Arsène Wenger, his coach at Monaco, predicted that Glenn would become an excellent manager for that very reason. Because he toiled long and hard to make it look like football came naturally to him, he understood the process. Wenger noticed how patient Glenn was when trying to help him knock the edges off the young, raw George Weah. He was a mentor to him.

More than that, Glenn knew his limitations. He was always appreciative of players who could head the ball or tackle better than him. Recognising and playing to the individual strengths of your players is a vital ingredient in team management. Nobody can do it all.

As a schoolboy rugby player, I had a penchant for kicking goals. Unfortunately, it meant that I was bumped up to a standard of play far beyond the rest of my capabilities. And certainly beyond my pain threshold. Fortunately, I had a team-mate that could do everything on a rugby field except kick goals. He thought I was awesome, so he made most of my tackles for me. That is team sport.

Football has an odd habit of categorising players like there is a requirement to find a specific shelf in its library to place them on. The more arts and crafts a footballer possesses, the more individual and self-centred they are perceived to be. And so we create the pigeon-hole labelled 'luxury player'.

It is almost as if grizzly, grumpy old managers become so sceptical in their thinking that the most highly-skilled players seem too good to be true. They can't possibly be trusted and relied upon like workaday jobbers with a tenth of their talent. Chiefs and Indians.

Former Tottenham captain Danny Blanchflower was once asked directly if he thought Glenn was 'a luxury player'. He replied, 'No, it's the bad players that are the luxuries.'

Life on the road as a co-commentator is not always luxurious. Tournament months are full of early alarm calls, delayed flights and long traffic jams. I can only really rate Glenn's capacity to be a team player in the context of our commentary team. Not only was he easy to work with and around but I always found him generous with his judgements on and off the mic.

The England team have given him any number of opportunities to be catty and disdainful about poor performances during the last few years, but his experience of managing the national side just seemed to make him more support- ive and sympathetic. I cannot begin to understand why ITV have chosen to replace his hands-on insight in their England coverage.

He is not the best co-commentator that I've worked with. No, not Glenn, not Andy Townsend, not Jim Beglin, not David Pleat, not Ron Atkinson, not even Gareth Southgate with whom I called a few games in 2010. Sorry, guys. The best co-commentator I've ever had is Brian Smith.

Smithy is an Australian rugby league coach. Whereas Glenn and the other football experts were talking me through the finer points of their game, Smithy had to help me with a lot of the basics too. I needed a minder. Not to mention a reminder of the laws of the game from time to time. He was the commentating equivalent of that school mate that made all my tackles.

I found rugby league a wonderfully welcoming sport. I had a working knowledge of the game when Granada acquired the rights to show some live matches in 1988 but no more. I made it my business to try to learn rugby league from the inside and the sport opened every door that I knocked on.

Widnes were the best team around at the time. I got to know their coach, a call-a-spade-a-bloody-shovel of a man called Doug Laughton. He was as straight as a Roman road, a perfect instructor for a commentator with L plates.

I asked him if I could watch a game from the coach's dugout area in order to get a close-up view one Sunday. He met me in the tunnel before the match and walked me out with his assistants and substitutes.

When we arrived at the bench, I asked Doug where I could sit. 'You're sitting next to me, aren't you?' came the reply. He lit us a cigarette each and proceeded to talk me through every decision and thought he had for the next forty minutes. That doesn't happen in football.

When Wigan began to challenge the Widnes supremacy, their coach John Monie proved every bit as helpful. I like to think that those top operators recognised my thoroughness, my professionalism and, most important of all, my thirst for knowledge. *Their* knowledge.

You can't busk it at the highest level of any competitive sport. I think and hope the same is true in sports broadcasting. My partnership with Brian Smith worked so well because we each knew what we could and couldn't do. He always wanted to know more about the delivery of the commentary, I always needed to know more about the game.

When ex-footballers first try their hand at co-commentary, my advice is to listen to someone performing the same role in a sport they like, but don't intimately know. Maybe a Nasser Hussain or a Lawrence Dallaglio. Both were elite performers but neither is guilty of elitist analysis. They impart their knowledge in words and ways that we can all understand.

Assuming knowledge is a dangerous practice in any kind of communication. To an extent, I was learning rugby league on the job and so Smithy's informed insights had to be couched in layman's terms for me to follow them. That only made them more accessible to the viewer. Result.

All I ever ask of a co-commentator is that they take the job as seriously as I do. That doesn't mean they need to arrive at the game armed with stats and biogs. I would rather manage and edit the data supply myself. I just want them to care about their performance as if they were still playing. I can count on one finger the ex-players that I've worked with that didn't give a toss.

I make only two rules beyond that.

1. We divide the pitch up into three thirds. The middle third is always free for comment and analysis but the two ends are danger zones where I would rather the co-commentator wasn't musing about high defensive lines as the ball flies into the net. You will get your turn when the replays start.
2. Rule One is not binding.

When Steven Gerrard lashed his 'oh, you beauty' of a shot into the Kop end goal against Olympiacos in 2004, it didn't matter that Andy Gray was bellowing all over Martin Tyler's commentary because it worked. 'What a hit, son, what a hit!' fitted the moment. It wouldn't fit every moment or every co-commentator but it was a perfect match for that one.

I may be in a minority but I'm not altogether comfortable with the current trend towards the co-commentator/fan. I don't expect Gary Neville or Jamie Carragher to totally hide their root allegiance to the clubs they served, but 'Mo Salah, you little dancer' adds nothing to the broadcast other than winding up the 'Anyone But Liverpool' viewers watching. Maybe that's the idea.

We are all in the entertainment business. Some of the most popular pundits are more entertaining than they are insightful. Gary and Jamie are capable of being both. They are headline acts. Hit-makers. The virtual back pages are full of the opinions of the suited and booted studio panels. Their votes count.

The likes of Neville, Carragher, Jenas, Dixon and Shearer take opinion beyond the decisions of the VAR and dig for the root causes of results. They are devout football watchers and inquisitive football thinkers. They prepare their cases like learned lawyers presenting exhibits that say more than words. They care. And they let it show.

I think it's important that the co-commentator brings his or her personality to the party because that helps build the sense of a relationship with the lead commentator that we can all tune into. Some chemistry, some rapport. But I'm not sold on the trend towards informal sports bar chumminess.

Conversational commentary can quickly become self-indulgent and rambling. It's not a buddy movie, not the Chuckle Brothers show. Too many voices and nicknames, too much familiarity and joshing can leave the viewer out of the joke. Once the banter begins to wander and waffle, you're heading towards Statler and Waldorf's balcony. I think the two roles are different and need some definition.

John Motson told me a lovely story about the early days of co-commentary when Jimmy Hill was first foisted upon a reluctant David Coleman. It wasn't a marriage made in heaven. Coleman agreed to the partnership on the proviso that there was only one microphone, and he had control of it. The tug-of-war would have made better viewing than the match.

Since Glenn is a good boy, I did let him have his own toy to play with but we tried not to talk over each other at any time. The avoidance of collisions was achieved by furtive winks and nudges when he had a particular point to develop. I tended to stand, he preferred to perch, so my ribs were at a perfect height for his elbow. It was a life of hard knocks working with Glenn.

It's good that there is such a range of accents and deci-bel levels among the different co-commentators too. Glenn's diction and grammar are a bit Eliza Doolittle but he is only speaking to us about football the way he spoke to Beckham, Owen, Shearer and Southgate when he was their England manager. The audience can forgive the odd syntactic lapse as long as the message is delivered with validity. When I cued Glenn, I was calling an expert witness.

The detail of the job is only that. It's trade talk. The bigger picture of the relationship is what makes it work or otherwise.

My function is to set a rhythm and tone that is in tune with the game, to build a sense of drama and occasion where appro-priate, to illustrate and amplify with relevant information, to editorialise and to make you feel a part of the broadcast, maybe even make you smile occasionally.

The co-commentator's role is to add qualified opinion and insight that raises your appreciation and understanding of what you are watching, to draw on the experience that he or she has and you can only wish you had. Their authority comes from that experience, their challenge is to translate it into something you can grasp and relate to.

If that all sounds more like a Home Office briefing than a formula for an on-air partnership, that is because we are actu-ally at work when we commentate.

There is a TV documentary about Peter Sellers in which Steve Coogan discusses the techniques that Sellers deployed to make him uniquely funny. Coogan looks like he's revisiting a murder case. There is a grave intensity about his analysis that seems at odds with the craft of comedy. But a craft is what it is. Comics take it very seriously.

I regularly get invited to speak to undergraduates on university media courses. Half an hour after I've arrived, they probably wish they hadn't asked me.

Communication is my business so I am invariably business-like when I discuss it. I don't have much time for students who ask me what is the best goal I've ever seen. I want them to be interested in the challenges of journalism and the obligations of broadcasting. They think they are getting a break from their lecturers when I turn up, but instead they just get the relief teacher.

I'm not particularly precious about myself or my reputation but I can get very cranky when I hear professional communicators passing up their opportunities and responsibilities to connect with their audience.

As children, we all yearned to be told a story. None of us ever grow out of that. To find a job that furnishes you with tales to tell to a captive audience is a privilege. The least we can do is choose our words with some care and consideration.

I'm a hypocrite. Who isn't? I don't always practise what I preach. I set myself up to be a defender of the language but it is not easy to get through ninety minutes of live commentary without mortally wounding it. When I listen back, I try to make mental notes about words I misuse and abuse but the last thing you learn is the first thing you forget under pressure.

Some lessons are indelibly learnt. Since Heysel and Hillsborough, I have never described a misplaced back-pass or a goalkeeping howler as a 'tragedy' or a 'disaster'. They are not, they are calamities and mishaps. The choice of words in the Oxford Dictionary is bountiful. Sports commentators are actually working with the same vocabulary available to Van

Morrison and Stephen King. Plenty of lucid scope to be dream catchers if we concentrate.

Stereotypes are landmines dotted across a football field for every commentator to try to plot a considered course around. That habitual categorisation of players within the game can lead those hired to narrate the action into dangerous ground. Stereotyping by gender or race is particularly noxious.

All I would add is that stereotypes usually have a source. They are not always created by an evil Stasi committee with the express intention of brainwashing the proletariat. The default of pigeon-holing is a tendency that silently creeps into conventional thinking. Halting its spread is a responsibility that professional communicators must take a lead on.

It is odd how many hackneyed phrases manage to survive in the journalese of our business. 'Often dubbed the Maltese Messi' etc., etc. Dubbed by who? 'Some people'?

We have got to be better with words than that. Lazy language quickly becomes hurtful language.

For some reason, the words that cause most discussion with the viewers and listeners are not the adjectives or the adverbs or even the compound prepositions. They are the players' names. There is a fascination with pronunciations that I've never quite understood. Many people mispronounce the word itself. Even more get my name wrong.

Glenn is a delightfully laid-back companion. He only really worries about two things. His health. And player pronunciations. For every game involving a foreign team, I prepared a phonetic guide that I emailed to him the day before the match. Half an hour before kick-off, he was still trying to write out his own version.

'Till-slee' . . . 'Tills-dly' . . . 'Tillser-lee'. 'Can I just call you Clive?'

In fairness, Glenn just about mastered that one, but anything remotely Polish or Serbian kept him awake at night. The most important thing to me is that we both adopted the same pronunciations, right or wrong.

It's the right and wrong that causes all the debate. Unnecessarily.

Ruud Gullit was part of the ITV studio team for Euro 2000 in Holland and Belgium. In rehearsal for the opening show, he corrected Des Lynam's accepted pronunciation of his surname, 'Hullit'. Ruud argued that we might as well call him 'Gullit' rather than 'Hullit' since neither of them was correct. The actual rendition of his name involved a guttural sound that simply doesn't exist in the English language. You can't make it without getting a mouthful of phlegm. Des didn't do phlegm.

He dryly pointed out that since Ruud had scored a goal in a European Championship final as 'Rood Hullit', it was maybe a bit too late to change twelve years on.

There is a story that Barry Davies was commentating for the BBC when Bjorn Borg began his third or fourth defence of the Wimbledon singles title. He started the knock-up by referring to the champion as 'Byorn Boryo'. A conversation with a Swedish broadcaster had revealed to Barry that the English-speaking world had been getting Borg's name repeatedly wrong for ages.

This time, it was his programme editor that whispered into Barry's headphones that he should 'stick with the mistake'.

We are in the identification business. If someone or something is known by a certain name, the best way to identify them is to call them by that name. Occasionally, a footballer may have cause to request a change of name in mid-career, but Andy Cole had scored more than 200 goals before asking to be called Andrew. Sorry, too late. My job is to pick him out by the name that our TV audience is most familiar with. I've got to serve them, not him.

If that sounds dismissively flippant, I promise I do try very hard to establish the correct version of a player's name when they first come onto our radar. It's the kind of sad conversation commentators make. I do prefer to sing from the same song-sheet as my colleagues but I draw a line at attempting those exotic accented intonations, modulations, reverberations and superciliations that are just not part of our twang. I'm English, I anglicise.

The conundrum surrounding pronunciations was best summed by the case of James Rodriguez at the 2014 World Cup. The young Colombian touched down in Brazil as plain 'James Rodriguez'. I recalled covering a couple of his games for Porto in the Champions League the season before and telling the tale of how he had been christened in honour of his father's love of James Bond movies.

Before his opening game of that World Cup, a BBC preview feature had referred to him as 'Hamez'. The player had chosen to display his given name on his shirt and was apparently asking to be known as such. Jetting around Brazil on a daily basis, I wasn't aware of this when I landed in Belo Horizonte for Colombia's first fixture. I called him 'James Rodriguez' and he duly scored their third goal.

Judging by the reaction on Twitter, you'd think I'd called him James Bond. My initial reaction was amusement, then bemusement and then bewilderment when I received a call from a newspaper reporter back home asking me if I was going to apologise for disrespecting the Spanish language.

I certainly wasn't about to apologise through the pages of his tawdry publication but I was both shaken and stirred by the suggestion. I needed counsel.

By chance, I bumped into the former Spanish international full-back, Albert Ferrer, at an airport the next morning. He immediately began to laugh when I told him of the pickle I was in.

'You know that he was named after James Bond?' he asked me. I nodded.

'Do you think we call the movies 'Hamez' Bond films in Spain?' Albert went on before answering his own question. 'No. James is not even a Spanish name. We watch James Bond films just like the rest of the world. If he's named after Bond, he is James Rodriguez.'

Criticism by Twitter followers is in the line of duty. I get angry with the performance levels of politicians, presenters, entertainers and news reporters too. They are usually people I don't know and will probably never meet. My wife knows who they are. There are a million marvellous things about her but listening patiently to my moans about total strangers from the sofa is right up there.

I must confess to a pathological hatred of news reports on serious subjects that end with a crass quip. Those stylised 'walking shots' in which the reporter delivers a meaningful message into the camera lens about the possibility of a policy U-turn before glancing knowingly in the direction of a bus navigating a roundabout.

Tar and feather the culprits please. The public stocks are not good enough for them.

Incredibly, Mrs T usually agrees with me. She's probably just smart enough to know it's easier for her that way. There's nothing like a good rant in the privacy of your own home. Better out, than in.

What I don't get is the habitual need to share your hand-wringing with the outside world. We are all agreed that Twitter has grown into a monster, but it only grows because we feed it. And if you happen to be one of the minor celebrities on which the 270-character assassins feast, I cannot for the life of me understand why you would pull up your own chair to the dining table.

For two years and more, Danny Baker subjected Glenn to a vile level of social media abuse. It would have been putrid and spiteful if it had come from somebody with a genuine personal grudge, but it was actually just a series of disparaging opinions on his co-commentary.

As a fellow broadcaster Danny, like me, is a matter of opinion himself. Why would anyone in that position launch a cackling tirade of personal insults at a very decent man they don't know?

If Glenn was really getting so deeply under his skin, I imagine Danny's contacts are sufficiently good to have enabled him to hook up and put his grievances to him personally. Instead, he just yelled mocking bile in Glenn's general direction from the distance of his keyboard.

I get so annoyed with intelligent professional communicators that abuse the rare privilege of our cherished jobs. Parroting the same tone of scorn and derision with which football fans ritually mock opponents from the stands is not connecting with our public, our audience. It's just humouring the extremes of behaviour that football brings out in many of us.

If I watch a match as a committed fan, my opinions during the game rarely tally with those that I hold when I've managed to calm down and rationalise an hour after the final whistle. Football is like one of those games that spins you round until you're dizzy. It takes a while to regain your balance. Glenn and I were broadcasting to millions of unbalanced people. And that's cool.

The co-commentator is not there to be universally loved or even to be agreed with. Differences in opinion about football are as healthy as they are inevitable. Glenn and I had them. But you can't just loftily dismiss the opinion of a man with unique experience.

What gives weight to the opinion of the co-commentators and studio pundits are the miles on their clocks. They are the pilot who has flown the plane, they are the mountain guide who's been to the peak, they are the surgeon who has made the incision. Their experience doesn't afford them automatic knowledge or the clarity to impart it, but it does give them a head start on those of us with little or none. Their 'how' and 'why' is simply more informed.

I was in Windsor Great Park on the day that my partnership with Glenn was almost broken by his heart attack in 2018. I was looking out for my daughter, Hannah, who was competing in a triathlon. Mark Pougatch messaged me and I immediately returned to the car to listen to solemn radio bulletins that made it clear that Glenn's life was in danger.

He's a serious, spiritual man and I often wondered after the coffees we shared during his recovery if Glenn would come out a little different on the other side. More subdued, more sober maybe. I needn't have worried. I've already been able to tell him that if he ever gets tired of my company again, he doesn't have to be such a drama queen about it next time.

On his return to broadcasting, he saw his beloved Tottenham Hotspur reach a Champions League final in the most ridiculous manner in Amsterdam. He said that night that he just felt lucky to be there. No, the people for whom the occasion was heightened by his judgement and acumen were the lucky ones.

In football, there is no substitute for Been There, Seen It, Done it.

Learning from the master magicians. Glenn and I at Wembley.

Sir Bobby Robson Refugio Aboim Ascensao charity supporter (2004–21)

Soccer Aid for UNICEF supporter (2006–20)

Patron of Bobby Moore Bowel Cancer Fund (2012–21)

When somebody tells you that you can save people's lives, you've got to listen.

Stephanie Moore told me I could save lives in the reception of the Wentworth Club in 2005. The widow of Bobby Moore had been hosting a golf day in aid of bowel cancer research. I had been called up at late notice to act as master of ceremonies at the charity dinner.

There are very few sports that you can play in the same arena as the best in the world. A birdie on the West Course at Wentworth is like straight-driving a boundary down the Test wicket at Lord's or curling a free-kick into the top corner of a Wembley net. You are walking in the footsteps of McIlroy and Rose. Only with a few more unscheduled detours than them.

I played Wentworth that day as the 'celebrity partner' of three highly-qualified clinical surgeons. To a man, they kept on saying things like, 'I don't know how you manage to find the nerve to commentate live to millions of viewers.' Pardon?!

Three guys that routinely find the nerve to cut open human bodies and save lives were marvelling at my ability to remember the identities of Slovakian footballers.

I shout out names, they take out cancerous tumours. Each to his own.

My wife, Susan, has climbed the Eiger and my daughter, Hannah, has run the Grand Canyon rim to rim. The furthest I've ever ventured from my comfort zone was a bungee jump in Stockholm in 1992. I hated it and hated myself for being talked into it. It wasn't even for charity.

Every year, I meet up with proper 'A' list celebrities that all leave stage and screen behind for a few days to raise millions at Soccer Aid. I've hung out with Robbie Williams, Will Ferrell, Usain Bolt and Woody Harrelson. I just commentate as usual but the UNICEF officials are always keen to point out spikes in the evening's fund-raising after particularly poignant things I've said.

And that was Stephanie's message to me at Wentworth. By standing up in front of a room full of golfers and alerting them to the tell-tale symptoms of bowel cancer and the benefits of early diagnosis, I could maybe have pointed one of them in the direction of a test that would save his or her life.

I became a patron of Stephanie's charity in 2012 simply because I don't mind asking strangers to check their poo. Brilliant surgeons and many other infinitely more talented people than me may be spooked by the idea but I'm not. I can talk crap in public with the best of them.

Bobby Moore died of bowel cancer at the age of 51 because he was not correctly diagnosed early enough. That day at Wentworth, Stephanie told in her speech of how one of her late husband's unrealised ambitions was to play the West Course. Nobody ever opened their mouth to invite him there.

Words are uncut gems just waiting to be set and placed somewhere that they will make a difference.

13

FERGIE

I only went under the hair dryer twice. One time by phone, the other to my face.

When Sir Alex Ferguson is angry with you, it feels like he is waiting behind every door. You don't sleep. The sound of his ire follows you to bed, to work, to the loo and probably to your grave unless you can square things with him before the grim reaper starts his backswing.

I have stood toe-to-toe with Fergie in any number of post-match interview positions. It was never a fair fight. Like an undercard welterweight who had mistakenly climbed through the ropes to find Mike Tyson waiting in the other corner, I had no chance.

If you dared to pose a pointed question, his head turned ever so slowly to the side, his eyes widened and a bubble appeared above him containing the words, 'Are you seriously asking me that, son?'

My tactic at that point was to interminably lengthen the question in order to include a few thousand stuttering, stumbling back-tracking qualifications until I had left an opening for him to cut me short with a one-word response. Usually 'no'.

I was commentating for ITV's highlights show *The Premiership* when United were beaten 4–1 in a Manchester derby at Maine Road in 2004. As I arrived in the interview area, Clare Tomlinson of Sky told me that she was waiting to speak to the jubilant City manager Kevin Keegan live and that I 'could have Fergie if he comes out first'. So this was how a crash-test dummy felt.

Sure enough, the United boss appeared for cross-examination and was ushered towards me complete with the nervous cough that always seemed to accompany his darker moods. It is in such moments that you silently pray that the innocent TV sound recordist doesn't ask him for a level.

'One fuckin' two,' is the best you're going to get.

Sir Alex knew exactly what he wanted to say. He may be as 'old school' as Albus Dumbledore but he was media savvy throughout his extraordinary career and he understood the impact of a carefully worded thirty-second soundbite. I could have started by asking him 'what's the capital of Ecuador?' and the answer would have been the same.

His snarling message was that he wished he could bring some United fans into the dressing-room to let the players know what a derby defeat felt like to them. He wasn't speaking to me or to the viewers or to anyone other than Ronaldo, Van Nistelrooy and company a few yards away.

Fergie used every jagged tool at his disposal to manage like he did. I went through the motions of posing a few follow-up questions but the show was over. He had already given us our post-match clip. It was a public put-down designed to catch a morning headline and spoil a few millionaires' suppers if they were careless enough to tune into the evening highlights.

He had a habit of saying 'well done' to his interrogator after any interview that had ended without flashpoint. It felt like a pat on the head. A veiled compliment if ever there was one.

When Gareth Southgate first took over at Middlesbrough, Fergie was quickly on his case because of his lack of relevant coaching qualifications at the time. Gareth was actually glad of the needle. Fergie had large pockets. He loved filling them with his rivals.

Sir Alex always liked the power of television. He has had close friendships with several esteemed football writers but press conference quotes can be edited and repositioned between the notepad and the back page. The nuance and weight of the dispatch could often get a little lost in black and white. When you actually heard the venom in his voice and saw the fix of his glare, Fergie left no room at all for any interpretation.

Those brief comments he shared with Gary Newbon in the moments before the second half of a live Champions League match were no part of any contract with ITV. He gave his time willingly. They were a platform to speak directly to millions of fans about the state of the game. All part of the service. Nothing more, nothing less.

I inherited a trusting relationship with Sir Alex from my predecessor, Brian Moore. I became a welcome guest at the manager's off-the-record ITV briefing before big games. Along with Gary, our football editor Jeff Farmer and maybe Bob Wilson, Des Lynam or whoever was presenting the live broadcast, we were summoned to the empty Grill Room at Old Trafford around 4 o'clock to be given chapter and verse on United's approach to the challenge ahead.

Sometimes, his team news had half-a-dozen sticks of dyna-mite attached to it. Roy Keane may have tweaked a calf muscle in training, Ryan Giggs was going to start in centre midfield, David Beckham wasn't going to start at all.

'Injured, Sir Alex?'

'No.'

No further questions, your honour.

Why? Why entrust a handful of media men with such classified information, with the secret formula for the most important games of an incomparable career? Nothing about those hushed gatherings carried a trace of vanity or show. He was not trying to impress or woo anyone, he was merely looking to inform us of his intentions so that we could explain them to the watching millions with as much insight and intel as was available.

Often, we would all file back down the stairs with a shifty guilt hanging over us. It felt like a secret affair does. The level of confidence placed in our unspoken vow of silence weighed heavily. A wide-eyed fan might call across the concourse to us, 'Two-nil tonight. Becks and Keano to score?' If only you knew. If only David knew, for that matter!

Sir Alex has been really good to me. I was lucky with con-nections. He had a long-standing friendship with my first boss, Paul Doherty, and I worked at Granada Television with one of his sons, Jason. I'd also like to think that Fergie could see that I was as serious about my job as he was about his own.

The pristine match charts that I compiled for his two Champions League final wins hung in his office for many years. He made generous donations to charity and framed them for posterity. Often, when I was researching the data for the charts, I would text him a quiz question that he'd knock around his coaching staff before coming back to me with an answer.

I remember sitting in the press room putting the finishing touches to my notes at about 6 o'clock one match night when I received a text from him advising me of a late change to his line-up. He didn't have to do that.

When he hosted an exclusive dinner to celebrate twenty-five years at United in 2011, my wife and I were among the invitees. Mumford and Sons and The Script were the house bands. It was a bit of a do.

Our relationship was essentially a professional one, though. However easy Sir Alex's company became on long nights when I was privy to fond reminiscences about his playing days and early experiences of management, I never felt altogether at ease with him. It was the safest way. All of the kindness would have evaporated into thin air if I'd even once broken the trust he placed in me.

His rebuke of choice was 'deary me'. You couldn't afford to collect too many of those.

It was his capacity to turn in an instant that maintained the healthy respect which gave him the upper hand in any exchange. An association like ours may have benefited me greatly but it was conducted on his terms. Control is everything for a football manager and Fergie had control of everything on his watch.

The legal battle with John Magnier over Rock of Gibraltar back in 2003 must have been particularly difficult for him purely because he couldn't exercise that same control over events. It was a battle fought on a foreign field. The friend that became the enemy outranked him there. This time, Fergie was in a ring with a bigger puncher.

Single-mindedness and stubbornness are a short neck apart. The best football managers all wear blinkers. They can only ever write eleven names on a team-sheet. No 50/50s, no ask the audience. Final answer. They've got to know their mind.

They need bone heads with just the one eye in the middle. The manager is judge and jury.

In my brief experience of the courts, once the lawyers get involved they rarely bring you good news. Just invoices.

Sir Alex's name appeared alongside Sue Magnier's as joint owner of Rock of Gibraltar on the horse's Irish registration documents, so it is easy to see why he believed he had more than a nominal stake in its future. But once it became apparent that those papers had no legal standing, he was backing his barrister against theirs. And in the transfer market for learned counsel, Magnier and J P McManus could afford to spend every bit as big as Fergie. This was a more level playing field than he or United were really used to.

The game turned nasty. The Irish partnership began buying up United shares and then asking public questions of the club's financial propriety. The manager's control over the running of his own turf was being challenged. His job might even come under threat if Magnier and company seized control of the club's stock.

United fans rallied around their manager and railed against his assailants. A protest was organised at a race meeting in Hereford where one of McManus's horses was running. Planned disruption of the 2004 Cheltenham Festival brought everything to a head and a peace deal was brokered. It didn't give either party what they wanted but Fergie gave up his claims on the horse and the Irish investors sold their shares in United.

However strong their character, managers need to know when a game can no longer be won and how to settle for the draw.

It was as close to a truly damaging defeat as Sir Alex came as United manager. He may have lost a couple of Champions League finals but he never lost a power struggle. He wrestled with his first chairman, Martin Edwards, in order to establish his true value to the club. The regime he created spawned tough, uncompromising players in his own image.

Recent fly-on-the-wall television documentaries have revealed how perpetually demanding serial winners like Pep Guardiola and Michael Jordan can be. Fergie didn't suffer fools. He generated a sharp street wisdom in his players by squeezing and stretching them into his mould. It was like having Bear Grylls for a manager.

The stash of '92 was exceptional for the presence of three nuggets as lustrous as Giggs, Scholes and Beckham, but many of the jewels of Sir Alex's youth policy were self-polished gems. Butt, Fletcher, Evans and the Neville brothers. All granite-based, all intent on grinding every last ounce of potential from themselves in order to reward the manager's religious faith in them.

Chief executive David Gill became an important, measured foil for the manager's bullish approach to any kind of combat but Fergie set the tone, set the level for everything the club achieved during his time as commander-in-chief.

It was a command he felt born to. It was a position he defended ruthlessly. The trust he placed in his brother Martin and one or two close confidantes was fixed. The trust he placed in passing allies like myself was always expendable. Just a hint of doubt or challenge could be enough to terminate the arrangement.

Stam, Ince, Leighton, Kidd, Sharpe, Mrs Beckham, the BBC. No right of appeal. Gone, gone, gone.

I was the BBC's man in the Manchester United hotel near Windsor for the 1996 FA Cup final. Skipper Steve Bruce was a friend and the man in charge of the players' pool and therefore all of my requests for access and interviews. He didn't seem to be in the best of moods when we met up on the eve of the final, but then he knew he had already played his last game for United.

Not only did Fergie opt for David May ahead of him in defence, he didn't even find a place for Steve on his three-man bench. The manager told him that he thought Lee Sharpe would make a better substitute goalkeeper if anything happened to Peter Schmeichel. What he was really telling Steve was that, at 35, he'd served his nine-year usefulness. He was a Birmingham player within a fortnight. Gone.

Bryan Robson's exceptional United career was terminated similarly. Roy Keane was shown the door, too. John Motson got an earful just for asking about Keane. Unreasonable, maybe. Unequivocal, definitely. Control was Sir Alex's ultimate weapon. If he felt an occasional pre-emptive strike was required in order to maintain it, he was not slow to pull the trigger. The infected limb was severed rather than treated.

Megalomaniacal? Not a bit of it. Quite the opposite. Fergie's merciless culls were always carried out with an eye to protecting Manchester United. They were not stopovers on a personal ego trip, he was merely taking care of business. Club business.

A club like United splits loyalties due west and east. There are no inhabitants of the middle ground. Nobody 'quite likes' United or Liverpool or Bayern. The voting slip for the game's superclubs has only two boxes. For or against.

The first responsibility of the standard-bearer of such an organisation is to recognise and respect that. The second is to defend their organisation against the rest of the world even via the indefensible at times. That is all that Sir Alex ever did during his twenty-seven years in charge at Old Trafford. Fiercely, coldly, even mistakenly at times but always corporately.

Selling Jaap Stam was an error that he actually admitted to. Nine years later!

Not every day was a tirade of rants and pointed fingers. Fergie's reign was rule by godfatherly ways. He was very, very Vito Corleone.

A budding young manager, sacked by his Fourth Division chairman after a few months of thankless graft, often found the first consoling call they received was from a Manchester number. Fergie saw himself as the shop steward for his profession. And you never knew when favours granted could be called in further down the road.

'Do me this favour. I won't forget it. Ask your friends in the neighbourhood about me. They'll tell you I know how to return a favour.' *The Godfather II* (1974).

There is only ever so much you can control in football. Games that define careers and eras are often decided by the bounce of the ball, the view of the referee, the whims of destiny. All that a manager can do is try to control as much of their job description as they can. Pick their staff, pick their team, pick their fights.

The modern manager is just a charm on a chain of command. He or she is always answerable, rarely the ultimate decision-taker. Their control is compromised by chief executives, technical directors and heads of recruitment. Sir Alex was all of the above and more. He gave up control as readily as a dog with a bone. A rottweiler.

You might think the favours he did me with advanced team news were part of a veiled treaty. You may suspect he thought that if he fed me information that I would reciprocate with praise for him and his team. All I can tell you is that never once did he take issue with any view I expressed during the course of a commentary. Fergie didn't need to make deals with me. I was no threat to his control.

That didn't spare me the hair dryer, though. Oh no.

I'd like to believe that the two biggest rollockings of my life were part of some ritual initiation ceremony. A rite of passage, a test of character. But the truth is I think Sir Alex simply lost it with me a couple of times. Once at Halifax, the other in Barcelona. No discernible pattern there.

My saving grace was that I was innocent of the charges that were lividly levelled at me. Not enough to merit an apology in either instance – still waiting for those! – but sufficient for some element of reason to take root once the red mist cleared. With Fergie, that took days rather than weeks. Or it did unless you were found guilty at the highest court in his land. Then, the black cap was donned and you were cast into damnation. No return tickets from there.

Halifax Town were placed ninety-second of ninety-two clubs on the league ladder when Manchester United travelled to The Shay for the first leg of a Rumbelows Cup second round tie in September 1990. The home team had not scored in nine hours of Fourth Division football. So, when a slightly deflected free-kick looped almost comedically over Jim Leighton for a Halifax equaliser, United were facing one of those embarrassing nights that no amount of second leg insurance could divert from the back pages.

An underwhelming performance improved sufficiently to yield two late goals and a 3–1 win but not enough for Fergie to agree to a post-match interview when approached by Granada's floor manager, Nick Beaumont. I completed the climb down from the lofty commentary position to be greeted by the news that I would only be interviewing Halifax manager Jim McCalliog and United scorer Neil Webb. Phew!

Imagine my surprise when Fergie belatedly emerged from the players' tunnel into the empty stadium and made a businesslike bee-line for our pitchside interview position, complete with nervously irritated throat-clearing.

What I didn't know was that my boss had somehow managed to contact Sir Alex via the club office and persuaded him to answer a couple of questions on United's next match against Nottingham Forest that was due to be broadcast live across the ITV network the following weekend. Mobile phones were not standard issue in 1990.

You know what's coming . . .

I innocently began the interview with a question about the uninspiring cup tie that we had just witnessed. Fergie's first answer was so mumbled and vague that I felt the need to go in with a stronger follow-up. The manager's second answer wasn't so vague. He peered up at me as if I had just questioned his parentage, jabbed an index finger into my chest and spat the words 'you fuckin' chancer' into my face before turning tail and disappearing from whence he came.

At the same time as Sir Alex was storming back down the tunnel, Nick was emerging from the club office with full details of the strict terms on which Sir Alex had agreed to be interviewed. Ah, 'no questions about tonight's game'. That explains it!

The silly thing is that I drove home confident that if I phoned the manager first thing the next morning I could account for the misunderstanding and he would see the funny side of our little contretemps. Wrong again.

My well-meaning call to the private number on his desk at The Cliff was met by a storm of loud invective that pinned me to the wall of my quiet suburban bedroom and woke the neighbours. I was banned from anywhere in Fergie's gaze for the foreseeable future. Persona non grata.

My sentence was later reduced on appeal by character references from my boss and my friend, the United physio, and I was allowed to remain somewhere on the planet.

There is an old Monty Python sketch about a violent gangster called Dinsdale Piranha who nailed people's heads to the floor by way of punishment. One of his victims conceded, 'He had to do that. I had transgressed the unwritten law.' That was my crime too.

Managing football clubs is a job of unwritten laws. Issues of right and wrong are fudged by the constant, overriding need to produce results. Managers of major clubs like Manchester United cannot afford to waste time dealing with potential distractions in a fair and equitable manner. If a famous captain axed from the starting eleven was not entitled to a full, reasoned explanation for his blackballing, then I certainly wasn't.

Perhaps Sir Alex's greatest single quality as a manager was his ability to move with the times. The world was a very different place when he finally gave up the job in 2013 than it had been when he arrived at Old Trafford late in 1986. Britain got through five prime ministers in that time. Across Manchester, fourteen City managers came and went.

Fergie managed Ryan Giggs differently to how he managed Cristiano Ronaldo. He had to. The thick protective blanket he wrapped around a shy, skinny Welsh teenager in 1991 would not have fitted the bolder, brassier version that arrived from Portugal in 2003. The spotlight had grown brighter, the wage packets had grown thicker, the temptations had grown scarier.

Sir Alex secured Ryan's signature by knocking on the door of his family home in Swinton on his 14th birthday and persuading his mum that United would look after him better than City. When he signed Ronaldo, it was Jorge Mendes that he had to persuade. Managing young players had become as much about managing their agents' expectations as their own.

Fergie could simply ban his first fledglings from any media activity until he felt they were ready. When he gave me permission to interview Ryan on the pitch at Wembley before the 1992 League Cup final, I thought I'd landed an exclusive. Only when I saw the player's eyes widen during my first question did

I realise that Fergie was standing directly behind me listening in. Today's teenagers manage their own media.

Sir Alex may have gradually loosened his iron grip but he was never far away. He could still get his hand back on your throat in a trice, he could still pick fights that others wouldn't dare to. The way that he refused to speak to the BBC for seven years was in direct defiance of Premier League rules on co-operation with media rights holders but I'm not aware that he was ever fined over the omerta.

His insistent boycott became so deep-rooted that it was difficult to recall what triggered it. A little-watched BBC Three documentary that portrayed his son Jason in cartoon form while repeating previous allegations about the player agency he ran. Allegations that United investigated and answered before 'Fergie and Son' even aired.

From the outside it looked like a bloody big sledgehammer to crack a tiny nut, but any attacks on his family resounded deep inside Sir Alex. Maybe parenthood was the qualification that enabled him to move with the times and adapt his management style. All three of his sons were of a similar age to the players he was schooling at Old Trafford. Darren actually played thirty times for his dad at United.

It is as the head of the family, the figurehead of Manchester United, the unofficial father of the chapel of the managers' union that he has always been at his strongest, his most strident. He loves to lead, to take control. When he finds a cause, he fights tooth and nail in defence of it.

Football is a hard school. If you are not prepared to accept the rough justice of the dressing-room court, you will be shown the door. Time has put better support mechanisms in place but not before there were victims. Roy Keane likened footballers' careers to cattle in a meat market. Bought and sold to the highest bidder then finally loaded onto the truck. Roy is hard to argue with.

Sir Alex enjoyed the rare luxury of loading his own truck. He had it revved up and was ready to go in 2001 but ended up serving twelve more years before succumbing to the word he hated. Retirement. Still had more hair to blow, I guess.

My next time to get some of Fergie's lift, volume and bounce was in November 1998 in the foyer of the Grand Marina Hotel in Barcelona. It's a long story.

Manchester United were in town for a Champions League group game and I travelled to Port Olimpic from the ITV hotel near Nou Camp in a taxi with Bob Wilson for our lunchtime briefing from the manager. I was soon on the way back.

Three days earlier, a preview of the game had appeared in the *Sunday Times*, written by the press doyen that was Hugh McIlvanney. Hidden amid the bard's flowing prose was a very strong hint that Wes Brown would be preferred to Phil Neville at right-back in order to combat the height and physique of Rivaldo on the Barcelona left flank. Hugh's long friendship with Sir Alex meant there could be only one source for such speculation. This was gen. Brown's name was already on my team chart.

The evening before the game, I happened to step into the lift at our hotel at the same time as Neville Neville, the father of the famous footballing brothers. In a conversation lasting no more than a dozen floors, he confided that Phil was worried for his place in the team and I tried to console him by saying there could only be a change if the manager was worried about Rivaldo's height. No reflection on Phil's ability. Night, night Nev.

Nev did not go straight to sleep that night.

By the time I marched into the team hotel the following lunchtime, dad had told his boys that Clive Tyldesley thought Phil would be dropped. Er, not quite what I said. Phil had told Gary and Gary had confronted the manager at breakfast about ITV knowing the line-up before the players did. I walked straight into a bloody ambush.

'Who told you the team?' Sir Alex asked me menacingly before any pleasantries were exchanged.

'I don't know the team,' I replied in all honesty.

I can't recall the precise detail of the next line of the conversation. Or the next. Or the next. I only remember their seismic reading on the Richter Scale and that my own part in the conversation was well and truly over. R2 had been pressed.

In a crowded hotel reception area, my character and fidelity were being noisily ripped apart by one of the most recognisable and widely respected men in all of Europe. Fergie didn't lay a hand on me but the ferocity of the verbal assault was such that I limped out of the hotel battered and bruised a few seconds later. My ears were ringing for days.

I don't know who coined the phrase 'hair dryer' to describe one of the manager's infamous rebukes but the blast of scalding, scolding hurricane air that came my way certainly made a few locks stand up on end. Not so much a talking-to as a talking-at.

Gary Newbon and Jeff Farmer were just climbing out of their taxi as I made my dazed retreat. It is a measure of the strictly professional use of his trademark hair dryer that the manager proceeded to welcome and brief the others as if nothing had happened. Brown at right-back, Phil on the bench.

Fergie's use of his Dyson Supersonic became more sparing as his career wore on. That instinct for adapting to the changing times kept his management techniques contemporary but the big old cannon was always loaded and ready to fire if ever the heavy artillery was needed to wrest back control of the battle.

Sir Alex Ferguson only lost control of his temper when his ultimate control was threatened.

Rubbing shoulders with the greats. Best job in the world.

Writer and Columnist

1999–2008

Writing for the *Daily Telegraph* was almost as much of a starry-eyed ambition realised as working for the BBC.

Much as I disagree with the publication's politics, its sports section was always my paper of record. To see my byline rub off on the readers' fingers alongside those of Paul Hayward, Sue Mott and Sir Michael Parkinson was a weekly source of pride.

Thirty years earlier, I had filed school rugby reports for the *Telegraph*. Now, I was dictating my own opinion column and match reports to their quick-fingered copy-takers.

'Peschisolido. That's P-papa, e-echo, s-sierra . . .' etc, etc.

In 2008, there were changes at the top and I was told that I would no longer be covering games for the paper. The sports editor said he wanted 'more young scufflers out in the field looking for stories'. Not sure what Donald Saunders would have made of that policy.

My weekly column was retained and in the build-up to the Champions League final between Chelsea and Manchester United, I was asked to make a case for Avram Grant getting the sack irrespective of the result. Sebastian Coe had agreed to write a counter argument.

I told the editor that, while it was my opinion that Grant would indeed be moved on or maybe 'upstairs', I couldn't write a piece actively calling for his dismissal.

He had stepped dutifully into the breach left by José Mourinho's departure in September. He deserved better.

By 2008, I was filing my copy via 'Send/Receive' rather than 'P-papa' and that Friday afternoon I duly despatched my 800 words into the ether and waited for a call from a sub-editor looking to question a few strands of my argument. Unusually, I didn't get one.

Instead, the whole column was changed. Just about the only part of the published article that I recognised was my name at the top of it. Complete sentences had been added in that name to give the impression that I believed Avram Grant was responsible for Chelsea's narrow failure to catch United in the title race. I'd written nothing of the sort.

The blazing telephone row that followed on the Monday morning marked the bottom of the page for my newspaper career. The end.

Well, not quite. *The Times* courted me to pen a column for their venerable pages at the start of the following season and actually published my first offering. I'm still waiting for payment and the return of any of the numerous calls I made to their football editor when he suddenly went quiet on me.

Situation still vacant. Lonely words seek empty pages.

14

GARETH

Gareth Southgate is the best man for the England manager's job.

I have met seventeen of the people that have taken charge of my country's national football team and come to know eleven of them reasonably well. Of all the incumbents, I believe Gareth is the best man for that job.

I can't tell you that he is the best coach or the best tactician or the best motivator. I am talking about the man. The bright, astute, tactful, thorough, contemporary man.

Of those seventeen managers and interim coaches, only one was invited to my wedding. Gareth. So maybe I am biased.

The bad news for my good friend in the hottest seat of all is that it never ends well for the England manager. Never. The job comes complete with a suicide pill. It is so hazardous an occupation that Gareth may even have become part of its horrible history by the time you read this.

All I can be sure of is that he didn't leave the job because he was entrapped by a fake sheikh or had expressed his views on the afterlife or become embroiled in a High Court fraud case or been seduced by a Football Association PA.

If the *Sun* ever revealed that Gareth once stole a Crunchie from the school tuck shop, I'd be shocked and horrified. His sheer decency may just have saved the England manager's job from itself.

The charge sheet attached to the position looks more like a catalogue of crimes and misdemeanours levelled at the manager of a Mafia strip club than a football manager. It inevitably raises questions of the people that appointed his predecessors.

Gareth rather fell into the job. He wasn't really appointed. Perhaps that's why he's such a good fit.

Not for him the covert drive through the Oxfordshire countryside behind the cloak of blacked out Mercedes windows to clandestine talks with FA head-hunters in a secluded stately manor house. His interviews were conducted before 80,000-strong panels at Wembley Stadium. A very public trial. An *X Factor* audition.

Promoted from coach of the Under-21s team in 2016 and given four games to see if he could handle yet another national emergency, he steered the senior team to a World Cup semi-final within two years. Maybe handling emergencies should be the future template for selection. England are certainly experts at creating them.

In my lifetime we've had the patriotic ones and the foreign ones, we've had the special ones and the safe ones. We've tried good cops and bad cops, popular choices and professional choices, veterans and rookies, turnips and Swedes. Now we've gone for the nice guy.

In the cold-hearted, cut-throat world of *The Apprentice* and *Dragon's Den* there is no room for nice guys. Peter Jones wouldn't let Gareth into the lift. But don't be fooled by the shy, toothy grin. This England manager not only knows his mind, he uses it continually. He is as smart as his World Cup waistcoat.

If I were so brazen as to share with you the most shocking things that Gareth has said to me within the privacy of our friendship, they would not be poisonous put-downs of fellow managers or saucy secrets about boys being boys. It would be his bluntly forthright verdicts on players. No minced words, no veiled compliments. He knows exactly what he wants from the men in his charge and whether they can deliver it or not. Realism is his chosen specialist subject.

Just about the first thing he said to me on his hero's return from the World Cup in Russia was, 'We are definitely not the fourth best team in the world.' Within a year, seven or eight of the players that took part in the semi against Croatia in Moscow had been cut from the team or the squad. Nice.

Not forever. Nothing is forever when you are a realist. Gareth is single-minded enough to show any player the door if he thinks there are better alternatives, but he rarely shuts that door behind them.

When only twenty per cent of the players regularly selected by England's most successful club sides are English, you are not quite at the stage where you can be leaving out Jimmy Greaves or Paul Gascoigne, but Gareth is always looking forward rather than back with his team and squad selections. He has named some of the youngest teams in modern England history. He always wants to know what happens next.

A measured man but with a restless, ruthless urge. When you think about it, there are no nice centre-backs, are there?

Between being a centre-back and England manager, Gareth was a television pundit. At the 2006 World Cup, he became my regular co-commentator. Watch Joe Cole's volley against Sweden and listen. He was going to be my running mate four years later but ITV needed him in a studio in South Africa and our partnership was prematurely ended. What might have been.

He can communicate. And that has given him a head start over several of his predecessors.

I confess I became so disheartened by the inability of true English football lovers like Graham Taylor and Kevin Keegan to make the earth move for me that I rather welcomed the appointment of an outsider in 2000. I thought a different accent, a different angle might just demystify the job. In truth, Sven wooed Nancy and Ulrika rather more than he beguiled me. But we'll always have Munich.

His English is an awful lot better than my Swedish but it soon developed a comedic ring to my ears. As Gareth himself said of Eriksson's half-time address during the 2002 World Cup quarter-final against Brazil, 'we needed Churchill but we got Iain Duncan-Smith.'

For me, Sven always brought to mind Peter Sellers' character Chauncey Gardiner in *Being There*. A man whose smiling silences convinced many into believing that he knew more than he was saying. Management always seemed to be happening to him, rather than by him. It all ended in smears.

One glimpse of the altar was enough for Phil Scolari to flee the aisle and, after Steve McClaren was caught in a downpour, the FA opted for a man with even less mastery of the English language than Eriksson or Scolari (or indeed McClaren) in the shape of the particularly unsmiling Fabio Capello. The antidote to a manager who called the players by their nicknames was one who couldn't say their names at all. Or even wanted to. The England job was stumbling from parody to parody.

International football is full of successful coaches foreign to the players they are in charge of. Hired hands with no emotional baggage that are just doing their next job. They don't sing the anthem or kiss the badge. They are not only immune to any charges of favouring one club ahead of another, but they are also deaf to the white noise that swirls around the white shirt from media and public alike.

On the evidence of all we saw from Eriksson and Capello, I was mistaken to believe that model could work for England. We are too emotionally attached to our national side to offer it up for adoption. It is in our blood so we want it to be in the boss's blood too.

After Sir Alf Ramsey and his legacy, Terry Venables and Sir Bobby Robson are probably the two that have got the nation's circulation going best. I have been fortunate to work with both at ITV. They could communicate too.

Terry was the original salt and pepper pot tactician. If you sat down for a hotel breakfast with him, you knew your cereal spoon was going to disappear down the French right flank at some stage in order to engage Lilian Thuram. He always had a new system on the go and, more importantly, he always explained it in a way that I could understand its workings. If he could show me, he might even be able to make Gazza see it too.

Terry was an argumentative sod, though. There are occasions when I am sitting at the feet of the elders that populate our studio when I might make a passing remark in order to try to offer a tiny contribution to the high-level talks. Rather than gently humour my relative ignorance, Terry was forever challenging me to justify my opinion. Great company but never relaxing company.

England are probably still the most popular football team in the country. They routinely fill Wembley Stadium, they attract bumper television viewing figures.

All of the most famous faces of English football have won their places in the hearts of the nation in an England shirt. Quite something when you consider how often that shirt has been swapped in anti-climactic defeat. It has become a symbol of different things – some less noble than others – but it remains a uniform of belonging. A replica birthmark.

From Matthews and Finney. Moore and Charlton. Beckham and Gascoigne. Lineker and Shearer. Pearce and Barnes. To Rooney and Kane. Even the three European club champions in that list are more associated with what they did in national colours than in a club shirt. Look at the directory of footballing knights of the realm – Hurst, Ramsey, Robson, Brooking, Winterbottom et al.

A cavalry of knights, with just one sighting of the holy grail. The mystery of the missing trophies. We very nearly lost the only one we won. Thank goodness for Pickles.

There are more theories about England's recurring underachievement than there are about JFK. No magic bullet has yet been recovered. So long and laboured has been the national debate that some have managed to convince themselves that Gerrard, Shearer, Scholes, Cole, Hoddle and all the other members of the gold, silver and bronze generations weren't quite as good as they were cracked up to be.

I saw them all play. They were plenty good enough.

I blame the Russian linesman. Since Tofiq Bahramov pointed towards the Wembley halfway line and nodded his head in 1966, England have barely got a decision. But then you haven't bought this tome to re-read the register of injustices that befell Lampard, Beckham and Campbell at the hands of gods. And nor do you really believe those dodgy calls are more than a fraction of the tale of woe.

We have been the *Mary Celeste* of football. Drifting, deserted and unexplained.

The most difficult game that I've ever had to commentate on was the Euro 2016 defeat to Iceland. But only because I wasn't at the mic for the goalless draw with Algeria in 2010. Or the one with Morocco in 1986. And. And. And. At least there was a masochistic compulsion to keep watching the Iceland match in Nice. There were no good reasons to see some of the other England let-downs through to their bitter ends.

Roy Hodgson took the hit for the loss to Iceland. No sooner had he lay down and resigned, than he took another kicking for his performance in the tortuous post-mortem media conference. 'I'm no longer the England manager. I don't really know what I'm doing here,' he said rather haplessly to the gathered press pack. It wasn't twenty-first-century varnished and veneered crisis management but Roy had a point.

In all those emotive, emboldened statements read from the steps of the Old Bailey, no one expects the guy that's just been sent down to come out and explain himself. He's heading down to the cells, his time in the witness box is over.

I'm sure that Roy would have loved to have called to the stand the two senior players who passed up their designated marking responsibilities on the Iceland throw-in that greased the slippery slope down which England skidded towards the exit door. They know who they are and how long the coaching staff worked in training on combating that most obvious of threats during the two previous days. They each had one job.

Roy and his coaching staff were there at the pavilion door reminding all their batsmen that Iceland's attack had but a single wicket-taking delivery. Block it. One after another, England's finest fell without offering a stroke.

From the equaliser onwards, an England team full of good players careered helplessly into bad habits. It was like watching a contagious epidemic spread in time lapse. A heavily poisoned chalice was being passed around the team. The ball certainly wasn't. The buck soon was.

In no time, technically adept players like Sterling, Kane, Alli, Rooney and then substitute Wilshere looked like they were trying to control the ball on a sloping corrugated roof, looked like they were trying to run through paddy fields.

As soon as they saw previews of the morning headlines in their minds' eyes, thought bubbles formed above their heads containing the words, 'I'm a celebrity, get me out of here.' Iceland had asked an all too familiar question of an England tournament team and there was nobody in white that even dared to put their hand up and offer an answer.

No wonder Roy hesitated so long before exposing 18-year-old Marcus Rashford to the toxic fumes that were choking the talents of his most seasoned players out in the middle. When the rookie was belatedly introduced from the bench, he played with an innocent freedom that the others had long since given up. He had no mental scars. Yet.

That most thoughtful of sportswriters, Paul Hayward, once likened an England player at the front of a press conference to a captured airman. Fresh off the water board, led into the interrogation room and straight under the arc lamps for the whole world to get a good look at the fear in his glazed eyes and his blank bewilderment. Name, rank and serial number then just read the prepared statement.

Twitter abuse isn't nearly good enough for a disgraced England team. They are taken to the stocks for Piers Morgan and Katie Hopkins to throw their properly pompous outrage at. Snide asides at the start of *The Jonathan Ross Show*. Debates about grassroots football on *Loose Women*. Questions in the House. Calls to bring back hanging and national service.

No, it wasn't the Russian linesman. We have created our own monster since 1966.

Brave Sir Gareth is the latest to tackle the dragon. Rather than fight it, he has tried to domesticate it. At the last World Cup in Russia, the England manager made himself and his players more available to the media mob. Darts matches between members of each squad were arranged and, to the shock and surprise of some journalists, the players actually threw their darts at the board and not at the scribes.

It was a little reminiscent of the Christmas truce football games played along the Western Front during World War I. Maybe not quite that friendly.

What was described as a 'charm offensive' on press hostility by Gareth was actually just an attempt to return some sanity to the circus that travels with the England team. Less human cannonball and high wire, more fire swallowing and lion taming.

Having assembled a team without schisms and ego trips that the fans could more readily get behind, the manager trusted the players' harshest critics to get a little closer to them.

The balance is a delicate one for both sides. Whereas political correspondents seem content to be briefed and brokered by party press offices, sportswriters tend to bite back at any attempts to make them sit or heel.

The press corps that often calls for greater diversity in football isn't very diversified. Most of the lead writers are men. Men that I know and mainly like individually. But, like most of the species, men that can lapse into a pack mentality when placed in groups. What is it about my gender that encourages sense and sensibility when we are left to our own devices, then lures us into acting like we are at Oliver Reed's stag-do when more than three of us get together?

England managers have woken up in even worse places than Reed after a bad night on the touchline. The back page flak aimed at Sir Bobby and Graham Taylor in the past was execution by firing squad. Personal, brutal, malicious. By any judgement, it was uncalled for and unacceptable. I don't think it could happen now.

Two extremely decent men were caught in the crossfire of the circulation war between the *Sun* and the *Daily Mirror* in the early 1990s. Neither newspaper has the power or the agenda to repeat those banner atrocities now. The hard cases and hatchet men that were groomed and sent into the field to pen the poison that brought down England managers have disappeared along with typewriters and ash trays. New media has diluted their venom.

You wouldn't want to cross Martin Samuel. The very best

of the tabloid sportswriters can still shred a man's reputation in one incendiary paragraph, but they take more of a sniper's aim than the 'all guns blazing' commando assaults of Brian Woolnough and Nigel Clarke in another era. Martin takes prisoners, his predecessors didn't.

The sound of the street corner paper seller has been drowned out by bespoke iPhone ringtones but the top hacks still have a voice on social media and beyond. Some of the lead writers do more radio and television than I do. I'm faintly amused when I drive away from an England game listening to the scholarly verdicts of journalists on phone-ins, knowing full well that they've spent much of the second half with their heads in their laptops bashing out match reports.

'What happened there?!'

Because helpful press officers and personal representatives are engaged to put unhelpful obstacles between their men and their media, the information flow is interrupted by all manner of locks and dams and weirs, so exclusive stories are hard to come by without a bank transfer. Truly investigative journalism like Daniel Taylor's chilling exposé of the sexual abuse of young footballers is more and more difficult to carry out.

There is a recent trend towards a lyrical, learned style of football writing that hopefully reflects more youth, more women, more graduates among the Fourth Estate. They still find it much easier to write cutting criticism than heartfelt praise, but there is now more reason and rationale in contemporary writing.

Gareth can do both with the best of them. He wears the FA blazer well and can act as a dignified and diplomatic spokesperson when called upon, but the journalists know that he won't hold back a weighty opinion when it is needed. The level of debate about the racist abuse suffered by his players in Montenegro and Bulgaria during the European Championships qualifying campaign was raised a significant notch when the England manager said that we needed to repair our own glass house before we started throwing stones at others.

It is not always easy to see the bigger picture when your own worried face is filling the camera lens. Gary Neville set up a system of social media monitoring at the full-time whistle of England games so that Roy Hodgson had an idea as to how the performance had been received by the chief football writers and was prepared for the kind of questions coming his way in the post-match grilling. Gareth just has a nose for fallout. He is rarely thrown during interviews, he never misses much.

His attempts to manage the media are not so much to save his own face or skin, but to try to keep the atmosphere surrounding his team at room temperature. He watched those good England players melting under the spotlight against Iceland as intently as anyone. You may recall he succumbed to a moment of supreme pressure himself once upon a time. Been there, seen it, done the pizza advert.

His England didn't win their penalty shootout against Colombia specifically because of the frequent practice sessions he organised for them but they didn't lose it by making the same mistakes that he did in 1996. Gareth couldn't wait to get his fateful spot-kick against Germany over with. He began his hurried run-up almost before the referee blew his whistle. He was trying to escape the moment.

The England players in 2018 had been schooled in the art of taking ownership of the entire process of their penalty.

Many of their training drills had been carried out at the end of sessions when their legs were 'match weary'. There was no 'who fancies one?' involved in the selection of kickers. Each taker knew his place in the running order in advance.

Jordan Pickford was the ringmaster for the whole shooting match. It was part of his job to collect the ball after each Colombian penalty and hand it to the next team-mate up to the oche. In that way, they could each take control of the timing of their part in what was conceived as a team operation rather than a sequence of individual contributions.

A lot has been said about the character-building by-products of Gareth's own individual torment. He himself has talked about the resilience and inner strength it drew from him, but penalty-taking is a footballing technique not a life challenge. Putting yourself in a frame of mind whereby you can then execute that technique under duress is a thought process. It's a heart bypass. Something you learn. Something Gareth taught from experience and research.

His bigger project is to transfer that mentality from the shootout to every minute of every match. When you read that he has flown across the pond to see the Super Bowl for himself, it's not for show. Gareth is a student of his profession. His eyes and ears are always open to new ideas and revised thinking. The England team has been stuck inside the same maze for too long to ignore any route out. Our *Groundhog Day* has become a horror movie.

The only sympathy for the team that lost to Iceland came from those that trod the inside of that same hamster wheel before them. Every tournament flop is chronicled by the very same memoirs with a different cover photograph.

Knowing Gareth, he's probably read them all in search of another percentage point of insight and understanding. Knowing Gareth, he's probably decided that defeat is not ultimately down to how many ketchup bottles there are on the canteen table or how often the players get some up and down time with their wags.

Baden Baden Bling.

He will be the first to tell you that he inherited healthy roots. Roy Hodgson will always be portrayed as a pair of safe, stolid senior hands, an old school pragmatist. The truth is that he blooded the likes of Alex Oxlade-Chamberlain, Raheem Sterling, Harry Kane, Dele Alli and Marcus Rashford long before many observers thought they were ready. Roy's squads were already pretty young and free of divisions.

The most unfortunate aspect of Sam Allardyce's brief dalliance with the England job was not so much the cheap newspaper scam that he fell for as his unkind words about a sincere and able predecessor. It was also the only stale whiff of pantomime scandal that the England job has been tainted by since the Capello Index. Gareth has certainly thrown open some windows and let some fresh air blow through.

He has had some breaks. It might have been a very different World Cup if England had started with a draw but Harry Kane's timely winner belatedly accounted for Tunisia. Two years earlier, Hodgson's team conceded a late equaliser in the final minute of the Euro '16 opener. The modern history of the England team has been chronicled in moments.

Gareth has earned the benefit of any doubts with his disarming grace and refreshing openness. He has brought a renewed sense of credibility and virtue to the job. He has won both a trust and respect that no England manager has enjoyed since he was playing. Not squeaky clean, but clean.

He has shown how much he cares at triumphal fist-pumping times but he has also found an ethical responsibility and gravitas. It is like a young David Attenborough has taken over.

How much of that stock he built up in 2018 will survive a run on reason in the wake of a few bad results remains to be seen. England managers are like celebrity marriages. They never last. We see to that.

It is like we become rather bored with the very qualities that suit them to the task in hand. Their strengths turn into their perceived weaknesses. Too sound, too sensible, too sane for this particular psychiatric ward.

If you're waiting for Gareth to start throwing teacups and storming out of press conferences, you are going to be disappointed.

He doesn't do illusion or slapstick. He will not shy away from dealing with misdemeanours and mishaps but he won't make a fly-on-the-wall documentary of them.

An awareness of the burning issues of the day are secure in his hands. No England manager has had to deal with lockdown breaches before, let alone half-a-dozen of them, but when landed with problems that were not of his making, he struck a clear balance between sanction and understanding that neither press nor players could take serious issue with.

When Jack Grealish became a cause célèbre for the amateur team selectors, Gareth faced the flak while quietly easing Grealish into first his squad and then his team on a timetable of the manager's own choosing. I don't know how many substitutions he has made since taking the job but I can't recall any player throwing a strop at one yet. In Gareth they trust.

No England player has to think twice about knocking on the boss's door to discuss racism or mental health. They know he will not only listen but act.

He will do all that he can to make sure that it's a pleasure as well as a privilege to play for England on his watch, and all that he can to avoid erecting security fences in order to keep it that way.

Whether we will let him is another matter. It's too early to say if we have kicked our addiction to melodrama. When you have seen as many tragi-comedies as England watchers have, it can be difficult to develop a taste for hero movies.

Gareth will have to draw on some more of his Euro '96 experiences to prepare the players for the gaudy glare of a tournament staged mainly on Blighty soil this summer. England may be the ancestral home of football but that waspish sense of entitlement can become a burden as easily as it can provide a boost. The idea that by lustily singing the national anthem in unison we will scare off any foes is a tad imperial.

Sections of the media will lead the hearty chorus. I am never quite so uppity as to try to separate us from them. The lines between platforms are increasingly blurred. Television does as much tub thumping as any other.

A tournament summer creates a nightly TV narrative better than any soap opera and returns mass viewing figures for national men's and women's teams. In turn, that creates separate stages for kit manufacturers to screen epic ads and Charlie Brooker to take the piss out of them.

Newspapers hate international breaks as a rule. Website hits and likes tail off as fans of the Premier League giants take umbrage at having their fun interrupted by one-sided qualifiers, but tabloids and broadsheets alike soon catch the deranged mood of a major Championship finals.

Silly cut-out hats become de rigueur. Psychic powers of prediction are bestowed upon random zoo animals. Eileen Drewery gets her own column. The office cleaner draws Germany in the sweep with a shrug of innocent shoulders.

And, as a commentator on England games, I actually get to say 'we' very occasionally. Impartiality is given the month off.

My very first England commentary was the second leg of the Euro 2000 play-off against Scotland at Wembley. The BBC broadcast the first match at Hampden and Paul Scholes scored twice in a 2–0 win. The return was expected to be a formality but Scotland dominated the first half and Don Hutchison halved the aggregate deficit.

From the outset, Ron Atkinson alongside me had been calling England 'us' and Scotland 'them', and the programme editor in my headphones was calling on me to get him to stop. Several scribbled notes that I passed to Ron were brusquely scrunched up and tossed onto the floor between us. He wasn't having it, but then neither was the editor. I was commentating live to 15 million people and refereeing a fight at the same time.

Half-time arrived and, before I could get an off-air word out, Ron was wagging a chiding finger at me and beginning his defence.

'Am I saying that "we" are playing well?'

'No,' I conceded, 'you're saying "we" are playing crap and "they" are all over us, but "we" are being heard in Scotland too.'

'And is there anyone listening in Scotland that doesn't know I'm English?'

'Certainly not now, Ron!'

'So, they all know I want England to win, right?'

'That's pretty obvious.'

'So I'm biased, everybody knows that. But I'm being objective. I'm calling it as I see it. They are better than us and I'm saying so. I'm not kidding anyone. I'm paid to be objective, not to be unbiased.'

I think a good contract lawyer might be able to argue that claim for a princely fee but Ron had a point. And it's one that I've often argued with myself at major championships. If I make 'serving the audience' my professional priority, then why not serve the heightened patriotic fervour with a nod and a wink in the direction of openly wanting England to win?

As long as I don't start conducting the *Last Night of the Proms* I see no issue with recognising the different audience and the different level of audience involvement that there is with an England World Cup semi-final.

You must never ham it up. There's no need to. Not when that audience numbers 20 million and more. Not when it's appointment-to-view television.

The very occasional 'we' is not xenophobic, it's simply reflective of the national-occasion status of the event. It's not actionable. As long as you're prepared to say 'we are crap' if we are!

Balance is awkward to keep when football shows even the slightest sign of coming home. That's where having Gareth in charge comes in handy.

Xenophobia is a phobia. Phobias come complete with fears and insecurities that need addressing and treating. The England manager has just got to keep the dressing-room door sufficiently ajar for his players to hear the mass chorus of support but not the strains of delusionary pomp.

It only takes a couple of Jägerbombs and a couple of verses of 'Jerusalem' to turn an England fan into an England lout. Euro '96 was a long hot summer of fun until the German cars on our streets started getting torched after the semi-final.

We want a team that shows our opponents respect while the rest of us show them none at all. The manager must promote confidence but not over-confidence. Expectation but not expectancy. Fervour but not fever.

Gareth has his hand on the throttle of a powerful superbike that could roar to victory or slide into a ditch with one excited twitch of a muscle. We can be excited, Gareth can't. He's got to keep his eye on all of the balls we have given him to juggle.

Managing England has never been quite what it said in the brochure. You turn up for work on the first day in a tracksuit and they immediately fit you for a blazer, a dinner jacket, a psychiatrist's white coat, a hard hat and a camouflage jacket. It is a hundred jobs in one. You can lose the other ninety-nine for a mistake in any single one of them.

You will spend about forty or fifty days a year with your players. Oh, and they are not really ever your players. When they are kind of your players, you are expected to ensure that they not only play football like gods but behave like deity too. On national service, they are the nation's property and must act like role models. Only not role models like anyone else of their age in the entertainment industry. Trappist monks off the field, hell raisers on it.

The football media treat the England manager like a nephew to begin with. We want what's best for him but we also think we know what that is. And a little better than he does. We await our moment to tell him and the rest of you.

Judgemental is the new normal. Gareth will need more than an umbrella if the acid rain starts to fall.

I remember commentating on an FA Cup tie at Middlesbrough in 2009. Gareth's team were in the Premier League drop zone. We had half an hour alone together in an empty dressing-room in late afternoon. He was three months away from relegation, eight months away from the sack but he already looked outwardly pale and drawn. I didn't like what I saw.

I liked what I heard, though. His thinking was as sound and balanced as ever, his spirit was strong, his sense of humour was intact. He admitted he had problems but didn't offer excuses, only reasons and solutions. Gareth's body clearly wasn't enjoying the pressure but his body language was full of clarity and certainty. If he'd handed me one of the red shirts hanging limply from the pegs surrounding us, I'd have done my very best for him that night.

Gareth has taken on a solemn duty of care and custody of the national team. The crown jewels feel as safe and secure as they can be. A luminary is in control of the asylum.

The excesses of football guarantee that some kind of batshit is never far away. The most electric young talents in the squad are starting to plug into the traps and trappings of wider fame and fortune. They are taking more managing as they do.

The England team's results will determine whether Gareth's next gig on the managerial tour is at Barcelona, Barnsley or Bahrain. History tells us that control over those results may not always be in his domain. Only responsibility for them.

When the time comes to head-hunt his successor, the chairman or woman of the FA will line up the usual suspects and consider which of them is the best match for the endless brief. They will advertise for a new national coach but they know they will need a lot more.

Beaten football people always look to cling to the consolation that they have 'learnt some lessons' in defeat. They rarely do. It is human habit to repeat mistakes. Of all the England managers I've known, Gareth is the one with the best chance of breaking that habit.

It's not what you know, it's who you know.

MEMBER OF LABOUR PARTY

1978–2012, 2020–present

It is not very fashionable to admit to ever having been a Blairite, but the first seven or eight years of Tony Blair's premiership were the most optimistic I've ever felt about British politics. I was a homeless voter at the last General Election.

Champagne socialist? Maybe more of a red wine Remainer.

I hosted a number of Labour Party events during Gordon Brown's time and became friendly with the likes of Douglas Alexander, Andy Burnham, Alastair Campbell and David Miliband. I was the on-stage adjudicator for a couple of the public leadership hustings in 2010. For me, we elected the wrong brother.

As much as I can accept the outcome of any mass vote, I just don't understand Brexit. Perhaps I've travelled too widely and too fondly to be an isolationist.

The low point of the whole political pantomime season in 2019 was Jacob Rees-Mogg's crass tweet about England not needing Europe to succeed after a dignified Irishman had led a diverse national cricket team to victory in the World Cup. If you don't get sport, stay out of it. Put your feet up on a Commons bench and fantasise about handing out prefect detentions again.

Maybe I should stay out of politics. Maybe Marcus Rashford should but thank goodness he hasn't.

There should be some cause for concern when 'you can't believe what you see in the papers' is part of common parlance, when we need a website like fullfact. org to translate what we read and hear.

I've been openly critical of television news coverage for failing its audience in recent years, for humouring and trivialising conceit and deceit. I've gone as far as to suggest that an important football story would have been covered with more gravitas and depth by the sports media than the Brexit issue was by the political correspondents.

I just felt the likes of Robert Peston and Beth Rigby allowed the country to become disengaged and bored of Brexit by portraying grave matters of state as knockabout reality shows.

Too many smirking pieces to cameras, too many film reports with trite pay-off lines, too many vanities massaged by 'Westminster sources'. Lobbyists and think tanks. Paid briefers with party lines to spin. Glorified ad men and PR reps. Professional liars. The electorate couldn't relate the content of news bulletins to their own lives.

Sporting action connects with the nation in a way that PMQs and *Question Time* cannot because the contest is honest, serious and easy to engage with. There's less bluster or sham. You can't dodge the issue. And the first person to honour and console the loser is usually the very person that has just beaten them. Respect counts.

In all of my dealings with Kick It Out, I have constantly argued that the biggest single source of discrimination in our society is not colour or gender or sexual orientation, it is wealth. Sport promotes social mobility more than any other sector. It is talent-based, it is barrier-breaking, it is international.

I was in Paris on the day of the 2016 Referendum, working at the European Championship finals. On the morning of the vote, I received a surprise call from my 87-year-old mum, Freda, asking me where she should put her cross.

'That's up to you,' I said to her before quickly adding that my wife and I were solid Remainers.

'I'm not bothered about you two,' Mum told me like it was. 'How are the children voting? It's their future. I'll vote how they're voting.'

However much you love your parents, they are always still capable of doing something that makes you love them more. If only everyone had a mum like mine.

15

WAYNE ROONEY

('REMEMBER THE NAME')

Frequently asked questions:

1. *What's the best game you've ever commentated on?*
2. *Which is your favourite goal?*
3. *What do you think is your most famous commentary line?*

Answers:

1. *I don't know.*
2. *Haven't got one.*
3. *You decide.*

The best things in football are over in a flash. They come without warning, they leave in a cloud of dust. If you're not careful, you can miss them altogether.

In 2006, one of my very favourite footballers blatantly head-butted an opponent in a World Cup final. I had one of the best seats in the house that balmy Berlin evening and I didn't see it. The red card was airborne, Zinedine Zidane was walking and I was falteringly searching for an explanation until the replay flashed up.

Live commentary is a staring competition. Blink and you might miss something. Every moment is a possible game-changer, every game-changer belongs in its moment. If it changes its game decisively, you will remember it and revisit it and reminisce about it forever. The commentator gets one take at capturing it and becoming a small part of your memory of it. Moments.

You can't compare and rate them any more than you can the lovers and the cars in your lifetime. The noisy banger you learnt to drive in is as memorable as the Explorer Sport Deluxe you aspired to because it was special to you at the time. Commentary is words for the time.

'Remember the name. Wayne Rooney.'

When I shouted those words from the rickety Goodison gantry at a chunky 16-year-old scouser in 2002, I got lucky. Imagine if Wayne had turned out to be a one-hit wonder. The name in question was in camera shot on the back of his Everton substitute's shirt as I invited several million strangers to make a mental note of it.

Not only had Wayne just scored a comic-book late winner, he had become the Premier League's youngest scorer and ended a thirty-game Arsenal unbeaten record in the bargain. I managed to find the words to communicate all of that in the following seconds but the three little words by which the moment is remembered I stole from somebody else. As much of a crime as David Seaman's ponytail that day.

The previous season, I attended a testimonial event for Alex Young at Goodison Park. During the evening, a striking man with a pointy beard approached me to whisper 'remember the name, Wayne Rooney' into my ear.

The name of Rooney was already buzzing around Merseyside football circles. He scored a mountain of goals for the Liverpool Boys team, then excelled in Everton's run to the FA Youth Cup final to the point that he made it onto the first team substitutes' bench in the spring of 2002.

Nevertheless, when Wayne came of age with that defining goal against Arsenal in the October, it was the words of the tall, bearded stranger that came to my mind and out onto the soundtrack to the moment. Rooney very nearly scored an even better goal a couple of minutes later. That would have spoilt everything.

A few months on and I was attending another function at Goodison when I suddenly caught sight of my mystery scriptwriter across a crowded room. His unmistakable features had become bathed in a proud smile long before I reached him to say thank you for the prophetic prompt. And would you believe he now had two more names for me to remember?

'John-Paul Kissock,' he said sagely. 'He's the next one. And Wayne's brother John is going to be even better than Wayne.'

This was quite a revelation since 12-year-old John had recently been released by the academy at Everton and picked up by Macclesfield Town. Both Rooney junior and Kissock have subsequently had decent careers around the lower leagues without ever quite living up to the premonitions my chief scout had about them.

If only he'd left it at Wayne . . .

Whenever I have been fortunate enough to extract a few apt words from the fluffier parts of my brain at a trending moment, the first question that usually follows is, 'Did you prepare them in advance?' Given that nothing in art or entertainment is original, the honest answer is, 'Yes, but I didn't realise it.'

Preparation is not just about compiling commentary charts, it's an ongoing process that absorbs material from every game you watch, every commentary you hear, everything you see. Not least because your audience are seeing the same things too, and your job is to communicate with them.

I'm always amused when artists and writers list their influences. If you possess any trace of creativity then everything you encounter in life should influence you one way or another. Following a few set texts is not being influenced, it's being brainwashed.

I can't tell you that the bearded wonder has been an influence on me but he somehow got inside my head when it mattered most.

There are no manuals, no works of reference that tell a commentator what to do and when. No 'Hey, Siri'. I can't give you a recipe I follow in the seconds after a goal is scored, only a list of some of my essential ingredients. And even they may not be to your particular taste.

I do believe that preparation for a commentary involves more than looking up facts and figures. You should also be thinking through the different possible scenarios and outcomes for the game ahead, asking yourself what their significance would be and how you'd go about expressing that.

You should be trying to do that throughout the match, too. If you're watching a thrill-ride of a game that is locked at 2–2 entering the final minutes and a free-kick is awarded in a threatening position, you need to be asking yourself, 'What am I going to say if this flies in?'

The fact is you can ask a search engine any question you like but you've still got to choose the answer that is right for you and the circumstances you find yourself in. There is no such thing as a diagram of the anatomy of the perfect goal commentary, but the perfect goal does deserve chosen words.

I obviously knew that a Rooney goal that day in 2002 would make him the Premiership's youngest scorer and so it would have been remiss of me not to ask myself what words and thoughts would best adorn the record goal if he scored it.

But when the goal is also an act of sorcery in its own right then you respond to its sheer wonder first and foremost. The new league record is secondary.

My first words were, 'Great goal, brilliant goal.' Nothing lyrical but basic outpourings about the startling audacity of this cocky kid, still too young for a driving lesson, whipping one over the England keeper and in off the underside of the bar. You go with the moment.

Only then did I look down at my monitor to see his name above the '18' on his back as he ran away from me in celebration. Cue my man's words, plucked out of the thin air of a chance meeting in the very same stadium months ago. 'Remember the name, Wayne Rooney.' Pause. But a pause for thought. What comes next?

Breath. 'It's Premiership history.' Breath. 'The big league's youngest ever goal scorer signals his arrival on the big stage with a breathtaking goal to end Arsenal's unbeaten run surely in the final minute.' Bit garbled, bit jumbled but most editorial bases covered, and I've even managed to smuggle a 'surely' in there as insurance against Thierry Henry equalising in stoppage time.

Still no replay on screen, so time for another line of rhetoric. 'Five days short of his seventeenth birthday, Wayne Rooney has just grown up.' Hmmmm. Just in time to spare the audience more corn, up came the slow-motion replay to show us all 'and how!'

I didn't have a co-commentator in tow that day. It wasn't a live broadcast, just a highlights edit for ITV's *The Premiership*. The words I shouted out at the moment the goal flew in at Goodison could have been doctored in an edit suite before being broadcast. Thankfully, the producer on duty left them alone to air as I said them.

None of Rooney's 208 Premier League goals were screened live on terrestrial television in the UK. None of Shearer's, none of Henry's either. At the start of 2021 there were still far more households in Britain with no access to Sky Sports or BT Sport than there were homes prepared to pay for their television sport.

From the inception of the Premier League in 1992, not a single match was shown free-to-air in the UK until last year. Not legally anyway. It took a global pandemic to create the circumstances for a few exceptions to the rule that is now firmly back in place.

It is a viewing landscape that we have come to know and largely accept, and one that has benefited the top end of the domestic game to the tune of the millions and millions we hear about every time a player's contract enters its last two years. How many unseen debits there are to set against those headline credits is a matter of debate, a question of the balance.

What is beyond debate is that television pay-walls marginalise the viewing of Premier League and now Champions League football. Viewing figures don't tell you everything but

BBC and ITV will attract an audience three or four times that of a subscription channel for one of their live FA Cup ties or England friendlies. Not a boast, not even an alarm call, just a fact.

Pay-per-view television football will be the next test of how much fans really value the traffic jams and the scalding pies.

Few products in British commercial life enjoy the level of customer loyalty that football clubs do. For every frustrated fan that tears up their season ticket, there are a dozen more crawling around on their hands and knees trying to pick up the shreds and piece them back together. Supporting a team borders on addiction. If you can't get your fix in person at the stadium, the blanket coverage enables you to feed the craving from your sofa or your local.

Unless we are in lockdown, the blankets are not free, though.

And neither are the rights. There is an argument for saying that the sports channels have become as hooked on the same drug. Premier League football is costing them in the region of £10 million per game. That includes Burnley versus Palace. I am not a media marketing expert but I know that only a fraction of that is recoverable on a match-to-match basis. And the consumer is now leaning more and more towards match-by-match 'on demand' buying.

The football economy's reliance on television money is clear to see in the match scheduling. The old fixture computer has been dumped down at the recycling centre. Some kick-offs are set to the clocks of time zones thousands of miles away. Football has acceded to the media moguls' own 'on demand' buying. The Premier League prides itself on being a successful global 'brand'. Brands depend on the existence of a sustainable market for them.

Most analysts will tell you that BT created their sports channels just to try to staunch the bleeding of broadband sales to Sky. The likes of Gary Lineker and Rio Ferdinand in front of the camera may have a passion for football but that doesn't mean their big bosses necessarily do. If some other form of entertainment emerged as a more effective loss leader, BT might change horses in mid-streaming.

Backing horses, backing first goal scorers, backing two raindrops dribbling down the smoked windows of an executive box have become essential revenue streams for the football economy. I am not a betting man but I'll have a cheeky fiver with you that there will soon be laws passed to reduce the promotion of gambling. Betting is tomorrow's nicotine.

I have no sermons to give on the perils of having a flutter because it is one of the few vices that I've not succumbed to. Sorry Ray, I loved you in *Sexy Beast* but the notion of responsible gambling has always seemed a bit of a contradiction to me.

So, I would not enter into a commercial partnership with a betting company myself and when I dutifully read out the sponsors' odds during a TalkSport commentary, I try to pay more than lip service to the obligatory plug for the support and advice website.

It's not my issue with gambling that is the problem going forward, though. It is the moral blood that it is leaving on the hands of football clubs and broadcasters that will imminently be wiped away by legislation. Erectile dysfunction ads will not make up the shortfall on Mr Murdoch's balance sheets.

It's got to work financially first and foremost. These conglomerates do have other divisions, they do have shareholders. And they do have competitors.

The power struggle is not confined to the rival television channels. There are tugs-of-war going on between them and the Premier League's own in-house productions, between international rights holders, between the established platforms and emerging streaming sites. And clouding the whole picture is a new power player on the scene. The consumer.

A generation of committed football viewers have had little option but to go with the flow and stump up their subscriptions every month since Sky and the Premier League woke up in bed together alive and kicking one morning in 1992. The second generation of pay-to-view customers are not used to paying for their media. Millennials want it faster, shorter, freer. And they know where and how to find it.

Football needs to adapt not only to a changing market place but to a smarter media consumer. The game has taken its public for granted. It has sold itself to the highest bidder on the assumption that its flock will keep following. The model hasn't changed much in twenty-five years, but all other media models have. The goals collages are edited to Kendrick Lamar tunes rather than Simple Minds hits now, but it's still the same direct debit patent. It may have had its day.

The reach of Sky Sports stretches beyond the hard facts of the viewing figures. Martin Tyler's bawl of 'Aguerooooo' is as iconic a commentary moment as any in the modern era but it may not be quite as famous on the outskirts of the football village. The viewing figure for it was about three million. A week earlier, the BBC attracted three times that audience for the FA Cup final.

If election and referendum results have taught us anything about the art of messaging in the last few years it is to make damn sure that you are connecting with those that feel disconnected. If you don't, they will vote you out. Don't waste too much time listening to your own echo. Burst your social bubbles so you can see through to the real world.

The Premier League quite probably is the strongest domestic football league in the world, but its 'partners' don't half spend a lot of time reminding it. The competition existed before the brand, the sport existed before the competitions. Football was a game before it became a spectacle. Viewers watch football, not leagues. Fans support teams, not events. More and more younger fans have more affinity with a particular player than his team.

What makes Martin's rendition of the Aguero goal that decided the title in 2012 such an outstanding piece of broadcasting is the naked emotion in his voice, followed by the arresting statement, 'I swear you'll never see anything like this ever again.' Big call, correct call. No brand promotion of the Premier League, just an unimaginable twist of sporting fable awarded the cachet it deserved forever and a day.

I was sitting with Peter Drury at ITV's Paris studios when Michael Owen scored his famous free-running goal at the 1998 World Cup. For five or ten seconds after the ball had squirted into the Argentine net, a dozen of us were still jumping around and hollering joyfully in celebration.

When we all settled down again, I said to Peter, 'If either of us are ever lucky enough to call a goal like that, we now know we can say anything we like in the seconds that follow because nobody is listening.' Brian Moore's reaction was lost to us in Owen's vapour trail.

Most of the content of a commentary dissipates like a vapour trail. Hot breath on a cold day. There one moment, gone the next. Some may marvel at our words for the patterns they leave in the sky, others will call them pollution. Little of what we say lingers for long.

The harder we try to leave our mark on the vista of the game, the more likely we are to leave a cloud on it. As a young commentator, I probably spent too much time chasing rhyme rather than reason. Too much greetings card prose, too smart arse by far. Slogans and catchphrases galore.

Over time and over a few glasses in the company of Brian Moore and Reg Gutteridge, I've hopefully toned down my act to let the true entertainers down on the field rustle up the drama, and limit myself to leading the applause. Good football doesn't need cheerleaders. It creates its own sense of theatre.

Like actors, like musicians, commentators need good material to work with. If the scripts for the 1999, 2005 or 2012 Champions League finals had been presented to commissioning editors in TV drama departments, the writers would probably have been told to go away and make them more believable. And maybe a bit easier to follow.

They were all ten-part suspense stories with only a couple of good episodes each. Slow burners with bloody big finishes. In Barcelona, the two most important characters weren't even introduced until the closing scenes.

That 1999 final between Manchester United and Bayern Munich was simply the most consequential night of my broadcasting career. It was the final game of my first season as ITV's successor to Brian Moore. If I'd messed up, this book would have concluded quite a few chapters ago.

Brian commentated on an era of European football in which an English team abroad commanded a level of support from fans of many other clubs. The early continental triumphs of United, Liverpool, Forest and Villa were heralded as national success stories. 'Our brave boys' versus 'Jonny Foreigner'. By 1999, club football had got more tribal, more rancorous.

I remember walking back from Nou Camp to our hotel after United's improbable comeback and wondering to myself if I had overplayed it, whether my words of florid praise had grated with every fan of a warring club. When I turned on *Sky News* in my room before going down to take Rioja with the rest of the ITV team in the bar, I sensed a retro mood of national celebration in the film reports from home.

The European Cup had not resided in England for fifteen years. It seemed longer still since we had seen a German team humbled in that way. United had completed a unique treble and done it in their own unique way. Maybe I was horribly wrong but I got the impression that, for one night only, even their most embittered rivals wouldn't begrudge them any praise that came their way.

'Don't wallow in it because you'll get dog's abuse when you come to our place next season, but fair play to you.' Plaudits spoken from beneath a curled lip, but plaudits nonetheless.

As legendary matches go, it wasn't a very good final. Either for United or for me until the very end. With a few minutes remaining of my grand audition in front of a judging panel of 20 million viewers, not only was there a hollow ring of anti-climax to the whole occasion but I had made a botch of the one goal scored.

I blame Peter Schmeichel. He may just have been the best individual player in that United team, so when Mario Basler's early free-kick left him rooted to the spot, I assumed that he had been fooled by a fiendish deflection. I assumed wrong. The shot bounced past the United keeper unaided. Doh.

Commentary is no business for perfectionists but we do all dwell on our mistakes. We try not to. We try to tell ourselves and each other that they are occupational hazards as inevitable as own goals and penalty misses, but every time your eyes deceive you or your tongue trips you up, it leaves a bruise.

There should be birch twigs in every commentary position so we can give ourselves a good thrashing and move on.

I made a bit of a horlicks of the incident that led to Jens Lehmann's dismissal in the first twenty minutes of the 2006 final and never quite got it out of my system all night. That wound can fester. The error rankles and rattles around the darker cupboards of your mind until you become tentative and wary. It's a fly you can't swat, an itch you can't reach.

By contrast, if you are feted with a good start to a game, it can carry you all the way to shore like the perfect wave. For some reason I cannot fully explain, I broke with tradition in the early seconds of the 2009 FA Cup final and declined to invite my splendid co-commentator, Jim Beglin, to add some overtures while Everton and Chelsea tuned up.

Louis Saha scored inside twenty-five seconds and I nailed it. I found the entry in my cup final records notes and found the words to accompany it. I never looked back all afternoon. My skeleton cupboard was beautifully bare. Jim and I were 'at it' tape to tape that day.

At last that 'FA Cup final records' sheet paid out on the hour after wasted hour I had invested in it. Every year, I compiled a page of feats and firsts relating specifically to football's antique club match. Hat-tricks, missed penalties, red cards, comebacks, fastest goals, white police horses, etc, etc. Every year, the existing records remained as untouched as my records page.

Until . . . Saha swung his left foot and I looked proudly down at my note of the only goal of the 1895 final scored by Aston Villa's Bob Chatt after thirty-five seconds. My 114-year wait for a faster goal was over.

The wait to atone for my early slip-up in Barcelona seemed to last for 114 years too. The '99 final was a bit of a grind. Both the game and my voice became stuck in a rut of deflated foreboding as time slowly ebbed away without offering a clue of the fireworks display to come. Fate is such a tease.

Fans of the two clubs won't thank me for drawing any kind of comparison but it was the sense of pre-ordained destiny that proved the most captivating common denominator of the Manchester United and Liverpool European runs of 1999 and 2005. An air of 'and so it is written'.

Footballers are an oddly spiritual lot. I'm not against divine intervention from any available deity but, as an agnostic, I am faintly amused by players that enter the field calling on the guidance of higher powers and then proceed to break most of the Ten Commandments before half-time.

Superstitions are even worse. Johan Cruyff used to insist on spitting a piece of chewing gum into the opposition half of the field before kick-off. The reason being, wait for it . . . for luck. Johan Bloody Cruyff. One of the most perfectly balanced and graceful stylists ever to bless a football pitch with his presence actually did that, actually believed he needed a form of uncouth witchcraft to succeed.

No, Johan, you are just better than everyone else. It's you, not the Wrigley's.

France did not win the World Cup in 1998 because Laurent Blanc kissed Fabian Barthez on the forehead before every game. There was more to it than that.

If I were a sports psychologist, I think I would want to be emphasising the hours of training and conditioning that the players have devoted to being the best they can possibly be rather than the order they put their socks on. If any success you achieve is down to some weird pre-match ritual, why point at the name on the back of your shirt when you score? Point at your lucky tie-ups.

And when you miss, whose fault is it? The same religious faith in the power of karma must logically invade the conscience when you realise that relegation is all down to you changing the pre-match playlist on your iPod. The pangs of shame, the stigma of knowing that a season's sweat and blood has been wasted because the all-seeing gods of football have punished you for allowing a guilty pleasure by the Jackson Five into your Beats. Blame it on the Boogie.

All of this hocus-pocus produces a troubled sense of pessimism in football people. Bad omens, bad vibes. This is a game where 2–0 is described as 'a dangerous lead'. I'm pretty certain that statistics would prove that it is an even more dangerous deficit but football always seems to fear the worst. Bogey grounds and former players coming back to haunt you. Hexes and jinxes. Results written in the runes.

And so it is that when a team is leading 1–0 entering the final ten minutes of a Champions League final and then hits the opposition woodwork a couple of times, an air of dread sets in. Oh no, not 'one of those nights'. And by the same bewitching formula, the team that is on the verge of losing takes mystifying heart from the fact that their hopes are hanging by an ever-thinner thread.

Bayern Munich teams are traditionally hewn from Black Forest oak and founded on rock mined in the Bavarian Alps.

They don't crumble or choke. For what seemed like centuries, hardened winners like Oliver Kahn, Stefan Effenberg and Lothar Matthaus had been taking medals out of English palms like the proverbial sweets from a baby. This looked a lost cause. Matthaus even went off to wash his hands ready for the trophy lift.

But then Scholl's chip hit a post, then Solskjaer came off the bench, then Jancker's overhead kick struck the bar. Then, then, then. One after another, a chain of events unlike any we had seen all night. A charm bracelet being linked together before our very eyes.

Even Bayern began to wonder. Every spin of the wheel was landing on red. Every roll of the dice was a United Flush. For the first time all evening, they looked like scoring.

'Can Manchester United score, they always score.'

My words before the first of the two corners that landed the great sting were more proverb than truth. They were factually incorrect. United had drawn 0–0 at Blackburn just a fortnight earlier in a critical league game. They didn't 'always' score. It just seemed like it.

Driving to Wembley for the FA Cup final the previous weekend, I'd heard Mark Lawrenson offering a prediction on BBC Radio Five. 'Well, it won't be United nil, will it?' he said when asked for a score line. Maybe that was the phrase that infiltrated my increasingly desperate ramblings as the clock ticked beyond 90.

There was momentum and there was previous. In the FA Cup semi-final, Giggs scored his giant-slalom of a goal against Arsenal when it was decisive. In Turin, Keane headed his captain's goal when it was needed. In the title decider, Beckham struck his pure equaliser after Spurs had gone ahead.

The stars just kept on aligning. One more constellation goal required.

The commentary position at Nou Camp is not far from the Moon. It feels like the viewing gallery on top of a skyscraper. There are three rows of sharply tiered tight-fit seats and narrow desks, a sloping ceiling and a partially-glassed front divided by grills. Sitting on the back row, you look down at the distant field through a kind of letter-box. You can see the pitch but you can't really see the stadium.

I wouldn't necessarily have chosen that particular perch for the most important three minutes of my career. But choice had left the giant building. Kismet had taken its seat.

Lennart Johansson, the UEFA president, was summoned from his seat in the VIP area to take the lift down to pitch side in order to present the trophy. Bayern president Franz Beck-enbauer accompanied him. When the elevator doors parted at ground level, they were informed that United had equalised. When the doors opened again back up at the VIP level, they were informed that United had won.

Neither of them witnessed either goal. Thankfully, I saw them both.

There were exactly 102 seconds between the two goals. My best work was done during the first eight of those seconds. I said nothing at all.

My best words all night followed that eight seconds of thinking time. 'Name on the trophy.' The great engraver-in-the-sky had long since gone to work on the European Cup. Teddy Sheringham's swept finish was only the equaliser but Bayern were beaten. They knew as surely as a boxer stopped in his tracks by a stunning straight jab that the knockout blow was on the way soon. It had been in transit for several months.

I'd like to tell you that I heard Reg's voice echoing around my head during those eight seconds. All of those breakfast-time phone reviews, all of his golden nuggets. 'What was the story, Clive?' 'Did you tell it during your commentary?'

The big red circle around United's date with destiny appeared to have been drawn long before they touched down in Barcelona. That was the story. Their name, their time.

It wasn't the whole truth of it. I'm not having that. I don't do horoscopes and Gypsy Rose Lee.

It wasn't luck any more than Cruyff's gnarled gum landing on the evening dew brought him luck. The winning goal was fashioned by the best ball striker in Europe finding the head of the best near post header in Europe finding the foot of the best poacher in Europe. Talent wins football matches, but fate's finger often seems to point them in the direction of victory.

'Football, bloody hell.' The greatest post-match television interview ever given. Sir Alex Ferguson's admission that he had no idea how his team had won.

Reg didn't call me for a couple of days after that final. He gave himself some of his beloved thinking time. When his critique arrived, it came with as much pride as praise. I had learnt well.

A few of the things I said in the eye of the cyclone have flatteringly become part of the screenplay to the night. 'Manchester United have reached the promised land', 'everything their hearts desired' etc, etc. If the big moment arrives on your watch it deserves better than 'amazing, fantastic, incredible, unbelievable'. It's actually happened, so capture and establish the moment. Make it yours.

Goals do belong to commentators. I was paid to re-record some of the audio accompanying United goals for the *Class of*

'92 film and the producer asked me to 'put a voice' on David Beckham's long-range missile against Wimbledon at Selhurst Park. I refused.

'No, that's Motty's goal,' I protested.

'It doesn't matter, does it?' came the irritated reply.

Yes, it does matter. It certainly matters to football fans to whom the goal matters. John Motson's BBC commentary is part of their memory of it. 'A goal that will be talked about and replayed for years.' Motty is the soundtrack to that goal like Travolta is the soundtrack to *Grease*. Anybody else is karaoke.

The most recited words I uttered in Nou Camp broke the cardinal rule of commentary. 'And Solskjaer has won it' committed the eternal sin of waving the winner across the line before the line had been crossed. If Bayern had somehow equalised and gone on to win a penalty shootout – and they would have! – there'd have been an effigy of me hanging from the entrance to the Arndale Centre by midnight. It would have been my fault.

The Sheringham and Solskjaer goals did not come completely without warning. Steven Gerrard's goal six years later did. Big Ron got a whiff of a comeback a couple of minutes before the equaliser in Barcelona and predicted that United would go on to win if they could find a leveller. In Istanbul, Andy Townsend and I spent half-time researching record Liverpool defeats. They were lucky to be only 3–0 down.

I have ached at the sides to the humour of some priceless story-tellers down the years but Andy is a stand-up comedy king. There are no Best Ever XI's, best games, goals or gaffes in this book but Ally McCoist is the best amateur singer I've worked with, Steve Kindon has the best football after-dinner routine I've heard and Andy Townsend just edges out Messrs St John, McCoist and O'Neill as a tale teller.

When Bryan Robson signed Andy for Middlesbrough in 1997, he moved him into Paul Gascoigne's house as a fatherly monitor. Believe me, there is a movie in the things they got up to.

As with 'all things Gazza', there is a sobering side to the binge life he leads and I'll never forget the day during the 2010 World Cup finals when Andy and I returned from a round of golf to our shared flat in Sandton. In the taxi, he told me that he had several missed calls from Paul. When we turned on the television, the Raoul Moat fishing rod and cooked chicken saga was in full, sad swing. Andy is the kind of friend people always reach out to.

He is a footballer turned broadcaster. That's all we demand of the ex-players that cross the great divide from walker to talker. If you want to work in television or radio, recognise it as your new job and care about it like you cared about winning football matches.

Andy was alongside me when Luis Garcia scored the Liverpool goal that won the 2005 Champions League semi-final by the shortest of short heads. He left Anfield that night as angry as Mourinho. Not because Andy was a former Chelsea player but because the ITV pictures had not been able to prove whether the 'ghost goal' had crossed the line or not. He did not have enough evidence to make a judgement call.

At the ITV hotel in central Liverpool, a fuming Andy tore into the match director for failing to provide definitive camera angles. John Watts is not only one of the most respected craftsmen in our business but also a lovely man. A delight to work with. Andy knew all that but he was locked on a professional warpath. He demanded to know why John hadn't positioned a camera on the goal line.

The answer was perfectly acceptable. Liverpool had been unwilling to give up the seats that would have needed to be emptied in order to accommodate a byline camera. Andy backed down, but the fact that he reared up in the first place told me all I needed to know about my co-worker. I had a poacher turned gamekeeper at my side. You only get angry when you care.

Andy wasn't best pleased at half-time in Istanbul. Not only had Kaka and Crespo just painted a Da Vinci of a goal to make it 3–0 to Milan, Liverpool were in disarray. The gamble on Harry Kewell's health was busted inside twenty minutes and his replacement wasn't even ready to come on. Andy was crying out for Didi Hamann and got Vladimir Smicer instead. Eventually.

He was telling it how he saw it. No need for extra cameras to work out that Liverpool were already in damage limitation mode. Their fans sang a loud, loyalist chorus of 'You'll Never Walk Alone' during the break but they were suffering with their team.

But then suffering always features somewhere in the plot of a good sports story. The essential narrative of any fanciful escape to victory demands that the triumph comes at a cost.

The conquering hero needs a tearful back story in order to appreciate the spoils. If they haven't lost a true love, lost a boyhood coach, lost a small fortune or lost their tiny mind, then what have they gained by winning?

I'm always faintly bemused when I hear the England fans' jubilant rendition of the theme from *The Great Escape* by way of a hymn of celebration. From memory, only three Allied soldiers actually get away from the prison camp in the film and only one of them is British. The movie should have been called 'The Nearly Great Escape' and then it really could be a truly fitting England anthem.

The main thing is that the characters suffered for the cause. The long and winding road to glory is the only route to the top in the Disney world of gallant and chivalrous sporting endeavour. We love the underdog, we love a storybook victory even when it's gained by a cast of scary hairy-assed bruisers from a horror storybook.

Not everyone lives happily ever after at the end of a football fairy tale. There has to be struggle and sacrifice for the drama to capture the imagination that sporting competition stirs in us.

It is no fun at all when Barcelona turn up at Wembley like they did in 2011 and simply win the Champions League final by playing near-perfect football for ninety minutes. Where's the box office appeal in that?

Just being better than your opponents is not much of a storyline. Real winners show defiance and hunger and nerve. They find turning points and omens. Their post-match interviews extol the virtues of digging deep and refusing to accept defeat. You've got to catch at very least a chilling glimpse of that defeat in order to enjoy the epiphany of finding a way to the winning post. There's got to be a journey.

Liverpool's journey to Istanbul was full of those oracles and signs that we can wisely point to with the benefit of hindsight. They had needed three goals in the second half of their final group game against Olympiakos in December just to reach the knockout stages. Two of them came inside the last ten minutes. The eighty-sixth minute decider by Steven Gerrard was a classic Anfield Kop end moment. They had been here before.

So, when Gerrard's looping header found its way into the Milan net nine minutes after the break, maybe I was entitled to promote the faint possibility of a comeback.

'Hello. Hello. Here we go,' I ventured as if someone had just handed me a copy of a new draft of the script.

I can think of very few instances during my career when a programme editor has tried to write my script for me. Entering the final ten minutes of the first leg of the 1997 Cup Winners' Cup semi-final, Liverpool trailed Paris St Germain 2–0. They stunk the Parc des Princes out that night. McManaman, Fowler, Redknapp, Barnes, Collymore. Good players having a bad, bad time.

Given that ITV were to broadcast the second leg at Anfield a fortnight later, a boss's voice in my ear suggested that I might like to lift the tone of my damning commentary to offer hope of an improved showing in the return leg. Dutifully, I combed my platitude collection to find a 'you never know what can happen on one of those famous Anfield European nights' comment. Essentially to keep my job.

No sooner had I spat it out than Jerome Leroy scored PSG's third.

I reached for the secret switch by which I could talk to mission control without the rest of you hearing and asked the big cheese, 'What now?'

I had no right to believe that a great escape was any more possible eight years later. Liverpool had performed no better in Istanbul than they did in Paris, their team line-up was arguably a weaker one and they were a long way away from Anfield with no return leg to come.

But Gerrard scored and all of a sudden, Steve McQueen was hurdling the border fence on his motorbike.

Smicer's snap-shot bounced past the keeper and Rocky Balboa was climbing to his feet to beat the count in the final round of the re-match with Apollo Creed. Within moments, Xabi Alonso equalised and Elliott's bicycle was soaring towards the sunset with ET safely nestled in the basket up front.

'Mission impossible is accomplished,' I blurted out rather prematurely. 'Liverpool are on terms. Yes, on terms.'

The year before, I called that England–France European Championship game in Lisbon. The one that dear old Sir Bobby Robson watched passively from the neighbouring seat.

Big Brother was still all the rage back in 2004 and *The Times* newspaper ran a feature whereby readers could vote an annoying presenter, pundit or commentator out of the tournament each day. I was the first to go.

England led 1–0 ticking into stoppage time when Emile Heskey conceded a free-kick just outside the penalty-area. I took the opportunity to spell out what a boost to the team's chances it would be if they could successfully negotiate this moment of danger. I definitely said 'if'.

Three minutes on, and Zidane had scored not once, but twice and England had lost on the opening weekend of the Championships. From public broadcaster to public enemy in seconds. All down to me. Guilty as charged.

I took the rap for Steven Gerrard that night. It was his blind back-pass that led to the late penalty that sealed my fate. Stevie made it up to me in Istanbul.

His own personal display in three different positions during the course of the match was astonishing. The team performance was fitful. I maintain Liverpool played better in the 2007 final and lost, but the individual contributions of Stevie, Jamie Carragher and a handful of others turned my hopeful 'here we go' into a prophesy.

It was a chance remark that caught the mood of the whole unlikely achievement. The creepy sixth sense that Liverpool were somehow champions by decree, by destiny, by divine intervention.

I'm not a dreamer, not a crystal-ball gazer. If psychics are so good at getting inside our heads, why do they have to put up signs outside village halls advertising their fairs? Why don't they just hypnotise us into going?

I'm a humanist. My match day bag is full of pens and charts, not pendants and charms. When I cock up, it's my cock-up.

I respect the work of sports psychologists but I don't subscribe. A golf professional once encouraged me to visualise my next shot before hitting it. I told him that my powers of visualisation were so strong that I'd won more Majors in my mind than Tiger Woods, and may even have celebrated them more disgracefully than he allegedly did. I can do fantasy, I'm just not so hot on swing planes and shoulder turns.

I'm an unashamed romantic. I still cry when Fran comes back to Bud's at the end of *The Apartment* and when I hear Karen Carpenter sing 'Goodbye to Love'. I was in floods when Nelson Mandela made his appearance in the stadium before the World Cup final in Johannesburg. I can be very touched by reality so I don't feel the need for an extra layer of spiritual explanation.

Nonetheless, I do think that momentum is the most powerful force in sport. When you find yourself running a sequence of green lights, the gear change can carry you a long way. Once the certainty starts to flow, it reaches the parts that other tonics can't. It creates an irresistible faith in your ability to make your talent count. No artificial stimulant can get you as high as confidence and self-belief. If only you could bottle bottle.

Liverpool had enough backbones in red shirts to stand up for themselves and not buckle once they found their momentum. It was the club's fifth European title. I had been lucky enough to be holding the mic for three of the previous four.

'Liverpool have their hands on the European Cup again, and this time it's for keeps. That trophy isn't going anywhere but Anfield.' Lines pencilled onto my notes the night before.

I didn't put a curse on them by preparing some words for the moment. I didn't tempt fate because fate didn't put the giant trophy in Gerrard's paws. He did, they did.

Preparing 'lines' for such eventualities is just part of my job. Football watchers tend to trademark commentators by a handful of the thousands of words we speak in the course of our careers.

'The crazy gang have beaten the culture club.' John Motson.

'Look at his face, just look at his face.' Barry Davies.

'He's going to flip one now. He's going to flip one.' Brian Moore.

'Some people are on the pitch . . .' Kenneth Wolstenholme.

They are our hits, the single taken from our album. The single is rarely the best track on that album but it's the catchy ditty you can't get out of your head.

Like Bowie, I wouldn't want to be judged on 'The Laughing Gnome'.

Like Bowie, we are performing when we are at work. Commentary is just an act. I didn't charm my beautiful wife by talking to her with the same inflected projection that I use when talking to the nation during an England game. 'Oh darling, that's quite, quite remarkable!' I'd still be single.

Unlike Bowie, I can't plan my whole stage set in advance. There is so little that the commentator can control once the game kicks off. You can't save 'Life on Mars' for an encore. You might not get one.

Unlike Bowie, you can't mix and remix your best 'lines' in a studio until they are ready for release. Every album is a live album.

All you can do is prepare for as many eventualities as possible. If you are commentating on a match in which a new Premier League scoring record may conceivably be set, it's not cheating to remember the name that someone whispered to you, and how they whispered it.

My best ever commentary 'line'? Easy!

For many moons I've written and hosted an annual sports quiz for a well-heeled Bobby Moore Fund dinner gathering in London, and one year I offered any phrase of the bidder's choice to be worked into an England commentary at auction. Basic error, Clive.

While my charitable work on the night pocketed thousands for cancer research, my television work was given the challenge of referencing the body contours of a barmaid in Kent.

'I can't say that,' I insisted to the ever-so-funny advertising executive who was prepared to donate £5,000 in order to use me to deliver a crude chat-up line to an unsuspecting employee of the Poachers Inn.

'A deal's a deal,' he countered, while also adding lairy layers of detailed vulgarity to the transaction. I drew the line at referencing her estimated bra size.

So, my best ever commentary line followed a Daniel Sturridge miss against Holland at Wembley. Hopefully, you missed it too . . .

'Got ahead of himself there. Got distracted. Like he was caught gazing into big dazzling headlights. Over the bar. Bouncing about. Known as a poacher, but never looked like scoring there, did he?'

Ker-Ching. That'll be five grand for charity, thank you.

The changing face of football commentary. 2020.

OUTRO

CURRENTLY APPEARING ON . . .

CBS Sports

TalkSport

Amazon Prime Video

Rangers TV

NBC Sports

ITV Sport

'Not for me, Clive' is an Andy Townsendism. An Ally Mc-Coistism too. You can make up ridiculous words like those in the easy-ozey, squeaky bum world of football. At the end of the day.

It's a show of dissent but not a yellow card offence. A beg to differ. A quibble, rather than a quarrel. It's what a co-commentator says after the fourth action replay has failed to persuade them that there was not enough contact for a penalty to be awarded.

It's a qualified opinion. How football opinions should be. Open to discussion, Clive

Both the former President of the USA and the current Prime Minister of the UK have regularly said things during the last few years that would have ended my career on the spot.

They are popularly elected leaders of the free world while I shout footballers' names out. And yet I am expected to uphold higher standards of decorum and propriety in my public utterances than they do.

Words are wonderful. They are a better invention than anything that science and technology has ever come up with. To work with words is a privilege. They are precious commodities and deserve better treatment than most of us afford them.

Football commentators are probably more guilty than most but we are not making keynote speeches. We work with our own little vernacular. We are no more than a bit of stuff-and-nonsense going on during a sporting event. Anyone that cares to dissect our every word and analyse them for public censure or to round up a hanging party needs to give their moral compass a good shake.

There is always a bigger picture than a football match. Or should be.

I am happy to take responsibility for the words I use as long as those that hear them take as much care over how they land on their ears and their sensitivities. Offence is anything that trends. Context is dead. Opening your mouth can be a dangerous business these days.

These days.

I hate to hear fellow football commentators talking about 'these days' as if nothing's any good any more. As if the game's gone. As if the crackdown on the tackle from behind marked the end of the Golden Age. As if muddy pitches were fun.

Nothing dates us like nostalgia. Nothing fools us like our memories.

One of the greatest moments in the life of any parent is when they catch their offspring listening to the same music they liked when they were young. We can't see the earth turning but it is. Little is truly original. We all owned the planet in our youth, so we all bequeath it grudgingly.

Experience is an underrated accreditation but it can make world-weary sceptics of us if we let it. It breeds a blinkered conviction that we've seen it all before, that we know how this episode ends.

Well, I haven't and I don't.

Experience should never be measured in years but in the experiences themselves and how they touch us. I want to be touched again and again.

I don't like rollercoasters. I am not into simulated danger. There is enough out there that frightens me already without paying to be scared senseless. I'm not thrill-seeking when I express an opinion or raise an issue in a commentary or an interview or this book. I want to provoke some thought and discussion but I want my mind to be stretched rather than your patience with me. I'm still looking, still listening.

The last year has come complete with a lot more questions than answers for all of us. We are continually breaking new ground. A lot of it is pretty shaky. I don't understand people that are so sure of themselves and their stance on everything. They accept cookies without thinking but they can't accept that there may be a counterpoint to their position on politics, gender, diversity or even pandemics.

I'm not the old, stubborn one. They are. They know no middle ground. To them, if you're not woke, you're a bigot. End of.

Life's really not like that. It's more enthralling, more suspenseful, more dynamic, more mercurial.

Most of our defining human emotions are felt in very personal, very singular ways. You can't model devout beliefs on them, you can't form policy around them. They relate overwhelmingly to the individual and to their changing circumstances.

My fears are your challenges. My turn-ons are your turn-offs. My idea of comedy is your idea of offensive.

We are a temperamental lot. Even our deepest feelings can be ephemeral. We fall in and out of love with partners we make solemn vows to. We go off people.

We all know how unfaithfully our minds are prone to change. Everything we think or say should come with a rider that we are human beings and therefore entitled to retreat from the position that we are currently defending so stoutly. We are revisionists by nature.

Communicators have got to try to connect with all of these different wavering personalities and viewpoints. It's quite a responsibility, quite a juggle.

It's easy to get it wrong with a live microphone in your hand. Even in a moment, hurtfulness can leave a lasting mark, an enduring scar. I've never delivered a commentary without uttering words that I'd like to edit or delete afterwards. It is not a scripted performance. They don't give you a map at kick-off.

Offence, affront, indignation, even violation . . . they are all as bespoke as joy and pain. They come in different shapes and sizes to different people. We have every right to complain and campaign about attacks on our own personal ramparts when they happen but we have no right at all to demand that our sensitivities get more consideration than those of others.

All that happens when a particular cause is championed beyond its natural reach is that a resistance movement forms. Chuntering, spiteful opposition mounts to something worthy purely on the grounds that it is being given undue attention. Creed envy.

Our fight is not necessarily the next person's. It may not even be our own in a year or two. Surely, the coronavirus pandemic has widened our perspectives and refreshed our priorities if nothing else.

In uncertain, unprecedented times, the emphasis on good communication is greater than ever. The journalist's job has never had more strings attached.

I am not quite finished learning this job. In order to learn, you have got to be free to explore. I explore out loud. You won't like everything I say or write. I don't myself, so you definitely won't.

Apologies in advance but I've still got more to say. More to learn too.

I know my age. I'm at a time when life starts taking things away from you. Things you are not ready to part with just yet.

There is a strange perception that you will give them up meekly in a dignified recognition that you've had your turn. Bollocks to that.

When Niall Sloane, my boss at ITV Sport, told me in a Zoom call last June that he was replacing me as his lead commentator after twenty-two years, I just hadn't seen it coming. Maybe I should have but I hadn't. There is a hole in my stomach just re-living the moment. I was in shock. Tearful, fearful.

Rejected, dejected. I told the people around me I was 'fine' but I wasn't. It felt like the beginning of the end because I was under the mistaken impression that I could still do the job as well as anyone else. But Niall didn't see it that way. And if he didn't, what was I missing here?

What couldn't I see that he could?

A lot of people proceeded to say a lot of nice things to and about me. As one friend commented – well, I'll name drop, it was Dara O'Briain – 'not many people get to see their obituaries before they die'. My inbox was full of support. Can after can of sweet-scented petrol was poured over my raging sense of injustice. I was very flammable for a while.

The furnace was stoked by a call from the producer of a future show that I was committed to. He asked me if I had 'health issues' or if I 'had done something' he should know about. I answered his suspicions in a short Twitter post. 'No' and 'no'. It had more than 6.5 million views.

I didn't bother to seek detailed reasons for Niall's decision. I wasn't looking for placation, I just wanted the job back and that wasn't going to happen. He said something about every organisation needing to 'refresh' from time to time. I'm afraid, that just put another log on my fire.

Hospitals don't refresh their panel of heart surgeons by bringing in junior doctors to keep the average age down. They tend to base their decisions on the specialist's ongoing ability to recognise the aortic from the pulmonary valve under pressure.

I look to refresh every single day. This job is about communication. It is the literal definition of networking. In order to reach an ever-changing audience, you need to constantly update and upgrade the connection. It's not about how many followers you have, it's about your engagement with them.

As it happened, other employers duly 'refreshed' by hiring me. Commentary's Harry Redknapp!

I really don't have time or room for injustice or nostalgia. 'These days' are right now. Every day should be part of the 'experience', and when you are lucky enough to have a stage from which to describe and explore an experience as formative as football is to so many lives, you've got to keep trying to seize the moments that the sport continually shapes.

I actively promote young broadcasting talent. I annually mentor six media undergraduates and I am happy to offer advice to anyone in the industry who asks me for it. And many have.

Too many of my generation sign up to a bitter, blinkered rear-guard action that digs in to defend the Empire like the Raj. I can only promise you that we don't all find Jim Davidson funny.

As I've already stated, broadcasters are all a matter of opinion, all a question of taste. To suggest those tastes are governed purely by age range is bizarre.

If you need a 25-year-old to broadcast to 25-year-olds, you are going to have to hire a hundred different commentators for every match. It's our national sport. It is watched by most of the nation's population. And that population is growing older, by the way. At least, I will be well placed by the time the BBC decide they need an octogenarian to relate to their care home viewership.

Diversity is vital to the balance of any branch of the communication industry. Diversity by social, economic and education background as well as age, gender and ethnicity. Counting in a quota from each grouping is merely Noah's Ark diversity. A good recipe is not about the ingredients but how they blend and complement each other.

I will vehemently challenge the idea that I am unable to relate to people half or even a third of my age. We have four 'children' in their twenties. They are among my best friends in the world. How dare anybody be so dismissive of their restless appetite for background and back story as to infer that they only want to hear from people of their own age?

Cosmetic changes to the cast of a radio or television programme are no more than a dab of perfume. Very often, the fresh blood continues to broadcast in the time-honoured style and tone of the people they've replaced. It's just like refreshing your Twitter page if you only get more of the same.

At least ITV have replaced me with someone that has a different approach to football commentary to mine. That makes it easier for me to process the decision and digest it.

Change has got to be tangible and progressive to be worthwhile. But change draws on experience, it doesn't leave it at the gate for the binmen to collect.

Some of the kindest messages that I've received from total strangers during the last eventful year have referred to me as a voice of their childhood. It seems like a rather veiled compliment when you are trying to fend off ageism but it's not. The voices of our childhood leave some of the most indelible impressions. We never stop listening to them.

The experiences that I have chronicled in these pages armed me for most of what even Messrs Trump and Johnson have thrown our way. The experience gained has given me perspective but not complacency. I may have more securities than insecurities, there may be less that is unexplained and so less to worry about but I have not closed this or any book.

For the final word, may I commend the *Daily Mail*? And before you sneer, it is probably the most influential source of information and opinion in our country. If you look upon it as a monster, ask yourself if it's you that's feeding it.

One of the greatest lessons that I've learnt from the *Mail* is that if it runs a headline that ends with a question mark, the answer is almost certainly 'no'.

Are fruit and vegetables actually bad for you? No.

Can dogs understand every word we say to them? No.

Could Kylie Minogue be the next James Bond? No.

Is Clive Tyldesley ready to call it a day? You get the idea . . .

No . . .

. . . but VAR will check that.

Everyone needs an escape.